very dark places

Also by Kristen Thomson Sheely

Blind Corner
Surface Errors

very dark places

*a memoir of grief, family, and learning to
survive unimaginable loss*

Kristen Thomson Sheely

The Derek Sheely Foundation
www.thedereksheelyfoundation.org

©2025 by Kristen Thomson Sheely, All Rights Reserved.

Hardback ISBN 979 8 9932570 0 6
Paperback ISBN 979 8 9932570 1 3
E-book ISBN 979 8 9932570 2 0

Library of Congress Control Number: 2025920629 (print)

Typeset in Garamond
Cover photo provided by the author

Printed in the United States of America

All proceeds from this publication will benefit
The Derek Sheely Foundation and its nonprofit mission.

The following pages are based on a true story.

Losing a child is traumatic and life-altering,
changing everything about you as a parent and a person,
including the will to survive.

People and events are depicted in this memoir according to the
author's present recollection. Certain sections are based upon
essays and poems written by the author and posted in her blog.
Some names have been omitted or changed to protect
the privacy of individuals.

Derek, You are my heart

Keyton, You are my reason why

Ken, You are the love of my life

table of contents

before

The framed photograph on my desk is of the two of us. Our faces are pressed together, and we're smiling. I'm wearing sunglasses, but you aren't; my face shades yours a bit so you're not squinting into the bright sun. I'm kneeling and you're leaning back against my thigh; my tanned arms wind around you; my right hand presses against your small chest, my fingers stretched open. Your left hand is on my other knee. You're wearing a black t-shirt with a howling coyote on the front. I remember the back read, *Ow Ow Owoooo*. You wore that shirt a lot, so many washings the black faded to a dark grey before you outgrew it. I still have it. The sun is on our hair, turning your curls blond and mine light brown. The sky is lit a curious shade of light blue – not quite blue, not quite grey, or perhaps the muted color is just because it's a faded photograph. Behind us are hundreds of yellow flowers, likely a weed, but still beautiful. Always notice wildflowers: They're small blooms on tallish stems, a clump, a bush really, some random loveliness in the rough grass. Behind the flowers is a low wall of ancient reddish rock. We visited a ruin that day; I don't remember which one. I should though. The builders of that jagged wall deserve at least that. Perhaps if I sifted through all of the photos from that summer I might be able to piece it together; after all, finding all of the photos of gorgeous sunny days when I wore a green shirt and flowered shorts shouldn't be that difficult. It's the looking at them that's impossible now.

My husband took this photo in 1991, the year we lived in New Mexico for three months.

Derek was two.

Flash forward twenty years, to 2011, when we got the phone call that is every parent's nightmare.

And now it's years later, and I'm trying to make sense of all of it – the time passed and lost – and none of it aligns with what I see in the photograph: My smiling little boy and me. I'm 22 there, the same age my son was when he died, and how I'm just now realizing this terrible truth I do not know. I've more than over-analyzed the minutiae of everything I can think of, every single thing he's left behind, every single thing that resembles a memory of him, but I failed to put this together until literally just now. I missed it. And this is the photo I look at – that I stare at – every day. What else have I missed? Tears do nothing to describe the feeling of despair that fills me. Our smiles didn't matter, and my arms wrapped around him didn't protect him. The one job a parent has: to protect the baby, and I failed. This is beyond survivor's guilt. Beyond what is ever acceptable. Beyond words. So beyond, that there's no word for it, no word for what to call someone who's lost a child.

There's no name for this grief.

part
one

I don't want to tell this story. But this is the story that overshadows all the other ones we have, because it's our last one, the one that shapes everything else, both in the Before and in the After. It's the story about what happened to our son.

Our son is dead.

How could we have let this happen?

I try not to think about the moment our lives changed forever. Or the seven days we spent in the hospital. Or the thousands of days since. But most days that's all I think about. What we lost.

monday

We got the call at 10:24 am on Monday August 22, 2011. A brief voicemail on my cell phone: "This is -----, one of the athletic trainers at -----. Derek has been injured this morning at practice. Please call me back as soon as you get this message."

My husband and I were driving home to Maryland after taking our daughter to college at Penn State, winding through the mountains with no cell signal. Scratchy reception meant we couldn't return the call for almost 40 minutes. My mind raced as the minutes plodded along, and I thought, Oh no, he broke his leg, he broke his collarbone, he pulled his hamstring. I had no idea what I expected to hear when we finally got a signal, somewhere north of Harrisburg, and I called the number back, numb, not really aware of what I was doing, like what was happening was in slow motion. There was no way we could prepare ourselves for a call like this. How could we? I pressed the last number and then *send,* and I felt so anxious I handed the phone to Ken because I knew I couldn't talk. As soon as he could, he whipped the car to the shoulder and slammed to a stop.

We had to get to the hospital as fast as we could. A neurosurgeon called immediately after we returned the trainer's call. This second phone call left us reeling, so shaken we didn't tell anyone for a long time what we were told: The injury to our son was so severe the surgeon doubted Derek would survive the emergency surgery. He told us that over the phone, with us almost three hours away. I wondered later, my thoughts folding over upon themselves, How long had Derek been waiting for this essential operation while we were unreachable? What care did he receive in the meantime? What's more, he was over 21 – did they really need parental permission to proceed with life-saving surgery?

Cinnamon was with us. She was our 11-year-old red and white Basenji. Really, Derek's dog, as he was in elementary school when we brought her home. Cinnamon calmed him when he was anxious, invigorated him when he was bored, and curled on his lap when he was lonely. They grew up together. We had to drop her off somewhere to be looked after before we could head to the hospital in the small city of Cumberland in western Maryland. My parents, usually available anytime to dog-sit, were out West somewhere on a two-week road trip with my mother's cousin and her husband. My sister had her own dog and was dog-sitting our parents' dog. So our next thought was Ken's mother. Though she lived in a dog-less household, she agreed without hesitation, and as she hugged us goodbye, she murmured in my ear, Derek will be okay; don't worry.

Worried did not describe how I was feeling: The surgeon had told us he doubted Derek would survive the surgery he needed. I was not worried – I was terrified.

Somewhere on the faceless interstate stretch between Mechanicsburg, Pennsylvania and Cumberland, Maryland, my cell rang again. Ken pulled over to hear from the neurosurgeon that Derek was out of surgery. But this news did nothing to quell our fears. I spent the remaining miles rocking in my seat, praying and crying.

I think I got out of the Escalade before Ken stopped it completely. I didn't know where I was going, and I never led the way anywhere – Ken always looked back to make sure I was following him, no matter where we were headed. I was in a daze, so Ken took my arm and we walked into the hospital together. It was well past two o'clock by now. A trauma nurse was waiting in the lobby for us. So was the neurosurgeon who had told us over the phone that Derek likely would not survive the surgery he just survived. He greeted us, shaking Ken's hand. But he did not shake mine.

We rode an elevator. I don't remember exactly what was said to us. Words like *serious, CT, midline, severe, white room, MRI, trauma.* Repeatedly, in different staccato sequences, like code.

They were talking about my son.

And suddenly there he was.

The only light came from the curtained window, and I could not stop looking at Derek, could not believe what I was seeing, my son. There was a white bandage on his head, and his eyes were closed, but to me there were no other indications that he was traumatically injured, let alone just had brain surgery. I shivered then, and I think now about what a craniotomy means. What it really means when it's done to your son – the slice of a thin blade, the sawing. As he's laid open, there's such delicate precision in the bare softness; isn't there? And where now is the piece of skull they took? Would he get it back? I could not stop myself from crying; hot tears just fell and fell. He was right in front of me, but they pronounced this to be a white room. No stimulus: No talking to him, no extra noise, and no touching him. His brain was trying to reset itself, they told us, so let it focus on the task.

I couldn't touch him?

I kept crying and shaking my head. This has to be a mistake. I stared at the ventilator, at the IVs. A monitor. I saw his heart rate, his respiratory rate, but I did not know what the other waves of colors meant. His arms were moving. Restless, like he couldn't get comfortable. I wanted to touch his arm, his cheek, to talk to him and tell him we're right here. *My son.* I stood frozen; I could not touch him.

What happened?

They said his arm movement was reflexive. A good sign, they said. They pinched him to make him pull away. They poked his feet to make him pull away. They yelled his name to provoke a response. They shined a light into his eyes. Not all of his reactions were good.

You said I couldn't talk to him or touch him.

The room was murky and dark around its edges, so I did not see exactly when one of the captains came in. He must have said he was Derek's brother to be allowed entry into the white room. He hugged Ken first, then me. He looked at Derek and then back to us. He was crying and shaking his head. One of Derek's best friends, they had graduated high school together and now were at the same college – alike in so many ways, even their heights, I likely thought, as I put my hand on the back of his head when we hugged. I don't remember what we said to each other; he probably said he was praying as hard as he could.

We would hear that a lot in the coming days.

21

♥ ♥ ♥

What happened? People like to say that things happen for a reason. That there's a plan. Maybe the people who believe this never lost a child. Maybe. But, no: There's no reason that could explain something like this. Nor could there be a plan. What reason could there possibly be to put anyone through this pain? What plan could there be to traumatically injure a young man like Derek who would have accomplished so much good in the world? If there were a reason, then every horror ever had a reason and was part of some ghoulish plan. Did an unexplainable collision of coincidence cause this? Or, was this a *Sliding Doors* moment? Bending down at the right moment to tie his shoe could have saved Derek. So could bending down to tie mine. Or, was this preventable? A split second sooner or later could have prevented what happened, right? A decision here, a decision there at any point could have changed everything. The permutations are endless. And that way of thinking makes me stumble with despair.

♥ ♥ ♥

The hit made his brain shift 11 millimeters from its midline. There was significant bruising and tremendous swelling. The craniotomy, the surgery Derek should not have survived but did, relieved some of the swelling, as indicated by a second MRI which showed the midline had shifted back closer to where it should be, but the impact had been so great it likely would not help for the long term. The craniotomy was a short-term solution by a small hospital to fix a catastrophic injury.

What hit? What impact? These vague hints dropped so casually left me numb. No one was telling us anything.

The small waiting room was full. We were led there when they wanted to examine and evaluate Derek further. I could not look at the people who were crowded in there – looking at their stricken faces made this all the more real. Derek's girlfriend stood next to three of his teammates. The head coach was there. Another coach. His position coach. The athletic director. My sister and her husband stood against the far wall, and I could barely breathe when I saw their familiar faces – how had I forgotten that I had called them on our way here? Soon a chaplain arrived. She sat right next to me and said words I don't remember. I was shaking as I sat, my legs jumping up and down, my hands crumpled into fists, my nails sharp and piercing my palms.

While we waited, someone I did not know from the school said they didn't recall seeing a big hit. That they didn't know what happened. That this morning at the early practice Derek was fine, then they changed from practice shells to full gear for the second morning practice, and at some point he said he didn't feel well, and then he collapsed. There were nods and murmurs of agreement from all corners of the small room.

I stared at the floor. My legs kept shaking.

He collapsed.

And then they were done – he was stable; we could go back to his room. I saw his arms still posturing – that was what they called the rhythmic movement his arms were making. I did not know it then but now I know that the kind of posturing we saw indicated a grim outlook. I prayed. My heart felt hollow. They still would not let us touch him.

A doctor came in. And another. The trauma nurse who had met us in the lobby when we arrived hours ago stayed with us. My eyes shifted from the floor to Derek and back to the floor. Another nurse arrived and she was pleasant and kind to us, but this one talked a lot. I thought we were supposed to be quiet. Why was she talking?

Sometime late afternoon, they told us they wanted to send him to the R Adams Cowley Shock Trauma Center at the University of Maryland in Baltimore. It was one of the best facilities in the country for traumatic brain injuries. Derek would be medevacked there and we would drive to meet him. They just weren't sure yet if he would be stable enough for the trip, or if there would even be a bed for him once he got there.

He will be at the best place with the best people. Put him in a hallway if you have to.

It took an hour to move him from the bed in the white room to a transport bed. Part of the delicate steps to accomplish before

23

carefully moving him to the helicopter was changing his bandage for a fresh one for the trip. Ken warned me not to look when they unwrapped his bandage, so I turned and faced the wall and cried. When Ken said, Okay, I turned back and saw Derek on the transport bed, a sheet fitted to his chin, grey seat belts wrapped to secure him. I want to say we were invited along onto the elevator to the roof where the helicopter waited, but we were not. We stood against the wall and watched our son be wheeled away.

Somehow, we told Keyton. I don't know how Ken made that call, but we had no choice but to destroy her life with the news about her big brother. And she was hours away at Penn State and completely alone when she had to face this news. What was she supposed to do now – first day of her freshman year, just go off to her next class like everything was fine? The worst thing a parent could do – fail to protect your child – and, though we had no choice, here we were, knowingly doing it again to our other child.

Then I had to call my parents and tell them. I think they were somewhere near Mt. Rushmore. When my mother answered, I think I was still trying my best to sound as if everything was still fine, trying to hold onto that feeling of safety, as if I knew this would be one of the last times I could speak and think with a sense that everything was in fact going to be okay. That I still lived in a world I thought I knew.

Take me off speaker, Mom. I heard my voice break. I could tell their phone was hooked up to their car. Assuming my mom's cousin and her husband were listening from the back seat, I probably first apologized for interrupting their vacation, and then somehow formed the words *Derek* and *hospital*. I don't remember what else I said, though I had to repeat myself because what I had to tell them was so unexpected and overwhelming they likely didn't grasp at first the gravity of the words I was saying. They asked if they should come home. *I don't know, I don't know.* Ken likely broke in with, We'll call you in the morning when we know more.

Ken called our pastor, who said he'd meet us at Shock Trauma. He confirmed both Derek and Keyton; Ken and I often volunteered for church activities over the years; I even edited the church's monthly newsletter. We attended church regularly then, and Pastor knew our family well.

Right before we got into the elevator, Derek's girlfriend asked me if she could ride along with us to Baltimore. I froze, thinking that I couldn't possibly take care of her, make sure she's okay, but wanting to nod yes. I hugged her and told her it's probably not a good idea right now, but we'd call her as soon as we knew something. According to Derek, their relationship was close, yet complicated. Even so, it was obvious she was upset; her eyes downcast, she avoided eye contact with us, and her face was unable to hide her worry and disappointment.

Ken made a quick call to his mother to update her, and then we got into the car and drove toward the highway, my sister and her husband close in the rearview mirror. My sister made me promise to text her when we got to Baltimore as we hugged at the gas station near the hospital. I glimpsed her husband over her shoulder, and he looked drawn, shaken, and was unable to meet my eyes.

The drive to Baltimore was a ferocious exercise in trying to arrive at Shock Trauma at the same time as the helicopter so that we would not miss anything. We did what we could, but not surprisingly, we lagged behind. It was after eight o'clock by now, I think. Maybe later. A day like this, time meant nothing. Traffic was a blur, and Ken and I barely spoke; the radio was off. Silence filled the car for the 140-mile trip. We were without a map, so we relied on road signs in the growing darkness to guide us to a parking garage next to the hospital. Ken found a space, and we walked away from the car, through a door or two, a metal detector, and just like that were inside the enormous hospital. Pastor was waiting for us – his drive from Gaithersburg was much shorter than ours, only about 40 minutes or so. Derek's here, he confirmed. He hugged us and showed us where we could sit and wait in a quieter part of the lobby away from the 24-hour restaurants and gift shop. We learned we would have to pass through security to get out of the lobby, and we were refused until "someone" called the reception desk "soon," which would be the required permission to allow us to go upstairs.

Soon was some three hours later, when Ken and I were issued pink paper bracelets that peeled apart and stuck together on themselves. These bands that encircled our wrists permitted us to pass through another metal detector, past an armed guard, and into an elevator. Ken took my hand. At some point we got off and walked through a brightly-lit and noisy corridor. A bearded man in blue scrubs led us to a curtained-off space next to a line of identical curtained-off spaces, so small it barely contained a narrow bed, beeping equipment, and chairs for us.

Derek was there. He looked as if he were sleeping. I knew he was not.

Someone cried nearby. Someone else moaned. Noise was everywhere. The curtains billowed between Derek's space and the next. It was clear he was not in a white room anymore.

Car accident?

What? Ken said.

Was this a car accident?

No. Football. Football practice. Pre-season camp.

I glanced blankly at the white coat, and my legs started to shake up and down. I looked down at my feet in the worn sandals I'd hastily chosen this morning for the car ride home. I'd just painted my toes a few days ago: homemade French manicure, a bit wonky here and there. I can still see those white tips. I will never paint my toes like that again.

Football? He wasn't wearing a helmet? A click of a ballpoint pen.

No. He was. He was wearing a helmet. Ken sounded terrible.

Why were they making us answer questions like these? Didn't the other hospital tell this one what was going on? What else were they about to ask?

Okay. He needs an MRI. Okay? Won't take too long. And then he'll get a room. Okay? We'll let you know when he's ready. Another click of the pen, and he was gone.

None of this is okay.

We looked at each other. I guess we've been dismissed.

We'll be right back, I told Derek as I touched his hand. His warmth, his silence, made my eyes burn.

Why we left on our own, I have no idea. After waiting over three hours, we should have stayed with Derek until we were kicked out. As we were to learn, *soon* and *not too long* and *shortly* meant nothing in a hospital. Back downstairs in the waiting area we checked with one receptionist after another every 40 minutes for five hours whether he had the MRI and whether his room was ready. We stopped asking only because no one was at the reception desk after three in the morning. I'm sickened to think that Derek likely lay there by himself for hours in that suffocating curtained room until he finally was wheeled to wherever the MRI machine was.

Pastor waited with us. He slept. Ken slept less. How he could quiet his mind at all I had no idea. Maybe driving so much today pushed him into sleep. I did not sleep at all. And I may never sleep again. All I was able to do was think.

This is not my life.

Just a couple of hours ago, it seemed like, we were out for breakfast at a local favorite that used so much butter the smell clung to your clothes for hours. Only yesterday we had moved Keyton into her dorm room for her freshman year at Penn State – an arduous task that left us exhausted but happy. We made trip after trip from the Escalade to her room, carrying box after box of books and supplies and suitcases of clothes and bags of snacks. We helped her configure her laptop with the campus Wi-Fi, coordinated extension cords and surge protectors, made her bed, and helped her trace her first day of classes on the campus map so that she'd have an easier time finding her way. She was set.

Ken and I talked about a lot of things over breakfast, but the one topic we talked about the most were the kids. We talked about Derek's upcoming graduation from college in December, what to give him as a gift, that we probably would buy him a car. How not even two weeks ago he had applied to the CIA before leaving for football camp, how great the summer was especially since he commuted to his internship in DC every day with Ken on the metro. That hopefully he'd get a job right after he graduated, but, I remember saying over my Greek omelet and home fries, I hope he needs to live at home for at least a little while first.

We talked about Keyton, that she enjoyed starting classes at Penn State early, for their summer session back in June, that she'd been more than ready for college, so done with high school and its whole scene for months prior to her graduation. Now it was fall semester and she'd be a part of the raucous student section at the football games; her dorm was in a perfect location on campus, near Rec Hall for pep rallies and the gym for workouts, near the Nittany Lion shrine, near almost all her classes. Her roommate, a nursing major, seemed smart and fun, and they had clicked immediately. How lucky Keyton was!

We talked about looking forward to being so busy every single weekend until Thanksgiving, either going to Derek's home football games for his very last season or going to Penn State games now that we had season tickets. We couldn't believe how perfectly the two schedules meshed. The only potential conflict was the week Derek would play at Salisbury for his last game ever, and Penn State would play at home against Nebraska. (There'd be no conflict, as I knew we'd sell the Nebraska tickets and travel to watch Derek play against Salisbury, a Maryland eastern shore school not terribly far from where we lived.) And then we knew that next year when Derek would be finished with school and football, that he'd want to attend as many Penn State games as possible, and would negotiate with us like crazy. We'd give him a hard time, and then off to Beaver Stadium he and Ken would go, just the two of them.

I remember wondering whether perhaps the four of us could take a trip after graduation, too, maybe back to Bermuda or the Caribbean. Or wherever Derek wanted to go to celebrate.

Hopes and dreams, that's all we talked about. Contentment. Gratefulness. Next chapter. Keyton in college, Derek about to be on his own, and Ken and me alone together.

And now this: Chapter completely destroyed, rewritten, shredded, thrown out, deleted. Gone. What would happen now to the hopes and dreams we have for our son? What would happen to his? And Keyton's? We're here, in this place, shocked and traumatized, waiting. It's even in its name: Shock Trauma. It's painful to wait like this, waiting to know the unknown. The unbearable helplessness of waiting. Time was broken, and all of the nights starting with this one would run together.

I tried to brace myself for what was coming even though I was already braced for what was coming. And still I could not sleep. I could not turn my mind off. It's strange that you're still able to think when you're too tired to sleep.

Derek was 22 and in the best shape of his life.

What happened?

VERY DARK PLACES

♥ ♥ ♥

It was just over a week ago when Ken took Derek back to college. The Escalade was stuffed, so full I didn't even fit. I'd been helping Derek pack since the end of July, running out to local stores for those last-minute must-haves for his final semester of college. He had signed a lease at a just-built apartment building that overlooked the football stadium and would move in two weeks before most of the rest of his classmates, the timetable to return for pre-season football camp. When Ken returned home that night, he laughed as he told me about the day: They'd barely arrived on the edge of campus and were still in the car when Derek was greeted by a slew of smiling teammates, shaking his hand and asking him about his summer. It was like he was the mayor, Ken said, the way he held court from the front seat.

Derek could have graduated the previous May, but he decided to stay one more semester to achieve a dual major in history and political science. Plus, that extra semester allowed him to be eligible for one more football season. He'd secured a position for the summer in the competitive paid internship program at the National Nuclear Security Administration's arm of the US Department of Energy, and this experience and his long-held interest in public service compelled him to apply to the CIA. This last semester of college and his last season of football would be like his victory lap on his way to adult life. And he had prepared for this victory lap for months: along with working all day, he endured that grueling 90-minute-each-way DMV commute, and then, he either went running in our neighborhood or met some of his friends at the gym for a lift session. Every evening. His goal was to get stronger and faster for his team, and he did. He got bigger too – I saw the grocery store receipts.

Between the end of his spring semester and the start of his internship, Derek's one-and-only free week of the summer, we planned a cruise to a handful of beautiful ports-of-call in the Caribbean to celebrate Keyton's high school graduation, and just as they had for Derek's high school graduation cruise to Bermuda four years earlier in 2007, my parents joined us.

29

Everyone eats too much on a cruise, and our family was no exception. I remember our dinner reservation time was late, 8:00 every evening, so in the interest of never allowing ourselves to feel hungry between lunch and dinner, Derek and I had a standing date at the sushi bar around 5:30. Fresh sushi, prepared right in front of us? Yes, please. He'd usually have four or five plates to my two. We'd eat our tuna sashimi and salmon rolls and stare out at the sea's limitless blue. Then he'd nod and lift his eyebrow, Are you done? And I'd nod back, Sure. We'd wander by the tea and coffee station, grab a mug and fill it with lemon wedges, and then head back to our cabins, three all in a row: Ken and me, Derek and Keyton, and my mom and dad. He'd follow me into our cabin, and we'd have a couple of quick shots of tequila, chased with lemon wedges. Beyond tart, but an easy and effective way to be a bit warm and buzzy while at sea. I'd smuggled the tequila within an extra contact solution bottle inside my luggage because I'm thrifty. Don't tell anyone.

Since we ate dinner so late, we caught the midnight shows, and the late-night comedians were our favorite. My dad would buy Derek a drink (he's not thrifty) whenever he asked for one, and Ken would smile and shake his head at every tall Long Island Derek downed.

I found out a few nights in that after these late shows, Keyton would call for room service, usually pizza and ice cream, and Derek would answer the door and accept the heavy tray. They had a system. Because they, too, never wanted to feel hungry.

I filmed Derek the day he discovered the giant two-story water slide at one of the pools. You couldn't get him off it. He waited in line with children half his size, this tattooed tall and muscular 22-year-old with a pretty bad sunburn waiting patiently among ten-year-olds just to slide down a ginormous slide. He tried to be stoic and super cool when he got to the bottom, but through the splash, all you saw was his huge smile.

Not even a week after we returned from the cruise, Derek's internship began. On just his second day was Keyton's high school graduation ceremony, and he had no idea if he'd be able to make it. Ken described to him in detail how to get from the Department of Energy to D.A.R. Constitution Hall, where the ceremony would be. Like her brother's class, Keyton's class plus guests was much too large to fit into the high school's auditorium, so the ceremony took place at a venue that could accommodate the large group. Most large high schools in Montgomery County, Maryland did this. I was skeptical and anxious: The whole idea seemed overwhelming to me. Derek had to get to work by himself via metro after commuting in with Ken and being shown which way to go exactly once, then excuse himself, Yeah sorry, I've got to go out for a few hours on my second day, see you in a bit, and rush over a mile across town on foot, past the Smithsonian Castle, the Holocaust Memorial Museum, the Museum of African American History and Culture, and the Washington Monument, to be at crowded Constitution Hall by 10:00 am? Mapped out, it was at least a 25-minute walk on a very warm June morning. I was more than skeptical, but I didn't want to put pressure on him as much as I didn't want his sister to be disappointed that her brother missed this milestone of hers. Maybe I shouldn't have taken today off and just gone in with him, Ken admitted when he saw my worried eyes checking my watch for the third time.

The venue was enormous, and filling fast, but somehow we found seats reasonably close to the stage for my parents, my niece, Ken's mother and her partner, and us. And one extra next to me.

The minutes ticked quickly to almost 10:00.

I felt nervous, and I could feel sudden sweat across my nose.

He's here, Ken said, nudging me.

And he was. I didn't know how he did it, but Derek made it to his sister's graduation ceremony.

I hugged him, I can't believe you're here!

Me neither, he shrugged. I walked as fast as I could to get here on time.

I laughed in disbelief and asked, How are you not all sweaty and out of breath?

He shrugged again. His blue dress shirt was pristine and his tie was square against his throat. No big deal, he said.

He went back to work after the ceremony, and we didn't see him again until Ken picked him up from the metro that evening. To celebrate Keyton, we all ate enchiladas and fajitas at her favorite restaurant followed by a decadent chocolate layer cake.

I have a photo of Derek and Keyton from that night. I took it after everyone left. It's now framed and sits on top of the wooden bookshelf my dad made for me back in 1975. My children are in our kitchen, standing in front of the refrigerator. It's a weird photo, with Keyton smiling up at the camera, her eyes knowing and wide, her head bowed a little. And Derek also has his head bowed slightly, eyebrows lifted, eyes wide, and he isn't smiling. The overhead lighting hits their faces just so, the bare floodlights painting shadows in the hollows of their cheeks. Why I took this odd photo, with them wearing old t-shirts and raggedy shorts, posing in front of the refrigerator of all things, instead of one with Keyton in her cap and gown next to her big brother in his dress shirt and tie, the way they looked just an hour before, I have no idea. I know only that it's the last photo I have of my son and my daughter together.

♥ ♥ ♥

I could picture him a week ago, and sometimes he's playing a video game, other times he's packing and checking his to-do list, and then I find him in his bed that last morning before leaving for football camp. I wake him up, gently, like I always do, by turning off the small fan next to his bed that helps him sleep. I tell him to have fun and to be careful and when I whisper, Bye, he waves me in, small waves with both hands, for a hug, and we hug.

The next time I saw him was a few hours ago, when he was in the white room.

I couldn't help but think that I should have done everything differently. I shouldn't have woken him up by turning off his fan. I should have gone with him and Ken back to school and helped him move in. I should have been there at the field to protect him when *we don't know what happened* happened. I shouldn't have allowed him to play football in the first place. I wanted to fix everything. Right everything for him. Give him what he deserved. Not this. He didn't deserve this. And I didn't even know what *this* was yet.

I looked at Ken, and I wanted to shake his shoulders, wake him up. How can you sleep, I screamed in my head.

Was it starting already? Not talking about the only thing I wanted to talk about?

32

I didn't know what to do.

And so I sat there, alone, restless and awake in the middle of the dark four o'clock in the fucking morning, staring at my exhausted husband, counting the ceiling tiles, and blaming myself, because what other explanation made sense right now? And it was always precisely what you never wanted to think about that crash lands on top of mind – *always the worst on the worst thoughts that you try to forget yet must remember you must remember every one of these horrendous thoughts over and over and over again.*

Maybe I had something of use, I bargained in my head. Slice me open; take my blood.

Take all of it.

♥ ♥ ♥

The lobby sounds all around me were rhythmic yet jarring, a strange continuous beeping coupled with a startling crash. Rolling wheels grinding across intermittent invisible bumps. Constant voices, lilting, dissonant, hoarse, whining. Coughing. Paper ripping. There was no droning sound that could lull me to sleep in a place like this.

Time meant nothing.

The bottled water Pastor gave me hours ago was tepid and left an almost withering tinge of metal behind when I finally swallowed a few sips. I leaned my head back and closed my eyes and squeezed them shut so tightly I saw a flash of light, and for a moment I felt lightheaded, almost out-of-body, a strange otherness that made, just for a split second, reality disappear and ether to take its place, and a warm calm settled over me like a mantle, and my eyes stayed closed, and what I saw in that flash of light slowed and slowed until there was nothing, and everything just disappeared, and what took up the space that was left was what let me sink and sink and sink and stop.

tuesday

Derek finally was in his own room. I had no idea what time it was when we got permission to go upstairs and see him. I tried to smooth my pants from hours of sitting, and then squeezed my shoulder blades together. My back was stiff and the muscles along my spine felt sore. A new day, so a new pink paper bracelet, this time with his name and room number written on it, then security, elevator, an exit onto a different floor than last night, only to find another windowless waiting area. Much smaller. Wood paneled. Chairs shoehorned around the perimeter. I did not want to sit. Sitting for a moment was the gateway to waiting for hours all over again.

Someone came to fetch us. We had to pass through locked double doors; later, we'd wave to the camera overhead and be buzzed through. We were recognized quickly. Derek's room was down the hall to the left and on the corner.

We saw him.

He was standing.

So tall in the middle of the room, his face handsome and unmarked, our son stood with his eyes closed like he was meditating.

♥ ♥ ♥

It's difficult to continue this story. The best version would be the one Derek himself would tell. It would be sincere and conscientious, like the time he got a voicemail from a college he had not applied to and had no intention of attending, calling to remind him of a visit he'd never scheduled. Derek being Derek, he promptly returned the call, telling them that they had contacted him by mistake and that they could free up his not-needed appointment time for someone else. The story Derek would tell would be honest and true, like the time we listed our house for sale, and during the walk-thru with the listing agent, Derek being Derek helpfully offered advice on how to close our floor-model refrigerator's door: you needed to use your foot to ensure the door was actually closed and sealed shut. He was 10. Because of his honesty and dry wit, though, you never knew when Derek could be playing a joke on you, like the time Derek being Derek convinced his friends he didn't have a sister so that they wouldn't befriend her, only to think later she was pretty and then make moves on her when she got older. A story told by Derek would be colorful with a detailed back story, full of dark and dry humor, and delivered with a straight face. Like the time he grabbed a friend's unattended laptop, quickly moved all the apps from the home screen, and downloaded an app that looked like a cracked screen. Derek let his friend suffer with fear for a few minutes over how to ask his parents for a new laptop, before he confessed the crack was fake. Yes, Derek's story as told by Derek would be calm, generous, compassionate, and with a little cynical wink alongside multiple historical references thrown in just for fun.

What *would* Derek say? He wasn't one who coveted being the center of attention, but, at the same time, he never was afraid to stand up for what he believed in. He was a fullback, the one on the football field who helped block and lead the way for the ball carrier, not usually the one with the ball who scored and basked in the glory. He was young, yet so sure of himself and what he wanted to do and how he wanted to live, that he acted mature beyond his years. That's what made him the center of attention, whether he liked it or not. Alone amongst his friends, he stood out. Quiet and unassuming, witty and smart, strong and kind; he was the mayor of his corner of the world, he was one of the good ones, and he would shrug his shoulders to hear that. Like it's no big deal. What's all the fuss about, anyway? He'd suck his teeth with disapproval, and then say something to make us laugh.

♥ ♥ ♥

Derek's middle school was grades six through eight. It's like everyone knows each other, he complained when he started there in late August 2000. He was a sixth grader, brand new to everything, since we had just moved almost 90 miles from York, Pennsylvania to Germantown, Maryland barely a month before school started.

Just a few weeks into the school year, the phone rang before eight o'clock in the morning. I almost missed answering because I was helping Keyton get ready for school. She was in second grade and got a later start than her older brother.

I heard a quiet voice ask, Can you come get me? It was Derek. I remember asking, What? Are you okay? What happened? And then I heard him start to cry. A woman's voice came on the line and she asked me to come to the middle school as soon as I could. Derek's in the main office. He's fine, but he's shaken up and wants to go home. Some older boys beat him up on the school bus. She said this as casually as confirming it was raining.

What? Who did this? What happened?

Derek rode the school bus, boarding and exiting just feet from our front door, and he liked riding the bus with his friends, laughing and chatting on the way to school every morning. He was average-sized as a young boy, maybe even on the smaller side of average. He didn't have his growth spurt until about tenth grade. But he wasn't ever skinny or frail – in a group of his classmates he looked pretty much like everyone else. Nothing about him said fodder for bullies, or at least that's what I thought. Like any other parent.

He was beaten up on the bus? Why?

Ken was already well on his way to work via metro, so I called my neighbor whose daughter was a year behind Keyton in school to ask if I could bring Keyton to her house and for her to make sure she got on the bus to the elementary school.

Morning traffic clogged the mile-long trip to the middle school, and so it felt like it took forever. I didn't know what I was expecting to see, but Derek looked like he always did, except for his red and puffy eyes. He got up from his seat in the main office and walked to my side. I put my arm around him and he said, I want to go home.

He gasped and tried not to cry when he told me everything in the car.

I get on the bus, and everything is fine, and then when the bus does this U-turn and comes back past our house on the other side of the street, these big kids get on, and they want to sit in my seat, and I say no, so they move to another seat, and this happened a bunch of times, but then today when they tell me to move and I say no, they say this is our seat, and I stand up and I say that I don't see your names on it, and sit back down, and that's when they put their coats over me and start hitting me and I know the bus driver saw because I saw her looking in the mirror and I don't know why she didn't do anything and I don't want to ride the bus anymore.

By now I knew he was more shaken than physically hurt, so I put my hand on his shoulder. I don't know what to say...that sounds terrible...I'm so sorry this happened to you. I remember tearing up as he said, It's okay. He patted my hand.

I drove him to school for about two weeks, which is what the principal recommended. And then it was Thanksgiving break. Could I continue to drive him until the new year? Give the incident (she didn't say *attack*) additional time and distance? Oh sure, yeah, I'll isolate my son while these bullies continue enjoying the privilege of riding the bus *uninterrupted*. Wouldn't want to inconvenience *their* parents. Ken and I pushed back, demanding consequences for the bullies, meeting with the assistant principal when the soon-to-retire principal was unavailable. Unlike her, he did not repeat the we-do-not-have-a-bullying-problem-at-this-school rhetoric, which we appreciated. And just when Derek bravely started riding the bus again, he came home with the news that those big kids were kicked off the bus for the rest of the school year. Other students reported their intimidating behavior after they witnessed Derek being threatened for a second time. I like to think that since he hadn't been afraid to stand his ground, even adding the challenging comment, *I don't see your names on it*, he wound up inspiring other kids to face their fears and do the same.

And now, here, in this room, I thought of him helping me through my own fears as only he could, and I felt overcome again.

He would hug me tight and pick me up, something he started doing as soon as he towered over me and realized he got an hysterical squeal and laugh out of me when he did it. He would talk to me in one of his thousands of voices, like Christopher Walken or Arnold Schwarzenegger, and make a goofy cross-eyed face; then I would laugh again. He would let me cry and not pressure me to stop. He would leave me alone when he knew I needed to be alone, or he would sit next to me and let me talk as long as I needed to. He wouldn't tell me time will help or tell me everything will be okay if you have faith or tell me to turn a tragedy into something positive or tell me we will meet again. Instead, he would tell me to scream and cry and throw things and go ahead and be angry and sad and hopeless. And he would try to take my fears away, because, Mommy, he would say, Let me do this for you.

♥ ♥ ♥

Gravity, they told us. They were using gravity to try and reduce the intracranial swelling. That's why Derek was standing. (And perhaps *standing* was not quite accurate, but I'd rather think of him that way, than to focus on my son strapped upright to a tilt table so that he hung there not of his own volition, a gruesome yet true description.)

Disconcerting was an understatement.

Cooling, too, we were told. Cooling wraps around his chest and legs.

Can you put it on his head, Ken asked. Wouldn't that help?

By any means necessary.

A lot happened that day, Tuesday, Day Two.

We met people, so many people. They all had names, but I remembered only Nurse. Nurse. Doctor. Doctor. Doctor. Doctor.

We learned more about traumatic brain injuries than we'd ever wanted to know.

Someone talked to us about the Ronald McDonald House nearby, that maybe a room might possibly be made available for us. Someone, my sister or Ken's sister or brother, maybe, had offered hours ago to pick up Keyton from Penn State and bring her here, and they would arrive any minute. I could barely think straight – how was I going to be able to help my daughter? What help was I supposed to give? I had no idea where to even start. Ken called his mother: They would come to Shock Trauma later today, and our dog was no trouble. And I was sure she wasn't, because like all dogs, Cinnamon was always in a good mood, ate when she was hungry, and slept a lot, finding the sun to bask in as it moved through the house. Pastor offered to bring us food from the lobby. There were

39

three different coffee shops, a couple of sandwich shops. We couldn't eat anything, but he brought something anyway. And my parents were on a flight to Baltimore, arriving sometime this afternoon. My mother hated to fly.

And then came the pronouncement that Derek needed another surgery. Another craniotomy to relieve the tremendous pressure he was suffering as his brain swelled against the inside of his skull. When *we don't know what happened* happened, the uncontrollable swelling was the devastating result. Hours of using gravity and cooling him just weren't enough.

Would you rather have a concussion or a traumatic brain injury? Trick question: They're the same. The very essence of football was hitting: linebackers hit the quarterback to prevent progress forward, offensive linemen hit defenders before they could reach the quarterback, ball carriers were hit before they reached the first down marker. Hit, hit, hit, hit, hit. And all of this hitting, whether it's helmet to shoulder or helmet to turf or helmet to helmet, very often resulted in a traumatic brain injury. (Or a concussion, the brand name.) The helmet protected the skull, but what protected the brain? Hit after hit could make the brain slosh around so much inside the skull that a family like mine stood in a room like this to hear Doctor say that my son's condition likely would get even worse, much worse, before it started to get better. If it would get better at all. Doctor compared it to a twisted ankle continuing to swell for days after its initial injury. But a traumatic brain injury was a far cry from a twisted ankle. What was before us was a terrible arc of waiting-and-seeing to be patiently endured. I wasn't in the room when Ken asked whether Derek could die if he had this second surgery. He told me later that Doctor had said, No. Even though we understood what Doctor had told us this morning when we were first allowed through security and permitted onto this floor, that the Derek we knew was already gone, we still had to try anything and everything to save him.

Already gone.

Already gone?

What was happening? How could we possibly understand this? I didn't understand any of this. I just hugged him goodbye a week ago. And we just talked to him. Sunday night. He called Ken to discuss the fantasy football draft they were competing in together. Ken asked about football camp, and Derek said only that he was tired. What could have happened that led him from that normal phone call 40 hours ago to the nightmare now?

Sometimes people could be wrong. Miracles could sometimes happen. Sometimes people got lucky. Sometimes prayers were answered. And other bullshit lies people like us told ourselves just to make it into the next moment.

I recalled some of the words: *stroke, medical coma, cranial pressure, frontal lobe.* And then: *organ donation.*

Nothing made sense.

My legs wouldn't stop shaking.

I wiped my eyes and saw Keyton standing in the doorframe. Her face was pale. How long had she been standing there? What had she heard?

♥ ♥ ♥

I didn't know who said it to us first, but it was starting already: Be grateful for the time you had together; take comfort in your memories; focus on the good times you had. All of this past tense made me tense. But no one cautioned us to be careful when memories were all we had. The weight of memory was heavy. The chill, still, bottomless pool of memory threatened to drown me. When I felt it coming, I knew to brace myself for the tidal wave and somehow breathe, because I was about to get drenched.

How far back can you remember?

Back and back to my 40s, my 30s, back to college, high school, first love, first heartbreak, middle and elementary school, first crush, first surprise birthday party, first pet, first childhood friends. I remember a lot, I do, and much of it I remember fondly. And much of it fucking sucked. We all were so awkward and hideous, thinking we were cool. Gen X before we knew what that even was. *The Breakfast Club* and *Sixteen Candles*, Friday night football games and marching band, Reagan and Iran Contra, crack, greed, big hair, AIDS, Bruce, Madonna, Michael Jackson, Prince. We came home to an empty house after school, played outside until the street lights came on, taped songs off the radio onto cassette tapes, and we knew nothing about self-care or mental health. My mental health was forcing a smile and saying, Okay! when I heard, *Wait till your father gets home*, and, *Stop crying or I'll give you something to cry about*, and, *Do what I say because I said so*, and, *Go to your room*. My self-care was taking the stairs two-at-a-time to my bedroom and slamming my door.

I was raised to be a good, nice, conflict-avoiding people-pleaser by two people who loved each other and my sister and me very much. They did the best they could. For sure. That I'm now a card-carrying democratic socialist who raised two democratic socialists of my own left my conservative parents wondering and shaking their heads. Good and nice, indeed.

I was in a comfy group of girlfriends – the JKLMs: the letters that started each of our first names. All through elementary school we four stuck together, confiding our secrets, passing *Forever* by Judy Blume back and forth to each other under our desks out of sight, not really understanding everything we were reading, at least I didn't (J and M had older siblings, so maybe through trickle-down osmosis they appreciated the nuances of certain risqué sections. I for one was so naïve back then I thought penis was pronounced *pen-iss*.). We stayed close through middle school, but advanced math in eighth grade separated us the whole school day except for lunch and band practice. We found a couple of new friends here and there in our disparate schedules, and sports took me to field hockey and L to track.

Then in high school, all of the JKLMs had a boyfriend except for me. I have a lot of other memories about high school, hazy snapshots, really, but this one stands out for sure. When you're 15 it's always hard to focus on small, insignificant things when that very specific and humungous thing was the center of everything. So there's me, 10th grade, alone with no boyfriend, while all of my closest friends were paired off with older boys, juniors with cars.

My mom assured me that the boys didn't know what they were missing. I would later tell my daughter the same thing, though I elaborated with a, You're an apple high up in the tree that the ordinary boys can't reach, so be patient until the right boy with a ladder comes along. Great, genius me consoling Keyton with a tale identifying her as a hard-to-acquire fruit only able to be plucked by a ladder-laden boy. Totally normal.

Naturally, I told myself a much different story: it wasn't the boys; it was me. My hair was too curly, my nose was too big, my butt was too round, I wore glasses, I was too short, I was too quiet. Also ugly. I was definitely too ugly.

And naturally, I coped like any other 80s kid would: I stayed alone in my room all-of-the-time. I wore black. I peroxided my brunette bangs and outlined my eyes with black pencil. I pierced my ear. I read Stephen King and played my cassettes at full blast, blaring The Cure and U2 and Duran Duran until my dad banged on my door. And I wrote sad, quasi-suicidal poems. Naturally.

When I was 16, thanks to the alphabetical world of homeroom, a boy whose last name also began with T sold me on applying for a job where he worked. He wasn't handsome or athletic, but he was funny and not gross, so I applied, and we worked together a couple afternoons a week. Working at Wendy's was a nice minimum wage distraction from my boyfriendless-ness. Within weeks I picked up a few hours every Saturday and Sunday, and that's where I met Ken one weekend. Maybe he was on the grill station and I was on fries, or maybe he was the cashier while I scrubbed the tables in the dining room – we didn't really have a so-called romantic meet-cute, our eyes meeting as I refilled the ranch dressing at the salad bar and he served a customer a large Frosty, especially since we were dressed identically, like we were in a cult: black pants, black shoes, striped Wendy's-issued shirt and navy blue Wendy's-issued visor. But I noticed the tall guy with the blue eyes and quick smile, and I guessed he noticed something about me.

If I wouldn't have started working at Wendy's, none of this would have happened. So goes my thinking.

I'd have to admit I'd never describe Ken as the most patient nor even the kindest man I'd ever known. But he's very smart, ambitious, funny, and yes, relentless. He could be as controlling as I could be emotional; he could be as unempathetic as I could be compassionate. For certain, what we had in common I probably could count on one hand, of which Derek and Keyton were two right off the bat. Maybe it's that we're both first-borns, or maybe it's the magnet effect of my being a Taurus and his being a Scorpio, our dark opposite stars aligned, or maybe it's something else. Still, we're very compatible. While he might decide where the ship was going and then was confident in steering it, at the end of the day, I knew all our passwords. He always said that Derek got the best qualities of our temperaments: slow to anger, like me, and quick to get over it, like Ken. Our daughter, however, was quick to anger and held a grudge. (Apologies to Keyton.)

Without a doubt, Ken took care of me. And this was far beyond the household and such. *He took care of me.* He was the one who made the terrible choices and decisions about Derek in the hospital and all the other places afterward when I couldn't bring myself close enough to the table to see what they even were. Everything, every day that week, was overwhelming, and Ken took care of everything. *He told me not to look when they changed Derek's bandage, and what did I do barely hours later but bitch and moan to myself about, How could he sleep at a time like this?* Stunned to think that I could possibly feel anything but love for this man, this husband of mine.

When we met, Ken was 19 and a sophomore at Shippensburg University, a small state school less than 40 minutes from our hometown of Mechanicsburg, studying toward a degree in physics. His parents had paid for his first semester's tuition, but after that he was on his own. Since no one in his family had ever gone to college – Ken was the first – no one had thought to save for college. He lived on campus during the week and went home to work at Wendy's on weekends (and over summer and winter breaks) to pay for school. Since I worked only after school during the week, our paths never crossed. But in December 1985, thanks to the timing of his winter break and mine, we worked together two weekends in a row. And that's all it took for him to make his move: He scrawled his phone number on a scrap of brown paper towel and told me to call him, teasing me relentlessly the entire shift. I still have that ripped piece of paper towel. Naturally.

Ken wound up calling me, and we went to see the non-award-winning classic *Spies Like Us* two days before Christmas. When he picked me up, he handed me a small gift wrapped in holiday paper. Wow – I didn't expect this, a gift from a boy. It was a cassette tape, Howard Jones. Yes, I still have that, too, but no machine anymore to play it on.

Who knew what either of us wore that night, but when Ken picked me up, he rang the doorbell. He also opened the car door

for me, a courtesy he performed for years, a habit that only ended
when he carried the baby from the house to the car and who needed
to be strapped into the car seat right behind the driver. I felt
nervous the entire time, yet I dreaded our first date to end. It almost
didn't: He drove me home and we talked for hours, parked in his
car along the curb in front of my house. I had no idea what time it
was (his 1981 Chevy Chevette was clockless, and I hadn't thought
to wear my Swatch watch that evening), so when the porch lights
flashed off and on I thought my parents were being ridiculous.
Turned out it was 1:30 in the morning. Later they told me they
didn't know what to do because they never gave me a curfew since
I'd never been out on a date before. My first date became an oft-
told tale at the next few family gatherings. I hated this, the attention,
all eyes on me as my dad exclaimed, And they were out until one-
thirty in the morning – *talking*, using his fingers as air quotes for the
punchline in a singsong voice. Relatives I barely knew smiled at me
and nodded knowingly. Kill me, I thought. Ask me about school,
the weather, the cows in the field over there, anything but this.

So, perhaps our first date didn't end, after all. We got married
three years later.

My mom took me to her doctor after it became clear that Ken
and I were serious about each other (I'm not one of those mothers
with her head in the sand, she declared), and on birth control I went.
Willingly, for sure. I didn't want to get pregnant in high school like
a few of my classmates – I saw pregnant girls in the hall now and
then like always and then *poof* they were gone, and they didn't come
back. There wasn't much support back in the 80s for girls who had
had babies and then wanted to finish high school, at least not in my
hometown. On this, you were pretty much S.O.L., shit outta luck.
I wanted to graduate and then go to college. I wanted to be a speech
pathologist and help people, either adults experiencing aphasia
because of a stroke or a car accident, or children with speech diffi-
culties, like those who couldn't say their Rs. Or even kids like me,
born with a cleft lip. That's how I knew what a speech pathologist
was in the first place.

I'd visited the Lancaster Cleft Palate Clinic twice a year until I
reached middle school, missing a whole school day to first visit the
plastic surgeon who'd done my original surgery when I was just a

few months old – people came from all over the country, even from all around the world, to see Dr. Robert Harding, and he welcomed the opportunity to follow up with all of his patients whose cleft lips and palates he'd repaired. I then visited the dentist, followed by the child psychologist, the speech pathologist, the audiologist. It was an adventure day, exiting one office and going right to the next. One of these offices had a huge mirror in it, and I wondered whether that was a two-way mirror like ones on television shows after nine o'clock at night I wasn't allowed to watch, like *Starsky & Hutch*. Was someone watching me read aloud and put puzzles together? The psychologist asked me question after question and recorded my answers. So did the speech pathologist. And then the audiologist steered me into a vault-like room with a heavy door that closed behind me. Princess Leia headphones on, I held up a finger when I heard various tones from across the speech spectrum, from the very low 150 Hertz all the way up to 8,000 Hertz, operatic soprano range. This was my favorite appointment of the day – trying to discern the mix of tones and putting my finger in the air felt like a test, and I liked tests. I wanted to do well.

The reasons for these appointments I was too young to really understand, but I never thought to ask my parents why I was there. Besides, asking *why* my parents were making me do something wasn't exactly a thing that was done, at least not by me. I saw other children in the waiting rooms, children with unusual faces, children with hearing aids, children wearing helmets, children who signed instead of spoke. At some point, though, probably when I was 12 or 13, a sudden awareness filled me: Why *am* I here? Am I different, too, like these kids? Sure, I wore glasses to see the blackboard and I'd need braces soon, but I didn't have hearing or speech or breathing or learning problems – I was even in the gifted program at school starting in third grade. After I complained to my parents about missing school and expressed embarrassment about the reason why, they finally stopped taking me to the clinic.

I was self-conscious of my cleft lip, of course, finding myself covering my mouth with my hand in class more and more as I got older. I didn't want anyone to comment on my scar, and actually no one ever did, even in the rude world of public education. Perhaps it was this habit of mouth-covering that served as an unintentional barrier for a prospective boyfriend when I reached high school. Perhaps. In tenth grade, about a year before I met Ken, I had three surgeries months apart: a bone graft where a sliver of bone was taken from my hipbone and placed into my upper jaw to close where the cleft left a fissure in my gums between my right front tooth and canine and to ready the area for a Maryland bridge, which was fitted with its matching tooth the following year; a rhinoplasty to straighten and narrow my nose; and a second cheiloplasty for further lip definition now that I was older. I don't remember telling any of the JKLMs about missing school for these surgeries, but maybe I did, or maybe my mom told their moms. Or maybe my friends just assumed I was sick, or maybe they didn't know that I was dismissed from class ten minutes early for a couple of weeks so I had extra time to slowly limp to my next class after the bone graft, or maybe they thought I was being extra new wave when I wore sunglasses to class for a few days to conceal my multicolored bruised undereyes after my nose job. Maybe. Why *did* I not remember telling my friends? Keeping these surgeries secret only reinforced my feelings of being different, and it was no wonder. My first surgery to repair my cleft was when I was not even three months old, and not only did my parents not take pictures of me until after I had my cleft repaired, but also my paternal grandparents offered valium to my dad to help him cope after he told them what to expect when they saw me for the first time after I was born. No wonder I felt different.

Long before high school ended, the JKLMs broke up with their boyfriends and were single for graduation, all of them, that is, except for me: Ken and I went to my junior prom and then to my senior prom. He came to football games to watch me play clarinet in the marching band, and then sat next to me in the stands. We went to plays and basketball games. He joked that he attended more school events of mine than he ever did at his own high school. He helped me with my trig homework. I proofread his college papers. And I graduated high school and went off to college at Bloomsburg University, another Pennsylvania state school. Ken finished his three years at Shippensburg, earned his physics degree, and then transferred to Penn State to complete his five-year program and receive a degree in chemical engineering from there.

Our schools were two hours away from each other. We didn't see each other much. In *Friends*-speak, we were on a break.

But we wrote letters. Lots of letters I still have. And planned weekly phone calls using a calling card – remember those? Reading off like 40 numbers to an actual operator for a long-distance call, but only after 5:00 pm, even better after 9:00 pm when rates were the cheapest, since we were billed per minute. We reconnected the day I got home for the summer after my freshman year. I'd learned on the car ride home that my parents had been separated for several months and were living apart, and I didn't know what to do. Why had this terrible news been kept secret from me? My sister was sullen and locked in her room, and Mom wasn't talking, so I called Ken. Yeah, it happened just like that. And like our first date, we talked for hours. And we saw each other the next day, and the next. He was home for about a week until he returned to Penn State for the rest of the summer where he'd continue working at Wendy's full-time for minimum wage until classes started back up. Penn State was a lot more expensive than Shippensburg, so he had to save as much as possible by the time the tuition bill was due.

I missed him.

One weekend in July, I asked to borrow the car and sleep over at a friend's house. Instead, I drove up to Penn State. I'd never lied to my mom like that before.

I wasn't on birth control anymore.

Well, I guess we'd better get married, Ken said when I told him a couple of weeks later. Looking back, there wasn't any pressure to conform or force our marriage into being. Nor my pregnancy. We were in love, and we were inseparable. My parents were back together again, reconciled after my mom forgave my dad for some stupid things that he did. Ever practical, they planned our wedding to be over our Thanksgiving break so Ken and I wouldn't have to miss school. In between morning sickness, going to classes, and studying, I sat at my desk in my dorm room and painstakingly sewed more than 140 pink satin roses by hand that would be filled with birdseed to be tossed our way for luck after the ceremony. Almost every Friday, my maternal grandparents drove two hours from their home to Bloomsburg, picked me up and drove me two hours to Penn State, and then drove two hours home. And then on Sunday, they did the reverse. My unbelievably devoted grandparents hated to see us apart, and my grandfather loved to drive, proving the adage repeated by my dad: They broke the mold when they made your grandparents.

Another practical move by my parents was inviting Ken's parents over to get to know them and to ask for a wedding guest list for their side. Like the oft-told story of our first date, this encounter was also told and retold: Her ass wasn't even in the chair yet and she declared, Well, we can't help, my mother scoffed with a shake of her head.

Yikes. When my mom, who rarely, if ever, said a bad word about anyone, spoke like this, you knew things were serious.

Our wedding was small and lovely, the chilly November air outside a vague mist. *Here Comes the Bride* was far too secular for my Lutheran minister, so *Trumpets Voluntary* was our chosen opening music, and as the first few bars played, my dad cried, which, of course, made me cry. Though there was no open bar, as I was underage (and pregnant!), the reception was a fun party: My new college friends helped me celebrate, and I was elated that the four JKLMs were back together. Good marital fortune also gave relief to some financial pressure: our wedding gifts totaled enough in cash and checks to pay the balance of Ken's Penn State tuition bill. Thank goodness we got married, right?

I withdrew from school at the end of the semester because I was due in April, just before my 20th birthday. It wasn't easy to walk into the registrar's office and ask for the form to withdraw from school. Filling it out was my decision, choice, whatever, *at least I had a choice*, but I wound up harboring deep resentment for years toward Ken. In my eyes, his life was staying on course: school, graduation, job, life. Mine, however, was not. I had goals, plans, and now, after being careful to not get pregnant in high school, here I was, dropping out of college. Not to mention I was the only one I knew to get married and be pregnant. Again, I'm the different one, the alone one, the other. I know now how immature and selfish I was to think like this, but then, I *was* immature, selfish, and a self-labeled victim, and it was all Ken's fault. Naturally.

After winter break, I lived with Ken in his apartment at Penn State for a month or two, passing the time reading and watching too much television, including every minute of coverage of the terrorist bombing of Pan Am 103 over Lockerbie, Scotland. Ken went to class, did homework, and worked at Wendy's. And he drove me the 100 miles home for my monthly obstetric appointments. At one appointment, I asked my doctor about the likelihood of my cleft being passed down to my baby. Though it's very common, it's not necessarily hereditary, she assured me. My mom said she thought it happened to me because she got dental x-rays before she knew she was pregnant. Maybe. Other environmental factors might have been to blame – you could smoke in grocery stores back then, cars used leaded gasoline, who knows. Fortunately, neither of my children inherited my cleft. I was more relieved than I could say. I never wanted my children to feel how I felt, believing they were different because of how they looked and covering their mouths with their hands.

Around February I stayed home to be closer to my doctor and avoid traveling hours by car. Since Ken was away at school, my dad took me to birthing classes. It was weird at the same time that it wasn't, and it's interesting that my mom didn't take me, though I could easily assume either she was reluctant to drive to the classes at the busy hospital across the river in Harrisburg at night, or, sadly and more likely, having a man with me would keep up appearances among strangers. Some pregnant people were there alone, some had their mothers with them instead of partners. Without a doubt, I was the youngest one there.

My April 2 due date came and went, and at my next OB appointment I was scheduled for an induction, a Pitocin drip to induce labor on Monday April 17. As she handed me the small reminder card, the receptionist joked, Still holding on to that baby? Yep, you got me: I'm 19 and this is the culmination of years of research on how to be the most embarrassed and uncomfortable: Get pregnant, have to live with my parents, go past the due date, secure an appointment for induced labor, in hopes of a comment like this one. Mission accomplished.

The first early pains gripped my attention on Thursday. I was alone in the house, in bed, reading. Pain after wringing pain. I stopped reading and tried to breathe like I was taught in class. Easier said. I found paper and pen so I could write down the time and keep track of the intervals of one contraction to the next. Guess what? I told my mom hours later the moment she got home from work, and she told me to call Ken right away. I told her I already did, and that he was on his way. I was nervous, afraid, and unsure what to do as I waited for him to arrive. This was finally happening!

Derek Thomson Sheely was born at 2:23 in the morning on Friday April 14, 1989, 12 days late, comfortable in his warm cocoon, just getting plumper with each passing day. He emerged an eight-pound 12-ounce beauty who promptly pooped on the receiving doctor. Would you believe that 812 was also our room number in the maternity wing at the hospital? Numbers became one of my many-focused-upon areas of minutiae. I didn't believe in signs, but numbers seemed different.

Ken and I knew nothing about babies. We had no idea how to change a diaper, and I had no clue how to breastfeed. As we buckled Derek into his car seat for the first time, we looked at each other, shrugged, and glanced back at the nurse smoking and watching from the curb give us a quick thumbs-up. We were young, terrified, and had no idea what we were doing. And the day after I came home from the hospital, Ken had to leave me and go back to school. He had almost a month left of classes and finals until he graduated. The day after he left, I mailed him one of Derek's tiny socks and a Polaroid of the two of us.

All day I was alone in my parents' house: Mom and Dad both at work and my sister a senior in high school. I had no idea what to do, about anything, really, and I was afraid all the time that I was screwing up. Was my baby sleeping too much or not enough? Was I holding him too much or not enough? Breastfeeding worked, until it didn't. Derek was constantly hungry, and it seemed like I just couldn't keep up, so one evening after making the switch to formula, my mom suggested rice cereal in a bottle, thick like a milkshake, for his last nighttime feeding. So we stabbed the rubber nipple to make a larger opening, added a little cereal, and shook the concoction together. Derek slept all night long, and finally so did I.

Ken graduated on a sunny day in May, and we drove up to Penn State with his parents and sister, his grandparents following along in their car. The photos from that day are from another lifetime. Ken's dark blue gown had sharp creases on it from being folded in its plastic packaging. You should've ironed it for him, his mother said to me. He told me later that this was the second time his parents visited him at Penn State; the first time was when they helped move him in to his apartment two years ago (although, to be fair, his dad did drive up to help him one time when Ken's car broke down). I took lots of pictures of the ceremony and hoped they turned out well; considering how poorly lit Rec Hall was, once they were developed, all the photos from that day looked faded and sepia-colored, Ken barely visible among so many other graduates of the College of Engineering. It was a long day, and I was exhausted when we got home. My parents met us at the front door, so excited to tell us that Derek smiled today and not to worry: they took pictures. I cried when I raced upstairs to check on him. I'd never been away from Derek before, and I missed his first smile.

Later that summer we moved to Frederick, Maryland. Not as abrupt as it sounds: Ken had been since graduation awaiting his security clearance to be finalized, as he'd accepted a job with the US Department of Energy back in February. We wanted to be on our own finally, so after we found an apartment that offered first-month's-rent-free, we decided to move before his clearance was completed. We still had no idea what we were doing, and to move 90 miles away from all of our friends and family was very scary. We had one car, one baby, COBRA health insurance, and thousands owed in student loans that would come due before the end of the year. It was difficult: after five years of college and two degrees, Ken made less than $25,000 a year as a federal employee. So it was generic everything at the grocery store, no eating out in restaurants, and zero vacations. But what was the alternative? Daycare all day every day for our baby just so I could work for minimum wage since I had no degree and basically only Wendy's as work experience? No thanks: I wasn't going to work at a job that paid just enough for daycare. If that. There was no question that I would stay at home with Derek.

But, it was hard for me to be alone all day in the apartment with just little baby Derek to talk to. Besides the long workdays during a regular week for Ken, not to mention his two-hour round-trip commute in nightmare traffic every day from Frederick to his office in Germantown, he also traveled a lot. Those first years of his career took him for weeks at a time to Vienna, Tokyo, Sydney, Rio de Janeiro, Moscow, and Buenos Aires. Plus days of domestic travel to California, New Mexico, Tennessee, Texas, and Washington. Incredible, to see that much so quickly, especially for a guy who didn't even see the ocean until he was 19. With 16-year-old me. So, for hours and hours each day, until his sister was born four years later, it was just Derek and me. During naptime, since we had no interwebs and certainly no smart phone, I taught myself to crochet, I read whatever I could find, I watched a lot of movies, and I even got into watching a couple of soaps. And it was a lovely reprieve that my parents and grandparents visited as often as they did. They took us out to dinner, and they even brought us groceries. But for the most part it was just the two of us. The pages of *Little Golden Books* I read to him, the miles we walked as I pushed his stroller, the oodles of games we played. I was 19 when Derek was born: We grew up together.

♥ ♥ ♥

We were alone in a small office across from Derek's room and down the hall. I don't remember exactly why we were there, maybe to sign the necessary consent form for his pending surgery that afternoon, but that's where we were when we felt it. At 1:51 pm an earthquake 5.8 in magnitude struck near Richmond, Virginia, about 140 miles away from Baltimore. It shook over a dozen states and a few provinces up in Canada – so many populous areas in the eastern US were rattled at that moment that this earthquake was felt by more people than any other quake in US history. Our earth must have been as outraged and afraid as we were over what was happening to Derek that it started shaking in violent protest.

I, too, was shaking, but not from the aftershocks that might possibly come. Who worried about an earthquake when larger fears lurked close by? When there's nothing a parent could do but watch and wait. What were we thinking, opting for another surgery? Hoping for a miracle, surely. Hoping for our prayers to be answered. Hoping for him to wake up, for this nightmare to end, for us to go back to normal. I wished Derek and I could've had one more conversation in a long string of conversations. But then *one more* would never be enough, would it? And I thought to myself, one more what? Conversation? Moment? Chance? To stop him from going back to school? To stop him from stepping onto that field? No, a moment was nothing. I wanted everything. I wanted my son to be okay. I just wanted my son to be okay.

♥ ♥ ♥

We lived in Albuquerque, New Mexico for three months in the summer of 1991. Derek had just turned two, and off we went on his first airplane ride. A temporary assignment, Ken was slated to work at DOE's Albuquerque Operations Office on Kirkland Air Force Base and for the occasional meeting might have to make the two-hour drive up the narrow mountain road to Los Alamos, birthplace of the atomic bomb.

We landed late, after nine, and had to drive to the pre-arranged apartment building in the dark. We were starving after our long flight, so after checking the phone book for ideas, Ken ran out to find food. He had no idea where he was, so he went a couple of blocks on unfamiliar streets to what appeared to be the closest convenience store, for pretzels and sharp cheese for snacking, and bagels and orange juice for the morning. Without GPS or even a map, he'd ventured a bit too far, as we learned later that this store turned out to be in the so-called not-so-great part of town, close to where the tv show *Cops* was filmed at times.

I don't remember everything about those three months, or in what order things happened. But the very first morning, I looked out our apartment window and was stunned by the unreal blue color of the sky and the otherworldly mountains that looked close enough to touch. Derek and I were together as usual all day while Ken was at work. We played with his cars, or swam in the huge pool that was almost always empty of other people, or went on long walks around the block. The apartment was a roomy two-bedroom corporate one, furnished with everything we needed, plus a weekly cleaning service. Pilar taught Derek some Spanish words, and his small yet confident voice pronounced *una mesa* as he pointed to a table and nodded seriously. *Muy bueno*, Pilar exclaimed. These lessons quelled somewhat my feelings of awkwardness as I sat with him on my lap and watched her clean. Cleaning was her job, yet I couldn't help but feel weird about just sitting there on the sofa. On the weekends when Ken was home we explored the area, shopping in Old Town Albuquerque, driving north along the Turquoise Trail, and especially navigating the twisty road up nearby Sandia Peak and hiking the many trails. The glittering view of the city and beyond was spectacular, parallel lines of neighborhoods inside a perfect grid of intersecting boulevards and wide avenues, surrounded by miles of literally nothing but blue sky. Derek turned into a mountain goat that summer, hopping around on rocks, exploring, noticing everything. We even crossed into Colorado one weekend and visited the Cumbres and Toltec Scenic Railroad, and all Derek wanted to do was sit on the grass and watch the engine move slowly along the track, a trip to nowhere. One day we were out sightseeing, somewhere south of Albuquerque, and Ken captured the photo of Derek and me amongst the wildflowers that sits on my desk. The photo of the two of us, my arms wrapped around him, that I look at every day.

One evening early on, we discovered a nearby New Mexican restaurant that delivered fresh sopapillas and honey to your table until you asked them to stop. Though always on a budget, we went there often, loading up on the fried dough and honey, as we waited for our orders of blue corn seafood enchiladas and crispy tacos for Derek. One night, a woman approached our table. Derek was content in the wooden highchair, coloring his kiddie placemat, as he always did when we came here. The woman told us that she dines out several times a week, and she just had to come over and tell us that she's never seen such a well-behaved child. I'm sure our faces turned red. We didn't know what to say, so we probably looked at each other and back at her and said, Wow, thank you. (And Derek being Derek, he probably said, Thank you.) Looking back, while I truly appreciated her taking the time to pay the compliment, it actually was a rare instance that Derek screamed or cried or fussed as a small toddler because something didn't go his way. One time a sandwich was cut diagonally instead of straight across; another time his balloon floated away. He was so easy he spoiled us, and I'm sure we took his easygoingness for granted.

My parents visited us for a week in June, and I remember that we pulled off the road on the way to Bandelier National Park to try and view the eclipse that seemingly everyone was talking about that summer. We weren't prepared for the occasion, and everyone (or almost everyone) knew not to look directly at an eclipse, so my dad had an idea based on a trick for safe eclipse viewing he recently saw on television. He successfully converted a Dunkin Donuts box into an eclipse viewer, as that was the only suitable thing we had in the rental car. Each of us took turns peeking into the sugar-stained box, and then one by one we got back into the car. The eclipse viewing was noddingly quick, like a harried Clark Griswold at the Grand Canyon.

My grandparents were next. They drove out for a week in July.

And then Ken's parents in August. By then, Sandia Peak was covered in a thin layer of snow, and when we drove up the road and reached the top to show Ken's parents the view, Derek jumped from his car seat and immediately scooped snow into a snowball.

Returning to our small apartment in Maryland that September was like Dorothy leaving Oz. Despite our short time out in the desert, I missed it. I missed the space, the sky, the air, the color, the light. I missed everything Georgia O'Keefe attempted to capture on canvas after brilliant canvas. Fortunately, Ken's job required fairly frequent trips back to New Mexico, and the next summer, our parents agreed to take turns babysitting Derek so that I could go back out with Ken. I knew I'd be alone and without a car most of the days while Ken was in meetings, so I brought a heavy library copy of *Roots* with me. With the Manzano mountains a beautiful backdrop, I read Kunta Kinte's story every day at a scuffed picnic table in the park near our hotel. I read so much back then. For years I even kept a careful record of books read, annotated and dated. And then I just stopped reading.

Keyton was only three months old the next time we flew to the Southwest. The four of us went to Phoenix first and then on to Albuquerque: Two business trips in one. Phoenix in July meant the tiles on the way to the pool were too hot to walk on, even on tiptoe, especially for Derek, who seemed to almost always leave his sandals back in the room while I had my hands full with baby Keyton. So instead we walked around the cooler grass-covered grounds, and he was amazed to see limes and lemons growing right on the trees. Four-year-old Derek was amazed with just about everything he saw.

Our next close interaction with Albuquerque was watching the early seasons of *Breaking Bad* together. Derek's colorful commentary animated the show even at its darkest moments (Ugh, too much Skyler, I recalled him saying with a comical eye roll).

Could I remember everything? Should I? Should I grasp every slant of light that comes?

I remembered reading to Derek. He wanted the same books read to him over and over again, books like *The Caboose Who Got Loose* and *Goodnight Moon* and *The Lorax* and *One Fish Two Fish Red Fish Blue Fish* – correcting me if I ever tried to cut the story short by skipping a sentence when I was tired. It wasn't long before he tried to read the stories himself, reading them like I did, with the exact same inflections, as we snuggled close in a bed in Albuquerque when he was two. We'd borrowed my dad's camcorder for that special summer, and we videoed some of our adventures. Now stored in plastic bins in the attic space at the top of the stairs, those fragile videos might still be playable, and I wondered whether our old video player still worked.

I remembered showing Derek interesting things in nature like my dad had shown me. Three different leaves on a sassafras tree, a twig broken off and chewed, its green tasting like root beer, sort of. Knowing that a poisonous snake has a triangular head. Identifying mint, a narcissus, a fossil. Laying a wide blade of grass along your thumb, pressing your thumbs together, and blowing through them to whistle, or trying to. Pulling apart a honeysuckle blossom to find the drop of sweet.

I remembered carrying Derek. Sometimes he grew so heavy I thought I'd have to put him down, so heavy I couldn't hold him one second longer, so heavy and warm with sleep he was, I would bend down and down as slowly as I could until I lay back on the couch, still holding him, trying to keep him in that perfect angle of sleep so he wouldn't wake from the nap he needed. Once I confessed to an ER nurse that my back hurt because I carried my son too much. She said, No, your back hurts because you have a kidney infection, dear. That's why you have such a high fever and why you need to drink more water.

And, of course, I remembered being angry, lonely, resentful. Angry my friends were still in college, on track as planned, lonely because I was with a toddler all day, and resentful, so resentful, of Ken. I was confined to our small apartment, I wasn't on track at all, so far from the inside lane I couldn't even see it whatsoever, blah, blah, blah. Poor me. And something small would set me off, like one time Ken and I argued about something now long forgotten and I stormed up the stairs to our bedroom, and I slammed and locked the door, just like I did when I was a child after being told something like, Don't talk back to me. I thought, I'll show Ken: I wasn't going to speak to him and I wouldn't open the door. My husband broke it down. Or one time I lost it at the end of a long week when Ken was out of the country on travel somewhere and I yelled and smacked my son's butt when he peed his pants. Derek was little, still learning, still having occasional accidents. Such immediate intense regret as I cried and apologized and hung my head in shame, and there he was, not even three feet tall, patting my shoulder and saying, It's okay, Mommy.

♥ ♥ ♥

Maybe it was the earthquake, or maybe it was something else entirely, but again, we were left waiting.

Derek's second craniotomy started much later than we anticipated, and by the time Doctor finally updated us that the surgery was complete and had gone as expected, a taxi had delivered my parents from the airport. Derek's girlfriend and her mother were there, too, and we all sat together in the small waiting area. The room stayed silent when Doctor finished speaking. Now all we could do was wait and see over the next who-knows-how-many hours whether his cranial pressure improved. More waiting. I kept scratching the back of my left hand with the nails of my right, a dreadful habit I'd first leaned on back when I was in college and under stress or pressure or plain anxiety. My skin was ripped and raw, starting to swell and grow numb. Blood might appear soon. But this was a wound I was comfortable with.

Waiting, praying, bargaining, begging, more waiting; what was next? What was left?

VERY DARK PLACES

♥ ♥ ♥

Before Derek started kindergarten, he had flashcards of dinosaurs and we played a matching game with them. But not only that, he learned the facts on each card and would spout these facts to anyone who cared to listen. Maiasaura means good mother, he proclaimed. She's a vegetarian. No, not Brontosaurus; it's called Apatosaurus now, the budding paleontologist insisted before moving on to another of the 40 or so cards left. He also had many tiny racecars and would position them in a long line and move just the one at the front about a foot, and then move all the other ones in the line forward. In this way he'd creep all around the living room, vroom-vroom-ing under his breath the entire time. Sometimes he wanted my help to relocate all the cars, and sometimes he didn't; on those days he wanted to drive alone, I guessed. After the dinosaur and race car phase came the fire truck phase, and we had trucks with sirens and lights in every corner and under every table. We never had enough batteries! This phase especially thrilled Ken's dad, a lifelong volunteer firefighter. For sure, when Derek was interested in something, he went all in.

And football was certainly no different. When he watched the games on television, Derek was completely absorbed in the Xs and Os, and his two favorite teams were the Penn State Nittany Lions and the San Francisco 49ers. So when he brought a flier home from school in third grade for football signups, we signed him up. He was so excited! We lived in York, Pennsylvania at the time, and our township didn't have its own team, so we were welcomed to the team in downtown York, Boys Club of York. Practice for the Boys Club Red Raiders was five nights a week, plus Saturday mornings, and games were on Sundays. The coach was about my height (barely five-two), and maybe only a year or two older than I, but he intimidated me. His demeanor was quiet and commanding, and he did not smile, not ever. He didn't yell, but as I found out, discipline on that team was incredible, which it had to be when it seemed like close to 100 third graders had to be herded and sorted and tasked with a common goal. If you sat on your helmet, take a lap. If you had to go to the bathroom during practice, take a lap. And so on.

Derek loved it.

His practice pants were too big, and there was no belt, so I taped him together with packing tape. I pressed the tape on his waist and he'd spin in a circle a few times until his pants clung to his shirt. The first week of practice he wore the same Steve Young jersey every night so that the coaches would begin to recognize him. Turned out we really didn't have to do that. There were only a handful of white kids on the team and only one with dark curly hair. Derek was memorable without wearing the same shirt every day. When he finally got a *Way to go, Steve Young!* for catching a pass, he continued to wear his Steve Young jersey to every practice, declaring it brought him luck.

Peewee practice was 3:30 until 5:30. Practice rarely ended at 5:30. I arrived on time, knowing practice wouldn't end on time, and did homework while four-year-old Keyton climbed into the very back of the 4Runner and read picture books. I was back in school at York College of Pennsylvania, earning a degree in English, while Ken still worked in Washington, DC.

Four years earlier, in December 1993, eight months after Keyton was born, Ken's dad died suddenly – a Monday morning heart attack at age 50 – and we felt we should move closer to home, so we sold our townhome in Frederick the following year and built a house in York, a city less than 40 miles from our parents. Ken started looking for a new job, as his stress and misery at work had been building, and he'd been thinking of leaving the government anyway. Unfortunately, and needless to say, he couldn't find a job in the York area in nuclear non-proliferation, his area of expertise. The situation was complicated by his being promoted soon after we moved to head a multi-hundreds-of-millions-of-dollars program to secure nuclear materials after the breakup of the Soviet Union. Change of plans: He dug in to his new role at work and suffered an insane commute: five hours round trip from York to DC. Every day. I was virtually a single mom, albeit with consistent financial support. I was able to go back to school and complete my degree, and we were close to family, just a quick drive a few miles away, but our own family life was far from ideal. The four of us rarely ate meals together during the week, Ken was exhausted and often short-tempered, and the weekends went by way too quickly. For nearly six years we argued about the same thing, then we made up, we argued more, then we made up. It's impossible to describe the heartache he suffered whenever he thought about all the time he missed with the kids that he could never get back. When we finally wised up, in early 2000, deciding that our family of four was more important than anything, we found a brand-new development in Germantown in Montgomery County, Maryland, when Derek was ready to start middle school and Keyton was beginning second grade. We built our dream house.

But back to peewee football.

Invariably, as the days grew shorter, parents turned on their headlights and lit the field, inadvertently extending practice at least another 20 minutes. For eight-year-olds! Derek loved it so much that sometimes after his two-hour-plus practices, he'd set up plastic chairs in our backyard to simulate the Xs and Os and practice running plays around and through the obstacles until it was too dark to see. These never-ending practices would be comical if they weren't so outrageous, but there was method to Coach's madness, for at the end of the season, we advanced to the championship game versus South York, and we overheard other parents in the stands refer to the game as *The Ghetto Bowl*. That term makes me wince now, and I hope we didn't call it that ourselves; I don't remember, and I don't want to give it the *oh, it was 1997* excuse. Boys Club won, and it was wonderful to see Derek and his teammates so happy to be on a winning team. We ordered the red and black championship jacket for him and he wore it everywhere.

The following year, as a fourth grader, Derek signed up again with Boys Club, this time in the next division up, as a rink – peewee was for the little guys, he said. And he also signed up for Cub Scouts. And soccer. Keyton was just starting kindergarten. I had graduated college and now worked part-time at my alma mater as a writing consultant, tutoring students in York College's Student Writing Center. Ken unfortunately still wasn't around during the work week to split weekday chauffeur, let alone parenting, duties, so they were all up to me. And since I was still intimidated by the football coach, I made Derek tell him every time he had to leave practice early (not early, on time!) to go to scouts or soccer. I certainly didn't want to have to run a lap! Derek cheerfully did what I asked; he had someplace he had to go and didn't mind telling his coach. But it was a challenge for him to change from his practice uniform, packing tape and all, into his neat khakis and scout uniform in the back seat of the 4Runner with his little sister watching and giggling. As hard as we tried, we were always late for scouts.

♥ ♥ ♥

I'd never thought of myself as fearful or as a chronic worrier, at least not about anything outside myself, nor a doom-and-gloom kind of prognosticator, nor a cock-eyed optimist. Too extreme, truth be told, to describe myself in that way. Perhaps I was one who constantly adapted as each moment unfolded, or maybe I lived each day in a constant state of blind naivete – either way, I'd always envisioned life like I was in the ocean and holding onto a life raft, and the waves were steadily coming, coming, coming; they never stopped, and all I knew how to do was just keep hold of my raft and ride those waves that lifted me up in a gentle way under the sun some days, and other days the sky darkened as waves changed and forced me down, plummeting down hard and fast into the sand no matter how hard I kicked until I nearly drowned.

Countless days of bobbing on the peaceful water in the sun and countless days of sinking underwater into darkness made up life. I was lifted up on the crest of a wave when I got married, had Derek, had Keyton, graduated college, adopted a dog, and I bottomed-out and crashed into the sand when Ken and I argued, my mom got breast cancer, my dad got prostate cancer, my childhood dog died, Ken's dad died, my grandma died. It's troubling to describe everything that happened to me when we got the phone call about Derek. I let go of my life raft and sank immediately. To be trapped underwater and without oxygen, and then adrift and lost.

And in a room like this, a small windowless room on a high floor in Shock Trauma, there was nothing else to do but think. Thinking about time, its meaninglessness. A moment ago, a day just like yesterday, Derek waved me in for that sleepy hug before he left for college. I told him to be safe and have fun. I pictured him like that so clearly it brought tears to my eyes. And just nine days later a phone call changed everything. I dug at the skin on the back of my hand and for however long forgot to breathe. Tears fell and I tried to find my footing, but my raft kept drifting out of reach. Why try anymore?

Let me sink.

♥ ♥ ♥

Derek was finally moved from recovery back to his room on the corner, and once we're permitted to go see him, Ken, Keyton, and I made the long walk together to his room on the end.

And I go back to that room a lot, because I can see him there so clearly, even with the machines and the horror and the fear. I go back to pick up fragments of myself I left behind. And I go there for him, and I find a seat and I sit with him. I lower my head and I lift his hand and place it on the back of my neck. Its weight, its warmth, anchor me, and with my head down like that, no one can see me cry.

Why did this happen to him? Of all the kids on the field, why him? Keyton whispered as she started to cry.

I couldn't pretend this didn't happen. Like what I tried to do when I covered my mouth with my hand, like my scar wasn't there. Object permanence. Pretending I was normal, pretending I looked like everyone else. Could I pretend again? Even now, with his hand solid on the back of my neck, could I pretend that none of this happened?

I am silent and screaming.

The respirator clicked and the machine that measured Derek's intracranial pressure beeped, its numbers glowing green, blue, red. I wished for something I'd heard about once – maybe it wasn't real at all, but who knows – electronic voice phenomenon, or speaking through the interference – the beeping machines, the clicks, all of it taken together – could it be code? Or music? *Or messages?* I shut my eyes and tried to listen, to concentrate, willing to hear something, anything. The curtain wafted side to side as a nurse brushed by him. The IV, the bandage, his closed eyes as he stood there were too much to look at in one pass, but I studied him anyway. His face looked scruffy with the beginning of a beard, and I remembered he hated to shave before football practice. He'd tell me that his face would burn with sweat inside his helmet, so he'd always wait until the weekend to shave his face. His hair was recently cut, freshly shorn short around his ears, so I assumed the friend who drove him up to Penn State one day last year likely gave him a quick trim a couple of days ago. Before the phone call.

♥ ♥ ♥

It was late April, perfect for tulips, but we were bundled against the chill. Ken and I huddled together under a blanket in the stands, turning away from the wind. Keyton was with us, along with my parents. My mother, in particular, was freezing. It wasn't actually freezing, but when it's April, your body adjusted its expectations for what spring weather was supposed to feel like.

That day happened to be my birthday, and we were up at Penn State for its annual Blue-White game, the kickoff scrimmage for the upcoming football season. It's free, fun, and something we tried to attend every year. We wanted Derek to try and come, maybe with a friend who had a car, but he lamented when we asked him about it a couple of days ago; he said he probably couldn't because all his friends were going home for the weekend or something.

We sat in the end zone, pretty high up so that the upper level jutted out over us to shelter us from the wind and the possible rain in the forecast. I usually didn't fret about the weather, and typically didn't mind the cold, but today felt absolutely frigid. My gloves were in the pockets of my winter coat, which was closeted away, since it's April after all. My fingers were numb, and I was ready for this scrimmage to be over before it even started. Ken kept reaching for his blackberry so much it was distracting; maybe he was reading work emails, or perhaps it was the draft weekend or something.

That thing was always in his hand, I thought.

That's what she said, Derek would say.

Before I knew it, Derek sat down next to me. Surprise – Happy Birthday! I think I heard as he hugged me.

My breath caught, tears filled my eyes, and I remembered nothing else having to do with the game.

VERY DARK PLACES

♥ ♥ ♥

Derek's hand heavy on the back of my neck, I closed my eyes and pictured future him: He'd leaned out, tall and strong, and he ran his fingers under his chin as he read through the news on his phone. His hair was very short, his blond curls he had as a little boy clipped and smooth, his hair now darker than mine. He texted his sister as he sipped coffee from a blue mug he painted for me one Mother's Day. He was so comfortable in his own skin; unlike me, he never covered his mouth.

It was hard to breathe once the tears started. This wasn't real, this couldn't be happening, I thought. My legs shook up and down, and I thought, my son liked Xbox games like *Assassin's Creed*; he liked hip-hop with the bass cranked up; he liked studying history, mainly to argue his points in an animated argument, like a good trial attorney would; he liked football and tattoos and lifting weights and eating good food and having fun. I wanted to remember everything he liked, like watching *The Daily Show* and *Justified* and *Archer* and *The Simpsons* and *The Office* and *Breaking Bad*. Movies like *District 9* and *The Town* and *Shaun of the Dead* and *The Shawshank Redemption* and *Good Fellas*.

I shouldn't be here, in this place, compiling a list of Derek's favorite things in my head, his hand heavy on my neck only because I put it there.

Derek? I whispered. He's within an arm's length of me, but I couldn't reach him. I whispered, Can you hear me? *Did he know we're right here? That we're doing everything we could to save him? That we would change places with him if we could?*

I had to believe he knew all of it.

But I cried anyway, wondering, as we left that night in a minivan driven by a volunteer for the Ronald McDonald House. Somehow two rooms were found for us and my parents. There was even a narrow cot in our room for Keyton. My first shower in two days, I was reluctant to wash Derek off me. I could smell him, or I thought I could. By the time I exchanged my contacts for glasses and put on clean clothes, I couldn't look at the bed.

I didn't deserve to rest.

wednesday

Once upon a time, there lived a little girl with blue eyes and curly hair. She lived with her mother and father and her little sister in a one-story brick house with a carport and a big back yard. She liked to read books and play outside with her black and white dog, and she thought she would never get married or have a family. Her name was Kristen.

But then the little girl grew up, and one day she met a tall blue-eyed young man who lived in a house on top of a hill. His name was Ken. They became inseparable.

Soon, though they were very young, they decided to get married. And almost right away, they had a baby. A beautiful blue-eyed curly-haired boy named Derek. And they loved him very much. A few years later, they had another baby. A beautiful blue-eyed blonde-haired girl named Keyton. And they loved her just as much.

Eventually, Ken and Kristen bought a house with large rooms and a green front door. They called it their dream house.

Time passed, and Derek and Keyton grew up alongside it. They both loved a cute mischievous dog named Cinnamon. They both excelled in school, had many friends, and played sports. They both learned to drive. Derek was a football captain his senior year of high school and was in the National Honor Society. He had a lovely girlfriend. Keyton played soccer, ran cross country, and was a captain on her lacrosse team. She went to her Homecoming dance junior year with six male friends who couldn't find dates.

Derek went to college. He played football.

Keyton followed him to the same university a few years later.

This is where I should write about a happily ever after. Finish the fairy tale properly. So desperate to write a story about what should have happened, I'd endeavor to leave out all the monsters and the evil and just focus on the happy ending.

I don't want to write about this.

But there's no other story to tell. Not anymore.

♥ ♥ ♥

As we walked the short blocks back to the hospital, gulls dipped and wheeled over our heads, their calls to each other startling and insistent. A catbird cried from its hidden perch up and to the left, and tears filled my eyes as I thought, I wish I could keep walking, far past the hospital, out of Baltimore, out of Maryland, could I just keep walking until I run out of land, to walk into the harbor and sink into the water. Out of this life, this unrealness. If I could keep walking, I thought, then I'd never have to face the truth that was waiting for us in my son's room on the corner. If I could keep walking, then maybe, just maybe, none of this would be happening.

There seemed to be a glimmer of light early this morning because Derek appeared to be doing a bit better. It was incredible news: His ICP had dropped since the surgery yesterday and was now steady, indicating the swelling – the intracranial pressure – surrounding his brain was gradually lessening. This was a significant improvement. Doctor told us they were readying to give him an EEG today, and probably another MRI, sometime late morning or early afternoon. Since he'd be out of his room for several hours, we decided to make a quick-as-possible trip home to Germantown for clean clothes and other essentials. We even sent Keyton back to Penn State because we understood that things were looking good. But regardless of whether Derek was improving or not, what were we thinking, sending Keyton away like we did? We weren't thinking. Not at all. We should have kept her close.

♥ ♥ ♥

They're very alike, Derek and Keyton. Similar dark, dry sense of humor. Very quick wit. Smart. Beautiful. Competitive, especially with each other. Not for parental nor academic attention, but just to keep up with each other: If one of them did something, then the other one wanted to do it too. And how they pushed each other's buttons; it drove me crazy. One summer day when Derek was in college and Keyton a junior or senior in high school, they were upstairs, and all of a sudden screaming erupted from Keyton, then laughter, then screaming, then Derek shouting, then laughter.

Thumping and more thumping. What were they doing, running in the upstairs hallway? I was reading, Cinnamon curled snug against me, and what I heard sounded completely insane, so I of course stayed seated and yelled for them to settle down. They stopped. I listened to the new silence. But within minutes they started up again: yelling, laughing, screaming, thumping. When I thought I heard hitting, I leapt out of my chair, startling our sleeping dog, and ran to the stairs and looked up. They were having a pillow fight. She hit him and ran away. Then he went after her. Back and forth. Aggravated, I watched for a few seconds, and again I yelled for them to stop and settle down and go outside. It was just too much. Okay! they yelled at the same time. And Derek swung his pillow toward Keyton one more time, to hit her that one last time, but his swing was too high and his pillow hit the almost basketball-sized cut glass light fixture in the hallway ceiling. The heavy orb came loose. He tried to catch it as it fell; it looked like he moved in slow motion trying to save the light, but it bounced onto the carpet and broke in half. Their eyes locked with mine.

I don't swear in front of my kids, but I did at that moment.

I was fucking pissed.

I made them both come with me to the hardware store, which they did not want to do whatsoever. I had to special order the light, which I told them through gritted teeth they would pay for. (I never collected.)

This was the last time I ever yelled at them like that.

I couldn't but I tried anyway to remember everything about that day, to picture their smiling faces, how they sounded so out of breath from running and laughing and being ridiculous and silly, how they played together, these two nearly grown people of mine. What I wouldn't give to have all of that back, all day every day.

♥ ♥ ♥

After the quick trip home, we returned to Shock Trauma and Ken stayed in Derek's room when rounds began, so he texted me line after line of what Attending Doctor said to the crowd of medical students. I was out in the waiting room with my parents and I read them his play-by-play texts as soon as they reached my phone, and for sure those hopeful updates, which was what they were, are still on the phone I don't use anymore.

That afternoon were hours filled with snippets, disjointed pieces, corners of snapshots, not whole colorful scenes and well-written paragraphs, as if my brain had been trying to protect me when later I couldn't remember everything about every moment. Sometimes the same memory appeared and then bled away quicker than before; some memories faded so fast all that remained was a guess. So infuriating and frustrating, this so-called *protection*: How was this protecting me when I actually wanted to remember everything? Protected? What a joke – I didn't deserve protection if I actually wanted to remember! My brain was betraying me.

♥ ♥ ♥

There's a warm and beautiful show called *Derek* (of course). And in an extraordinary and poignant scene, Derek, played by Ricky Gervais, describes his dad abandoning him and his mother back when he was a baby, a time when he most needed his dad to protect him because he was small and weak. That's what you should do, protect the baby, little baby Derek, his line goes, shattering me when I heard it.

Such a basic universal truth: Protect the baby.

Keyton carried potent antihistamines with her at all times. Appearing at random, then going dormant for months and even years, her allergies were weird, unpredictable, and undiagnosed. Apples, almonds, celery, orange juice (maybe), lavender oil (that time), the white wine I served that one day at dinner, and I'm sure there were others. From once afflicted with mysterious rashes with a fever, to convinced she had measles (vaccinated), then chicken pox (also vaccinated). Keyton breathed in what she called "weird air" at a bar once and started itching at her eyes; another time when her spin class finished and after she wiped her sweaty face with a clean towel, she felt the roof of her mouth start to itch. Hives randomly arrived, sometimes with nausea and headache. Her symptoms passed reasonably quickly, but every time she recounted an episode to me, I was literally hundreds of miles away, too far away to personally help, and I would panic inside because I couldn't protect her. This was our only clear job as parents, to protect your child.

I'd gotten the phone call once. I couldn't get another one.

♥ ♥ ♥

I stood in stunned silence as Ken's mother challenged Ken on the secondhand information about Derek she was given by who-knows-who versus what Ken had told her moments ago. I watched his face as he waited to speak, his head shaking slowly from side to side, his jaw clenching and unclenching. I closed in on myself and imagined him punching the wall right here and now, outside the elevator bank, his fist cracking into the plaster. His knuckles numb and bleeding, I'd hold his ruined hand in mine, my swollen and scratched raw one, and I'd pull us out of the hospital and down the street, me leading for once, on toward the harbor where we'd walk into the water. Instead, I blinked and heard Ken repeat word for word Derek's status. Why can't she just listen?

The next thing I knew was being obliging to the kind hospital volunteer who placed her hand on my shoulder, offering me a massage and meditation. To help me relax, she murmured. Why I agreed to this, to spend time with a stranger and be away from Derek, I couldn't say, except again, I did not know how to say no.

My first-ever massage took place in a curtained corner of an empty hospital room while my son was in a coma down the hall. I'm typically open to alternative medicine and the power of Nature, chanting and incense and oils, and all of that, but as I felt my neck and shoulders tightening further amid the bell-ringing – or was it a singing bowl – at the same time all I could feel was anxious, jittery, and lightheaded, like I'd been in a hot tub too long. Despite the dim light, her low om-om-ing, and gentle touch, I was not relaxed whatsoever. I actually felt worse, my limbs and belly tensed, my eyes and fists clenched shut. By the time I went back to see Derek, I felt like I had lost hours.

♥ ♥ ♥

Like all parents, I supposed, I'd always worried whether I was ever doing the right thing, and I seemed to do the right thing most of the time. Whatever I did or tried to do seemed to be enough. Derek was a curious and easygoing toddler, became a kind, polite, and intelligent student, and grew to become an ambitious, hilarious, and conscientious young man. Though I often felt like I was bumbling in the dark, I tried to do everything I could to be a good mother. I never knew till later whether it was right or wrong to ask him something, knock on his closed door or not, good or bad time to call. In parenting experiments, hypothesis to conclusion often took ages. What was I so afraid of? Of failing? Maybe I was right to be so afraid of messing up – no matter what my track record was, all evidence pointed to failure in the end. I shouldn't be surprised.

My wonderful son, but he was no angel. Derek himself would admit that. He wasn't perfect. And sometimes he could be a jerk – ask his friends. Or his sister. His clothes remained in a soft jumble on his bedroom floor where he dropped them; they got washed when they got *smelly*, the technical term he used when he had to distinguish between clean and dirty (or between when I washed his clothes and he did his own laundry). I told him once, and he oft repeated it to me, that I wished he came home from school more often because I'd do his laundry all the time. Big mistake by me that he took full advantage of with glee. He burped noisily when he wanted to really annoy me. Or his sister. And his music he played too loud and with way too much bass in the car, but he always turned it down or off when he drove me somewhere. He tolerated my music when I drove, usually making fun of it, however. All your songs sound the same, he complained. We could argue about that for days. How could Prince, Third Eye Blind, and English Beat all sound the same? And yet if I so much as implied that his particular genre of music wasn't as, well, *musical*, as mine because, I don't know, every third word was fuck, bitch, ho, or the n-word, not to mention nearly every hook was lifted from my Gen X well of songs, Derek insisted that I was being ridiculous. And he'd shake his head. Just ridiculous.

He particularly enjoyed using your words against you, and when he learned the term *hypocritical* when he was very young, it was all over. One day, on our way out to the grocery store, I asked Derek if he needed anything, and he said chocolate syrup. Fine. So off Ken and I went, picking up food for lunch and Derek's chocolate syrup that I knew he added to his protein shakes to make them more palatable. I grabbed two bottles so he wouldn't run out. Ken put the food away in the pantry and saw a bottle of syrup already there on the shelf. Why do we need three bottles of chocolate syrup? This is ridiculous! Derek! No one needs *three* bottles of chocolate syrup! No response. Ken was annoyed. About 40 minutes later, a bit bleary-eyed from playing video games all morning, Derek emerged from the study to have lunch. He stepped into the pantry, and started announcing in a high voice, Why do we have six bottles of salad dressing? This is ridiculous! Daddy! Six bottles of *your* favorite dressing? Ken started laughing right as I explained that I bought them whenever they're on sale. Well, it's still ridiculous, Derek replied. No one needs *six* bottles of salad dressing, and he sucked his teeth for emphasis.

Along with his effortless humor, Derek often showed his compassionate side. Once when he was a little boy, he heard his grandpa tell him a story about catching houseflies and pulling off their wings; Derek frowned and asked, But why? Always, Derek's been about helping the little guy. He captured crickets he spied in the dark corners of the basement only to release them, rescued lost ladybugs who somehow found their way inside the house, and sidestepped worms on rainy morning walks to the bus stop. I liked to think he got his well-roundedness from me, especially the saving critters part – my personal trophy shelf of imaginary accolades included my saving thousands of spiders, a baby bunny, and two bats. On second thought, when my sister and I were little, our grandfather walked around the lilac bushes in the backyard with an empty orange juice can filled with water into which he'd tap pesky lilac-leaf-destroying beetles, and when enough beetles were caught, he'd pour the water out into the street, so that my apparently murderous sister and I would crunch-crunch-crunch those nasty beetles into gleeful sparkly smithereens under our Thom McCann's.

♥ ♥ ♥

Later that afternoon, with hands laced together, Doctor announced the crushing truth: Derek's ICP was indeed steady, but somehow the monitor had been getting an incorrect reading for hours, so all this time the pressure was actually higher, not lessening like everyone thought. Ken and I looked at each other. We were numb. Looking back, fury and guilt filled me. Hope made us believe he was on his way back to us. Hope made us believe we were past the it'll-get-worse-before-it-gets-better stage. Not only did we send Keyton away, but we left Derek for hours this morning because we thought we had more time. Not to mention my pointless massage. My terrible knee-jerk thoughts multiplied, beginning with, How could this have happened? Was the machine malfunctioning? Hooked up wrong? Did no one check for hours? How in the hell was this missed in the best place in the country he could be?

There was a mirror above the sink in his room. I was afraid to look at myself, afraid that seeing my reflection would confirm that all of this wasn't a nightmare, that it was real, and afraid that I would rage and rage at what I saw.

This was not my life. This was not me. This was not what I should be doing.

I shook my head and clenched my fists as I recalled a couple of recent texts we got and wished I could change our bland thank-you-for-thinking-of-us response to, Fuck you for telling me to just think positive thoughts, Fuck you for admonishing me with, Count your blessings. What doesn't kill you makes you stronger. He was doing what he loved. Be thankful for the time you had with him. There's a reason. There's a plan.

Such ideas sickened me. They were dismissive and harmful.

Anger, rage, red.

Anger was active. Anger was doing. Anger was a fucking verb!

Punch the mirror! Do it!

Pastor brought some coffees from downstairs and his kindness added to the violence I was feeling. Why did some people say and do the right thing and other people not only misstep, but were arrogant, hurtful, and selfish? A mystery for the ages.

The coffee was too hot to drink, almost too hot for thought, and I returned to Derek's room, counting my steps as I moved down

74

the hall toward him. I remembered a random spring day when I took Derek to school with me because he was ill, likely the only time he ever was sick in elementary school. And my college class had to learn the beginning of Chaucer's "Prologue" of *The Canterbury Tales.* And then recite it in Middle English, no less. Derek sat next to me near the back row of the small auditorium, sniffling, slightly feverish, a Pokemon book in his hands, bored and apparently not listening much. But on the drive home, as I played the cassette to study, he began to recite with me, *"Whan that Aprill with his shoures soote / The droghte of March hath perced to the roote."* His memory was impeccable and astounding, and I tearfully lamented that now, connecting impossible dots, I knew that these rhymes clearly were the template for his penchant for rappers Kid Cudi, Three 6 Mafia, and Pastor Troy. Would that thought ever make me just smile?

Please remember this, I thought, as I sat next to him in his room on the corner, his hand heavy on the back of my head. I tried to will my memories of him into the air, higher and higher, until they landed across the bridge of his nose, dusting his eyelashes, his temples, phantom freckles he had when he was little, and then he'd remember – *he had to hear me* – and remember this.

Derek asked for a birthday sleepover back when he was in middle school, with pizza, cake, and video games, and I pushed this memory toward him. And chocolate-on-chocolate cake. So when I iced *Derek, you are so precious* in awkward chocolate cursive letters atop the chocolate cake, he smirked, and dove in with his fork, because that's exactly what he said I could write because no one would be able to read chocolate lettering on a chocolate cake. It always was a challenge to out-Derek Derek.

When Derek was ten, he lobbied for a puppy (it didn't take much convincing for me – I wanted one, too). He listed his categorized reasons on a sheet of notebook paper and presented his argument to Ken and me one Saturday afternoon. Six-year-old Keyton had co-signed. Ken unfortunately was allergic to most fluffy-haired canines, so I researched short-haired supposedly hypoallergenic breeds and discovered the Basenji, a small feisty barkless dog native to central Africa. I found a breeder in New Jersey who was expecting a winter litter, and we nervously waited for word. A red and white female was ours a few months later. Cinnamon was a perfect fit for our family, from the tip of her curled tail to her yodel-like voice, and both Derek and Keyton loved playing with her and trying to teach her tricks (Basenjis weren't known for doing what you wanted them to do, and Cinnamon was no exception. Case in point: If we threw the ball to play fetch, she looked from the ball to us as if to say, You threw it, so you go get it.).

Please remember this. Please hear me. Please be rolling your eyes.

Open your eyes, Derek, I heard Nurse say. I moved his hand off the back of my neck and lifted my head.

Open your eyes! Derek, open your eyes! She's shouting. Help me, she pleaded.

I don't know if I can; what if I can't?

Derek, open your eyes! Look at me, Derek!

Open your eyes! Derek! Derek, look at me! I finally shouted and squeezed his hand. Derek! I'm here! Open your eyes, please open your eyes, Derek!

He did what I thought he'd do.

♥ ♥ ♥

Maybe we ate at some point. Who cared. That massage from earlier was awful enough, but eating made me feel more guilty – guilty for taking the time to eat instead of sitting with Derek, guilty for eating when he wasn't, guilty for keeping myself alive with food. I ate very little. So did Ken. I lost ten pounds that week; he lost over twenty. And sleep made me feel even more guilty.

How much is too much? Feeling guilty, or looking out the window, or at anything on a screen, when did it become a problem? When it replaced the problem I was facing? Where then did the problem go when it's replaced? Maybe it became another problem, a problem^{problem} times infinity until it just canceled itself out. Would guilt like this ever go away? Would I want it to?

Narrator: If you lose a child, the guilt never really goes away.

76

♥ ♥ ♥

Everything, and that meant everything, went through my mind at a time like this in a place like this. Despite the grossly wrong ICP reading, Doctor wanted to move forward with the planned EEG and then another MRI afterward. To cover all the bases, she said. And when I watched a petite third-year medical fellow teeter on a small ladder on top of a milk crate reach up to affix electrodes to Derek, who towered over her as he stood against the tilt table in the middle of his room on the corner, so he was ready for the EEG, my breath rushed out in amazement. What a sight. I couldn't help but think that she looked like she was trying to decorate the upper boughs of a Christmas tree.

Once the EEG was completed and while we waited for him to be transported for the MRI, I tried again: Derek! Open your eyes! Open your eyes!

♥ ♥ ♥

Derek is behind a door.
Mommy! Daddy! Where are you? Help me! I'm trapped!
He pounds on the door.
I don't know what to do! Help me!
Where are you? Where am I?
I'm alone and I don't know what to do.
He pounds again.
Mommy! Daddy!
You said everything would be okay.
You said you'd take my place.
You said you'd help me.
What is happening?
It's dark.
It's so dark.

♥ ♥ ♥

Word traveled fast and visitors laden with flowers, cards, snacks, and random mementos appeared now and then all afternoon. A small manatee, its meaning written on a slip of paper, left behind next to a framed photo of Derek, his arm around a girl I didn't know next to a friend I did know. Whatever was left of me after the phone call sat in the quiet noise of Shock Trauma, lost in thought, thoughts about nothing. My mind wouldn't stop as it panicked and spun and found no safe place to settle. Shallow breaths kept tears at bay when I heard what some visitors nearby were saying: Their intent was to comfort me, but so many wound up doing exactly the opposite. Some said god wanted only the good ones. Some said god needed another angel. Some said this wasn't for us to understand. That last one was the only platitude I heard that had a kernel of truth in it, and I took it further: There was no understanding to be found in this. None.

Until visiting hours ended, I walked his friends down the hallway, made a left, and headed to his room on the corner. Teammates from high school, from college, friends from class, young men twice my size, numerous pretty young women. The guys towered over me, and I walked between them, a pair at a time, my arms linked with theirs. Were they holding me up, or was I supporting them? I smelled their cologne, so similar to Derek's but not quite the same. I felt them slow a bit when we neared Derek's room. Reluctant to see their friend like this.

Like this. This is all there is.

Some of his friends I knew and knew well. Some I knew only their names, and some I met today for the first time. And all of them seemed the same: tall, quiet, thoughtful, heads down, tears appearing immediately upon seeing their friend. I didn't ask, but I wondered later who visited tonight who was also there on the field and saw *we don't know what happened* as it happened. *Would they be okay?*

There were so many visitors to see Derek that the small waiting area was overcrowded, past full to overflowing, pushing visitors for other patients out into the hallway. Ken sought out a member of staff and asked whether a larger area could be reserved for our group. A conference room was found just for us, a gracious gesture, and that's where we gathered and where story after story was told. Stories that made us all laugh, stories I'd never heard before, stories that filled me with sorrow.

That Derek did in fact play practical jokes and make bets he knew he could win time after time that kept his friends entertained. That he was in fact a master of the art of bullshittery. One friend described the wager sophomore year in college when Derek bet friend after friend he could eat the most steaks on steak night, so friend after friend said, You're on, and surrendered their steak tickets to Derek. He won without taking a bite. Another friend retold the wager Derek made freshman year to wear just a t-shirt, no coat or sweatshirt, to every Penn State home football game with the loser buying the winner dinner. Except this friend didn't know two very important things. First, Derek selected the priciest restaurant in town and, second, Derek possessed an unnaturally high resilience to cold weather, wearing shorts and t-shirts year-round. Another friend chimed in with, You know shit's serious if Sheely's wearing a sweatshirt, in regards to the weather. Derek easily won this bet, even suffering through two brutally cold November games.

Derek was very serious when it came to these bets, but when it came to practical jokes, all bets were off. A friend described the time when Derek borrowed her car for a quick errand, and when he returned it, he parked it inches from another car, so close she couldn't open the driver's side door, so she had to open the passenger side door and crawl across. Through laughter, another person chimed in with the time when an unsuspecting freshman, new to the football team, asked Derek for directions to the weight room. Quick-witted and poker-faced Derek pointed, It's easy: go down there, then take a right by the football stadium, keep going, then another right, up the hill, keep going, keep going, then another right, and go into the first door, and it's on your left. Five minutes later, the poor kid made a giant loop back to where he started, and then he saw Derek shaking his head and smiling. Derek laughed, What did I tell you then do when you come through the door? The kid sheepishly said, It's on my left? Yep, the kid was just outside the weight room before Derek sent him on this crazy journey. How long had he waited for the perfect moment, for the perfect unsuspecting person, for this perfect prank? Another friend jumped in with the story about the time Derek outlined the plan that his Division III football team was going to scrimmage Penn State's JV team. He was so convincing with schedule details and bus departure times, his friend exclaimed, he had half the team believing it. Everyone laughed. He got us, too, all the time, Ken added. He was always so honest and such a good storyteller, that when he was making something up, we usually couldn't tell.

Story after story of rapid-fire laughter mixed with heartache overwhelmed me, and all I could do was wonder, How well did I really know him? I thought I knew everything – then I see all his friends, close friends of his with names I don't even recognize, and it's like he had a whole other life I knew nothing about. Of course he did! Normal, totally normal. But the only reason I was meeting these people and hearing these stories today was because we're in this conference room in Shock Trauma. The phone call on Monday obliterated any chance of Derek telling me about his relationships with other people, about his life that was completely separate from mine, and now it would be only through these strangers that I would ever learn about this side of him. And I didn't even know what questions to ask. I rocked in my chair and dragged my nails across the back of my hand. *This wasn't fair…this wasn't fair*

♥ ♥ ♥

The glimmer of hope that had been offered this morning was now officially snatched back: Derek was not getting better.

The MRI they'd done confirmed that. We were pulled into the hallway outside Derek's room and the explanation that came out of Doctor's mouth made utter despair take our hopes and throttle them. Despite being barely able to stand, I knew I had to. I leaned against the wall so I could stand there and pretend to be agreeable. To stand there in calm understanding, acting like, Yes, that makes sense, while whatever words were said to me were said to me. I heard Ken saying, I understand, a few times. I doubted he understood anything; I certainly didn't. And I didn't talk much, but I must have said *something*. Nothing made sense, but on and on I nodded like a dumb bobblehead, and as we walked back down the hallway I wanted to scream at everyone within earshot, his friends, the coaches, his teammates, to everyone else revolving in and out of the conference room. Ken. My parents. Most of all, myself. But screaming was unimaginable. Under severe stress and shock like we were, we barely remembered to sit down, let alone to question the authority of a white coat. We did what we were told, and we believed everything we heard.

♥ ♥ ♥

I decided to take Derek home. Yes, this could actually happen, I nodded to myself. I was sure of it. And I didn't want to hear Doctor tell me it would be impossible to take him home with us. Impossible? Like getting the phone call we got impossible?

I felt the energy of the idea course through my body. His bedroom furniture would fit in the study off the family room on the first floor. No stairs to negotiate until he was ready. A large window lit the room with morning sun, a beautiful maple just outside. This study was where he played his video games during school breaks – he'd be comfortable in that quiet familiar space.

I would do everything for him. I was his mother; I knew how to take care of him. We'd hire a home health aide for the tasks I couldn't manage. Plus, I'd studied for three semesters how to be a speech pathologist. I would address his aphasia with what I'd learned. They told us how healthy he was, and how strong, so slowly he would improve and start talking again. He'd laugh and re-learn how to walk and brush his teeth and hold a spoon and how to tell time and his colors and his numbers and use the bathroom and wash his face and recognize me and *oh my god when I screamed in his ear he couldn't even open his eyes he can't even breathe on his own oh my god what was I thinking?*

thursday

My sister picked Keyton up and brought her back to Baltimore. The conference room was filled: Ken, Keyton, me, my mom and dad, maybe Pastor, Attending Doctor, an anesthesiologist, probably additional ICU doctors, at least one nurse, and the liaison from Living Legacy. We were there to discuss next steps.

Next steps.

I looked at the small table below the window. It was crowded with flowers, cards, teddy bears, photographs. Caring gestures from caring people who didn't know what else to do. Next to the table was the chair I sat in yesterday evening when one of Derek's friends kneeled in front of me on the worn blue carpet, promised he was praying, that everyone he knew was praying, crying as he spoke. I sat there, holding a small magnet in both my hands, staring past him. I had only this magnet in my handbag when we got the phone call on Monday, a thin magnet I carried in my wallet to which I had scotch-taped a small photo I'd taken years ago of Derek and Keyton outside in autumn. They looked up at the camera, squinting into the low sun and half-buried in a pile of leaves. Four years apart, somehow they looked the same age in this particular photo. I had no smart phone in 2011 as I sat in Shock Trauma, no photos of my children ribboned in an endless scroll – only this magnet. The magnet, barely two inches by two inches, I held yesterday like a talisman.

I held it again now. Keyton had a lot of questions she wasn't afraid to ask. There was another surgery that could work, maybe, possibly, to relieve the intracranial pressure, which would relieve the swelling, which would bring Derek back. Perhaps. It would be performed today as soon as an OR became available. We wanted to try everything we could, so we signed the consent form.

Hope was a dangerous thing, according to Red in *The Shawshank Redemption*, one of Derek's favorite movies. For him and for his friend, Andy, hope meant freedom, but to focus on freedom meant they had to ignore their present circumstances, which was incarceration. This surgery, this hopeful possibility before us that might help Derek, kept my eyes and mind focused on his recovery, his future, and I had to ignore what I was told days ago, that the Derek I knew was already gone. Hope persuaded me to deny the present and instead believe in the future.

♥ ♥ ♥

Derek and I grew up together, but did he paradoxically somehow protect me from becoming an actual adult? We were a pair, sharing most everything: the same blue eyes, the same curly hair, the same smile, the same knife flick dimples. Even though I could hold a job, do our taxes, pump my own gas, I felt like I didn't know the first thing about being an adult – like I said, Ken typically handled the difficult stuff, and I couldn't even say no to a massage while my son lay in a coma. And now I stood in shock, numb to reality, wrapped in hope, because Derek, the other half of my pair, was three feet away yet couldn't protect me from the hard edges of reality. We're only 20 years apart – had Derek always been my shield instead of the other way around? I was supposed to be the one protecting him, but had I been hiding behind him all this time? Maturity wasn't magic – it was full of choices and decisions – Ken made the big ones, Keyton was more independent than I could ever be, and it seemed like I let life happen to me as I floated around on that stupid life raft – and life kept fucking happening. But no, absolutely not: What happened to Derek was not some lesson for me to learn just for me to grow up. There was no lesson in this.

♥ ♥ ♥

Derek's vitals were excellent. He was moved to a gurney and transported down a few floors for another CT – most patients suffer significant distress during a move like this, we were told, like elevated blood pressure, a drop in heartrate, but not Derek. He is so healthy, Attending Doctor exclaimed again, and so strong. I was

84

sure she thought her comment was helpful, good news, even, but it only made the whole situation worse.

He is so healthy. He is so strong. He's in the best shape of his life. What happened?

♥ ♥ ♥

I remembered jumping into the deep end. Holding my breath as long as I could, bubbles clinging to my skin, my feet, my knees, my hands touched the very bottom of the pool, my fingertips tracing the letters of my name onto the rough surface. I always tried to stay there as long as I could; down there at the bottom was complete silence, just my heartbeat in my ears that no one could hear but me. I fought the burning in my lungs, and I remembered thinking, *Just wait…one more second…one more*; I resisted the pull back to the surface, where the air was, where the sun waited, until the last moment, and finally I surrendered and let it take me back to the top of the water, weightless. I was maybe nine or ten.

I'd been in the soundless deep, holding my breath for days now. I'd acclimated here, sitting next to Derek for hours, and I rose to the surface when I could, needing to breathe, alongside my fear. The pull to see the sun was powerful.

I took a deep breath. Held it. Looking at Derek, I imagined trading places with him. I wished it. My dad hovered in the doorway, and I knew he wished the same thing. The CT had shown dreaded dark areas of stroke taking up more and more space and so they would come to take Derek to surgery as soon as possible. Could be in a few minutes or a few hours from now. Time meant nothing. Derek's hand was warm and rested on the back of my neck. I wanted to sleep, but I knew I couldn't. I had to stay awake. Maybe staying awake would jar me from this nightmare.

♥ ♥ ♥

Except for Keyton's questions and the answers that followed, it was mostly quiet when we reconvened around the conference table. My parents held hands and sat still with their heads down. The abbreviated presentation about organ donation I ignored as much

85

as I could, and I shuddered to think that it was first mentioned to us almost as soon as Derek arrived here. While I pretended none of this was happening, even wondering why another surgery was offered as a possibility if organ donation was part of the same conversation, Ken signed our consent. Years ago when I went with Derek to the DMV for his driving test when he was 16, he had agreed to be an organ donor quickly, almost as quickly as he accomplished the parallel parking part of the test. What will I need them for, he wondered aloud as he checked the *agree* box. It's good, and it's generous, and it's living beyond yourself. I'm an organ donor; I encourage everyone to be one, too. Look for the helpers, Mr. Rogers said. But I could barely process this kind of help. Despite Ken's firm hold on the pen and his quick signature, I knew he couldn't process it, either. Why did we have to witness our son become one of these particular helpers?

♥ ♥ ♥

I didn't know whether Derek's surgery would take 15 minutes or four hours, and I doubted I could last another five seconds in that conference room once visitors started arriving, with overhearing small talk about the weather (*did you hear about the hurricane on its way?*) and back-to-school (*can't believe back-to-school night is next week already, can you?*) and traffic (*no matter what time of day, isn't the beltway a nightmare?*). Then Ken's sister quietly told me she took photos of Derek. As he stood against the tilt table in a medically-induced coma in his room on the corner. That she'd print the photos, put them in an envelope, seal it, and write a warning on the outside. *For when I was ready.* I knew this was her way of helping, of being kind. I knew this. I also knew years ago she'd worked at the Air Force base at Dover, in the morgue, which could have compelled her to take photos of her own father in his casket; had she become ready to review those photos, even pin them to her fridge? Her heart was generous from the moment I'd met her. But would I ever be ready to view photos like those she'd taken of my son?

I then turned blindly toward someone handing me a stack of dollar-store puzzle books and fashion magazines (to pass the time, she said). I almost didn't come, a friend I used to know whispered as she hugged me, because it's so hard to see Derek like this.

I felt frozen and weak. Nauseated and empty. Numb. Yet I absorbed everything everyone was doing and saying in this conference room. The constant talking felt smothering – was that a headache? Yet another thing pressing down. Ken led Keyton and me out of the room and down the long hallway to Derek's room on the corner. He knew me so well.

And again I was stunned. Absolutely fucking stunned at the flurry of scattered thoughts that swirled through my mind. Embarrassing to think about my fairy tale ruminations yesterday, and how my life had been anything but a fairy tale, then about taking Derek home with us and helping him recover. How absurd, really, these ideas were. Just thinking again about how much resentment I held toward Ken for years, the numerous ways I acted like his victim, as if he were a villain who had locked me in an unreachable turreted garret. In reality, Ken had been the one who helped me survive this horrific week. Ken was not my captor. Ken was my partner. My knight. How dared I resent him for anything? How could I? When he saved my life? He made choices and decisions when I couldn't bear to even consider them. So I was stunned. Our parallel lives that intertwined into a stronger one together left me crying in disbelief that he'd stayed in my life when I used to almost wish myself out of it. For the terrible crime of being able to live his life as planned when I chose to abandon mine. To have Derek. And who said he got to live the life he planned? He never imagined to be married and have a child by age 22 – and to be 22, so young and as old as Derek was now. I didn't deserve Ken. He sacrificed himself over and over for me. I didn't deserve him.

♥ ♥ ♥

It's wait-and-see for the next few hours, we're told now that the surgery was over. Will Derek's pressure drop? Will it stay elevated? Will the reading even be accurate this time? Other words said by Attending Doctor and Doctor and Other Doctor, and I hung my head and capitulated and pretended to understand. I said nothing. They didn't have answers to the questions I couldn't even ask.

Hope sat close alongside despair, and that was a lonely and terrible place to be.

Whether early and still dark or very late in the day, I had no idea; I knew I'd been sitting next to Derek for hours, alone sometimes, and sometimes Ken was there with Keyton, my parents alternated, and nurses and doctors drifted in and out. Derek's hand rested on the back of my neck; my tears wetted my sleeve. Time meant nothing, and all I could do was let my mind drift.

♥ ♥ ♥

I knew if Derek could, he'd tell me to calm down. Not in a dismissive way, but likely the same gentle way he helped me when I drove him home from school last winter break, and it started snowing barely minutes into the two-hour drive, and I started freaking out because I hated driving in the snow, and I desperately wanted to pull along the shoulder and turn the wheel over to him so that he would drive instead, but we were in the Escalade, Ken's vehicle, which Derek had never driven before, not even to practice in a parking lot, and the idea of putting him behind the wheel of our behemoth SUV in a snowstorm was too nerve-wracking an idea in that moment. But I should have. While I drove white-knuckled on an increasingly icy interstate, Derek spoke to me in his quiet and calm way and just kept telling me, You're fine, Mommy, and, It'll be okay, Mommy. We were indeed fine and okay and finally made it up the off ramp, passing other cars actually stuck in the snow, and we drove slowly to the high school to pick up Keyton, and then we went home, and I pictured making cups of hot cocoa for us and sitting between the two of them on the couch as we watched *Christmas Vacation*, but I remembered Derek cajoled me into helping him unload the SUV so he could set up his television and Xbox, and Keyton was upstairs working on her homework.

Derek, you're the only one who could ever convince me that everything will be okay. And here I am, trying as hard as I can to make everything okay for you, and I don't know, I just don't know how it's ever going to be.

VERY DARK PLACES

♥ ♥ ♥

Today was endless with waiting and yet so suddenly brief. I sat alone as much as I could, Derek's hand on my head where I'd put it, heavy and comforting, and I willed all the hope that I had to wherever it would do the most good, though I knew my hopes evaporated as soon as they lifted out of me and floated toward him. He was right in front of me and I already missed his smile, his laugh, the sound of his voice. Derek made all of us better. He was right in front of me and all his promises and dreams were suspended and lost in the air. I felt lost, too, and I knew that when I left this place tonight, I would look for hope everywhere in the silence, in the darkness, and in the spaces between seconds.

To imagine what should be, *hoped for*, instead of what was, filled the hours, and not being able to talk about it with Ken or my parents because we all shared the same despair was isolating. I tried to think of what to say when I hugged Keyton before we climbed into the van that would take us back to the Ronald McDonald House, and I didn't have the words. Maybe I'd finally run out. What I couldn't say broke me in ways I couldn't understand, and what I couldn't bear to think about would come later.

friday

I froze when I saw him. Derek wasn't standing anymore; he was lying in the narrow bed. He didn't look the way he had all week: His face was puffy and swollen and not at all like himself. Maybe his medications were changed since last night, but I was too afraid to ask. For the first time, he actually looked injured when we stepped into his corner room.

We decided then and there to not allow visitors today.

It wasn't acceptance – There was no accepting the unacceptable.

It was resignation. A surrender. A hopelessness that went beyond ordinary hopelessness.

The surgery they tried last night hadn't worked to alleviate the intracranial pressure, as we pretty much knew it wouldn't. But it was that last-ditch attempt, that hail mary, that squeeze your eyes shut and pray our hardest to save our son.

And for Derek, all that prayer didn't work.

Friday was the day we knew all hope was gone.

It was over. Our lives were over. Our family was over. And we didn't know what to do.

So we were quiet.

♥ ♥ ♥

What should I have done differently?

The most obvious one was never to have let him play football, not in third and fourth grade, not all through high school, and certainly not in college. Not ever.

It's a conditional geometric proof: if-then: hypothesis/conclusion: I let him play; and therefore, he died.

It followed then that when I read about the terrorist attacks at the concert in Las Vegas, the Pulse nightclub in Orlando, the 4th of July parade in Highland Park, and so many more since, not to mention the mass shootings at school after school after school, all I did was think about the adults who put themselves between bullets and children. That's what you do: you protect your child.

What if I could have saved Derek? What if I could have taken his place?

I pictured the semi-posed photo of Derek's senior class, the one where some 440 kids are crowded into bleachers, too many to monitor, too many goofing around with tongues out or middle fingers stabbing the air. I knew right where Derek was, though not hard to find there in the front row with a huge smile, his dimples he often tried to hide on full display, his friends surrounding him, his life ahead of him.

His smile on my mind, how could I continue to think about the one true thing that was right in front of me: I did not do my job. I failed. Yet I kept trying to rewrite what happened, as if the closer I looked I could figure out what I'd been missing. What I couldhaveshouldhave done to fix it, from never letting it happen in the first place. And I knew very well I wasn't there on the field, on the sideline, among those watching. Yet from where I sat, both these disparate things could be true, because no matter what, this was all my fault.

But maybe the answer to just not let him play football wasn't so obvious. Maybe it's all the small things I should have done differently that would have protected him. Maybe they would have added up, compounded exponentially, and would have saved him. Different clothes, different foods, different toys and books, a different house, a different car. A different mother.

I wasn't enough to save him. My only choice was to rewrite the story until the words themselves blurred and rearranged into the proper order. I couldn't offer solutions or even sunny skies, but I still could read the revised sentences. And it was no fairy tale.

♥ ♥ ♥

Sitting in thought like this wasn't easy today. Waiting was exhausting. We're powerless in it. And could I call it anticipatory waiting? Is that right? This waiting and hoping for a miracle, a miracle that would never come, not for Derek, and not for us. Once our waiting was over, everything would be over. We would leave this place. Without Derek. And somehow after whispered phrases and tears and maybes and nevers, we made the decision to let him go on Sunday. Son-day, Ken said. Derek's birthday is 4/14, and Sunday would be 8/28, both numbers doubled – like his jersey number of 40, here were more numbers to remind me of Derek to look for out in the wild.

I didn't know what to do as I waited. Why should I *do* anything, anyway? My voice was quiet. I had questions, but I didn't want to hear the answers. I didn't know it yet, but grief would take whatever was left of my voice soon, and it would be a long time until I would start to regain the ability to speak.

How much and how often necessities passed unnoticed, like air or kindness, and how lost and suffering we became without them. When we went down to the lobby a few hours later, we spied Derek's roommate and his girlfriend sitting together off to the side. They were waiting to visit, and they had no idea we asked for no visitors today. I burst into tears as they hugged Keyton, then me. Apologies poured out of me, but they weren't enough. I couldn't look Derek's best friend in the eye. I felt terrible. They'd been waiting here for hours, waiting for permission from the receptionist to go upstairs. Ken explained today wasn't a good day for visitors, and they nodded and said they'd come back tomorrow. We told them what we'd decided about Sunday, and after another round of hugs, they left without asking to see Derek now.

Their action of leaving didn't seem like much, but it meant the world at the time. It's one of the first of many examples of graceful kindnesses given to us. No push back; rather, just doing what needed to be done. It reminded me of a poem I'd read in college by Scottish poet John O'Donohue, "Beannacht/Blessing," which goes:

> *On the day when the weight deadens on your shoulders*
> *and you stumble,*
> *may the clay dance to balance you.*

I remembered being struck by the idea that the earth should move to keep me standing, and not the other way around – and I thought of that now, that two of Derek's closest friends left even though they'd waited all day. They didn't pressure us to let them see Derek because they'd waited all day – that was the earth moving to balance me. I didn't have to pretend or hide or find my own balance to suit them. They lifted that burden off me. In the weeks and months and years to come, it became surprising, disappointing, and disheartening how often I would wish for effortless kindness like I'd been shown that afternoon in the lobby, instead of the silence I usually received.

And this kind of silence was expressed so clearly and repeatedly that it was deafening.

♥ ♥ ♥

Back to waiting. And as I looked at Derek, I thought again of what he'd say in all of this. I know for sure that he wouldn't be silent. Just like when he stood up for himself and faced those bullies on the school bus. He wasn't silent then. That thought was the rope I grabbed, coiled twice around my wrist, and let pull me along.

My son would be as strong as granite.

♥ ♥ ♥

Not long after Derek got accepted to Penn State, receiving the letter welcoming him to the class of 2011 the morning after a devastating loss one game away from the state championship, he started receiving invites from D-III schools to come play football, so we took him on recruiting visits to several of those schools, and we told him, if you like another school as much as you like Penn State and you can play football there, then let's talk about it. No pressure. He took his time making his decision, and then out of the blue a few months later, at Easter brunch, my mom asked him where he was going to college. There was Penn State and one other school in the running, a small private Division III school in southeastern Pennsylvania, that not only offered a sizable academic scholarship but also just built a gorgeous brand-new modern football facility. Penn State, Derek said. No hesitation and no sigh of resignation. I remember feeling a bit of actual surprise as I looked at him, and I smiled, my eyebrows lifted in astonishment, Wow, that's great! Ken reacted the same way I did, surprised and happy.

He enrolled in summer session at his dream school and thrived. But when autumn came and the air grew cooler and for the first time in four years Derek wasn't suiting up and practicing for hours with a team he knew so well and who also knew him, and then one by one of his closest friends started transferring from the schools they initially chose, he decided to make a change as well.

I hoped more than anything he didn't want to transfer because he wanted to recreate exactly what he'd had in high school, and I told him as much – you never want the best years of your life to be your high school years.

Now, were we being naïve if we ultimately, albeit very reluctantly, supported his decision to transfer from Penn State to play football? Maybe not naïve – because I argued against it, for sure, thinking at the time he was just following his friends, that he was trying to live in the past, trying to recreate the great times he had in high school, that he hated being a small fish in a big blue-and-white-forever Penn State pond, that I'd be just as opposed if he were wanting to leave to follow some girl to a different school. Desperate, I even asked my parents to intervene, that maybe a serious conversation with Grandma and Grandpa would shift his thinking. They took him to dinner and asked him to explain why he wanted to leave Penn State, why he wanted to try to re-live high school, or at least that's what it looked like. Like he told us, he explained that he missed playing football and he had only three years left in his entire life to do so. *Such chilling words: three years left in his entire life.* Ken resisted as well, putting a tremendous financial hurdle, a literal contract, in front of Derek, as well as a challenge to get the best degree from the best school that you can and the road ahead of you will likely be easier and much simpler. Hopefully. But Derek did not back down, and he wasn't about to be complacent.

Not long after Derek told us he wanted to transfer to play football, we visited him at Penn State for a long weekend. On one of our walks across campus and through the adjacent neighborhoods, we spotted a *For Sale* sign on a quiet street. We crunched numbers on the drive home and made an offer that week.

We labeled the house our long-term retirement plan. Blocks from campus, it was a Sears catalog house, built in 1945 but flipped, gutted, modernized, every trace of the hoarder who'd lived there for 40-some years painted over and replaced. Except the piano in the basement. That's still there. I thought it was weird and strange and random – who has a baby grand in the basement – so we kept it, broken keys and wires and all. Every note sounded flat. Derek had a party once in the basement and the dusty piano had been moved further into the corner, the lopsided wheels leaving telltale streaks of dust and dirt on the floor.

We turned this house into a carrot. When Derek wanted to leave Penn State to play football, we dangled the house in front of him. No longer would he have to live in a cramped dorm on campus – he wouldn't even have to find an apartment and pay rent – look, here was a beautiful home, move-in ready. Take the key! What could be better? Not to mention he was attending Penn State on the so-called parent scholarship – if he left his dream school and transferred to follow his friends to play football, the responsibility to pay the first $3,000 toward his tuition every year was his (we'd pay the remainder, which we labeled a loan). He didn't have that kind of money, and he'd never worked a job in his life. His job in high school was to get good grades. We were convinced he'd stay at his dream school and forget about transferring when faced with such a steep financial reality.

Ken drew up a contract. His intentions for the contract were to make it as difficult as possible for Derek to do this thing he supposedly wanted. To make it an unreachable task. We didn't want him to do this, so we tried to make it impossible. It didn't work. He agreed to our terms and signed. Our son said, Okay; deal.

Both Derek and Keyton signed contracts before, our way of motivating them to do well starting in middle school. Getting paid cash for good grades was indeed motivating, but I wish now we hadn't chosen this method of motivation. This contract concept is another nightmarish detail that haunts and shames me, and I wish I would've known then what I know now. I would've argued with Ken to forget the whole idea.

Derek bussed tables for minimum wage at a local Italian restaurant the first summer and had to tap into his savings to reach the $3,000. Then he found a better-paying temporary office job the next two summers, and the last summer before he was set to graduate, he was accepted into the highly competitive paid-internship program at DOE.

He did it. He did what he set out to do.

We were so proud and impressed that at breakfast that morning of the day we got the phone call, we decided to tell him we'd forgive the loans, give him a car for graduation, and plan a trip. We wanted to reward his hard work: He did very well in school, earning Dean's List five times, Academic All-American honors twice, and was about to graduate with a double major in History and Political Science. And he got to play football, suffering through losing seasons the entire tenure of his eligibility, despite the team's slogan, F.A.W., Find a Way – or, as Derek put it, *Forget about Winning*. Indeed, forget about winning, as he was there to play, to be with his friends, his brothers who elected him a team captain; he was there to learn, to lead, and look to his future.

♥ ♥ ♥

But I just sat, hopeless, unmoving, and silent, and stared down at my toes again, the homemade white tips chipped, stuck in the same old sandals worn every day all week in this place. I clawed at the back of my hand, feeling the rip of my skin, still tender and raw from earlier today or the day before or the day before that.

I held Derek's hand between my two and bowed my head. I thought about the early mornings all summer when he ate a frozen pastry before he left for his internship in DC. Chicken, cheese, and broccoli, and he called it breakfast. He turned on ESPN's *Sports Center* while his breakfast was cooking (i.e., thawing) in the microwave. He sat next to me on the couch as he ate the savory pastry alongside a huge glass of water. I drank coffee out of a ceramic mug he'd painted that had *Penn State* and a white helmet on a blue background dabbed on the outside and yard markings on the inside, like hash marks on a football field. He'd remark, Ah...I see you're down to the 40-yard line, once I'd taken a few sips. Some mornings I showed him a cartoon in the newspaper I thought was funny. References to *The Godfather, Star Wars.* Or politics. He'd usually raise his eyebrows and say, Oh yeah? But sometimes I'd get a smile and a wry comment, both well worth the wait.

♥ ♥ ♥

We decided to leave him for the night at some point after dark and head back to the Ronald McDonald House, and on the shuttle ride my dad tried to make small talk with the driver.

Grandpa, stop, Keyton said. Please stop talking!

He protested once and then silence again filled the van after my mom squeezed his shoulder and implored him to hush.

Keyton sat on my left and I could feel her closeness, her warmth. Did I put my hand on her leg? Did she lean against me, her head on my shoulder? Silence filled the van. Terrible to admit how absent I felt, unable to comfort my own daughter. I had no words to say that could help her. I had nothing to give her. I was silent. My own silence haunted me then and haunts me now.

saturday

A hurricane was on its way, the same day we invited everyone to visit. Not hyperbole. Hurricane Irene had weakened to a Category 1 and made landfall on the Outer Banks. But earlier projections estimated that 65 million people along the East Coast could be affected with power outages and much worse, and a state of emergency had been declared in Maryland two days ago in preparation for the monster storm. There were gas shortages as people closer to the ocean filled up and evacuated if they could, grocery shelves emptied in a panic, sporting events were postponed, and emergency shelters were prepared.

So, the earthquake on Tuesday and a hurricane today. The earth was heaving in all directions in protest for Derek. Yes. Yes, definitely. Maybe a meteor would be next. I kept my head down under my borrowed umbrella against the wind as we again walked the couple blocks from the Ronald McDonald House to Shock Trauma.

And today, Derek looked perfect when we saw him. His cheeks and chin were smooth, clean shaven. He smelled nice. He was lying back in the bed, his head and chest elevated, looking comfortable and restful. All of the swelling he had in his face yesterday was completely gone now. But whatever momentary relief that brought was overshadowed by the small stuffed bear propped onto his shoulder. Its chest read **Hero** and it had a bandage wrapped around its head.

Nurse said something like, Isn't that cute? They look alike now. She clapped softly three times. *She actually clapped.*

I looked at Ken. I felt like I was going to be sick.

When she stepped out of the room, Ken took the bear, threw the bandage into the trash, and set the bear out of sight next to the computer by the doorway. This wasn't a TV show, live in front of a studio audience.

The heavy rain and relentless wind were fierce, but the hurricane kept no one away today. We had texted a few people who then texted a few people, and the conference room was fuller than anyone expected, so Ken and I took turns leading friends and family to visit Derek all day long. It was a hard day, playing host, walking the line between being grateful that so many people came to show their love for our son and being resentful that we weren't alone in our quiet sorrow.

None of this should be happening, anyway.

My mother-in-law gave me a blank journal at some point during the week, in case I wanted to write about what was happening, she said. A kind gesture, it really was, and I tried to write a few pages a couple of days ago, back when I thought things looked encouraging. But then I stopped and started to rip the pages out. I couldn't face what was happening, let alone write about it. Putting words down made the unbelievable all the more real. So now this almost-blank journal I decided to share with everyone who visited. Please write something, anything, even just your name, I asked. No one will read it. Please, help acknowledge Shakespeare's plea to:

> Give sorrow words; the grief that does not speak
> whispers the o'er-fraught heart
> and bids it break.

The journal was passed around all day Saturday, its pages gradually filled with looping cursive descriptions of warmth and love, and I didn't read it until much later, and only once.

At some point I was led downstairs to the lobby by two women I used to know to take a break after a blurry few hours of meeting-and-greeting. We sat in a small café and they bought me a coffee. I cupped my hands around its warmth as I sat on a tall wooden stool that did nothing to support my shaking legs. So many people milled about the small restaurant, grabbing takeaway food and bottles of juice, a quartet of coffees. All oblivious to my broken life, just as I was to theirs; after all, here they were in Shock Trauma Medical Center just like I was. Who knew how much time had passed – watching people was lulling, and small talk with these particular women wasn't necessary, as the silence at our table was comfortable. Until "1979" came out of the speakers. Even though The Smashing Pumpkins played my preferred style of music, not

Derek's, I felt my heartbeat in my ears and thought of Derek immediately, hearing him sing along from the back seat. My breath caught as I teared up, and I had to, just had to, get back upstairs. What was I doing down here away from him? Wasting time, wasting time away from my son, time I did not have.

Couldn't I do anything right? For once?

I threw out my half-drunk coffee and walked toward the elevator bank. As I waited, I stared at the floor and shook my head, as if that would help me hold this dilemma in my hands in the first place: Knowing there was no hope for a miracle anymore and at the same time taking Derek home and helping him recover so he could keep on living his life. Impossible to wrap my mind around this, on this day, in this place.

And why put myself through this torture, beginning with the very first day, and to re-tell this story, looking for misplaced time, critiquing my word choices, spotting mistakes. How could I even think about this? What was I doing?

The elevator was slower than ever, and once I made my way back to the conference room, I resumed welcoming Derek's visitors and saying, *Thank you for coming we're so glad to see you,* finding a place for their umbrellas as they came in from the wet. These rote pleasantries and mannered movements marked me as shocked and numb to everything, and again I screamed to myself, *what the hell was wrong with me?*

Your dog is fine, Ken's mother said. She's so cute!

I blinked to clear the dim from my eyes and realized I hadn't asked about Cinnamon, hadn't even thought about our sweet dog. I couldn't see past, couldn't think past, my son in the corner room. I shivered.

Are you cold? You're just in short sleeves; why don't you have a sweater?

There was a bulletin board over her left shoulder: a flier for a support group for families of TBI. Were they success stories? Should we ask someone about this group? I stared at the bulletin board without reading anything.

We're not coming tomorrow, she continued. Just so you know.

I felt my eyebrows lift in question, but then I bit my lip and looked down and away from her, my soft sigh quiet. *Are you fucking*

101

kidding me – Doesn't she know that – Why wouldn't she be here – Tomorrow is Sunday, our last day with Derek!

I just can't be here for that; it's too much, I thought I heard her say.

That now familiar feeling of suffocating sickness filled me and I was flooded with green. I had to get out of this room. I scanned the sea of faces for my sister, but I didn't see her. It was too crowded, warm, and noisy in here. People had a habit of filling silence with directionless chatter when they're uncomfortable. This room was deafening. On second thought, I didn't want my mother-in-law's insensitive comments, which I should be used to by now, be the catalyst for my escape. I pushed her words to the side as best I could as I spotted an empty chair under the window and sat down – every single person in this room cared about Derek; they cared about us. That's why they're here. They hugged me, they took my hands in theirs. So many faces I recognized, some having names I couldn't think of right away but would later. And a blur of so many faces I didn't know at all. On the day of a hurricane, here in this small conference room, a room designed to hold maybe 15 to 20 people, more than 40 jockeyed for space while others were downstairs in the vast lobby, patiently taking turns to come up and see us and visit Derek. In all, more than 100, perhaps even 200, people visited him today. I thought, this young man, my son, Derek, truly made such a big impression on so many people in such a short time. Incredible: Look at all of the people in this room and beyond who loved him because these were the people who would grieve for him, remember him, and in that way he would live on through them. It wasn't at all what should be nor what any of us wanted, but it was something. *It was something.*

All his friends were here again today, and they were talking over each other until their voices shifted and a clear thread of stories began to be told. A friend re-told the story of how Derek sent a new kid in a big circle when he asked where the weight room was located. Then: Remember that time he sent those four kids in full gear to practice, when there was no practice? Everyone laughed. And that time he had a Super Bowl party – yeah, my cereal! Derek's roommate interrupted. I knew this one. Derek's roommate loved Frankenberry cereal, but couldn't find it in stores, so he had to special order it online. It was his precious cereal. But at this party, someone broke into the stash of Frankenberry, and Derek turned protector instantly and kicked the would-be thief out of the party. Speaking of parties, Ken jumped in with a story of our own. There was this time we were away for a long weekend, and when we got home, we noticed a few things looked a little different. Both Ken and I are a little OCD – everything always exactly in its place – so we are talking about noticing *micro* differences. The refrigerator looked out of place, maybe an inch or so too far forward. And one of our coasters was missing. Did he have a party? We asked Derek about the weekend, and after an elaborate detailed apology for breaking the coaster, which he said stuck to the bottom of his sweaty glass and fell onto the tile floor, breaking in half, so he threw it away, and as for the fridge, no, he hadn't moved it. Why would I have moved the fridge? he'd asked. Over the years we would joke to Derek about it every time we would go away – Please don't have a party when we're out; we can't afford to lose any more coasters. Ha ha. We always thought he might have had a party, but nothing else was out of place and Derek's story about the coaster was believable. Derek never had a tell and never confessed during numerous cross examinations over the years. No real proof, but to this day, we kind of think that maybe he had a party, but we don't know – Derek could get us too. As Ken finished speaking, about a dozen heads in the room dropped. I almost laughed out loud. There was the proof. Derek had kept this secret for years. Did you know? I asked Keyton. She nodded. I promised not to tell because he swore he'd make me breakfast every time you and Daddy went away. I took a deep breath and wiped away tears. I felt heavy hearing about this side of him again, this side I felt like I never knew, like here was a different person altogether, the one they knew, the one they came to see, the one they were crying over; so perhaps was the son I knew still somewhere around? Just not here? But somewhere?

♥ ♥ ♥

I had no idea what time it was. This conference room was like a casino: the lone window was dark with rain, so no sense of time or anything of the outside world. But there's no glitz nor tacky glamour here. Just hushed voices that seemed too loud. People who meant well. People who said they're praying for us. A coworker of Ken's on travel in Europe called to tell us a mass was said for Derek in Italy, and it should help us to know that people all around the world were praying for him. It should. Did Derek even know every person here? Did they tell him how much he meant to them or how smart or funny or kind he was before today? Did they tell him they loved him when he could actually see their faces and hear what they said? (Maybe he could hear them. I hoped so, and I kept thinking about this. When I rested his hand on my head, I had to believe he knew I was there. So, I had to believe he could hear too.)

♥ ♥ ♥

Despite the torrential hurricane rain, today blurred past with a revolving door of visitors. The conference room was always full, and we were always leading visitors down the hall to the room on the corner to see Derek. I realized that all week questions were being asked of me, questions like, How was he doing, What does this mean, What does that mean, but today no one asked me a thing.

The journal was passed around to countless people, cards and flowers were left behind, enough to cover the table and spill over to a second table. Cookies in a tin. A fruit plate. Someone even brought a case of water. Two former girlfriends of Derek's brought photos, prom pictures, printed that morning on printers that were running low on ink. That always seemed to happen, didn't it? Having to print the most important thing – *now* – and your four-color ink sputtered and almost managed to print a clear image, but inevitably there'd be a stark line running down the photograph a third of the way across, ruining it. Cyan, magenta, yellow, black, all half empty, all plotting together to make sure that nothing printed perfectly.

How are you doing? A smiling someone asked as she handed me a couple of dimes and pennies. I'm okay, I say with a half nod, *but I actually have no idea.* She smiled harder and said, Look what I found on the way here. She pressed the coins into my palm and covered them with her own. Oh, thank you, I replied, nodding but not understanding. Not enough for a Snickers, these, I thought. Derek's sending coins for us to find, she said. Oh, I repeated. I was dumbfounded. She said, Remember to look for cardinals and watch for rainbows and pick up coins because Derek would be sending signs all the time.

Before I could respond, she then launched into a story I remembered hearing at my grandma's funeral, the parable of the dragonfly. This should give you comfort, she began, as she described an underwater village of beetles that lived in the mud, until the day one of them crawled upward on a stem that led toward a lily pad on the surface of the water. When the beetle got to the top, the sun was so warm that she took a long nap, and by the time she woke up she had turned into a beautiful dragonfly, and she stretched her wings and flew away. See? she said, Transformation! Everlasting life! I knew this story, and I knew she left out key details, that the whole underwater village missed their friend and dragonflies definitely did not live forever.

I also doubted Derek would be watching over me nor sending cardinals nor coins…he was dying, and all I could do was stay alive and think of him and tell his story, so keep the coins you find in your pocket. Please. What signs, whether perched cardinals or cupped coins or found by dowser, could ever help me?

I felt so alone in this conference room filled with people, close and caring and bearing prayer blankets and crosses and hot coffee other people drank and sweets we didn't eat. Nothing made sense. Signs, stories, I wanted none of it. I tried another way. The dark way: The unlit endless path of everything that Derek was going to miss. What we're going to miss. We're being cheated. We're all being cheated. Especially Derek. Not a day would go by from now on, not a single moment, that these beliefs wouldn't grip me. Already the injustice of it all threatened to overwhelm; there was no relief. And I didn't want relief. And then a feeling so strong came over me, as strong as thirst or hunger, that I could think of nothing else: Derek came back, he was safe, we were safe, and all was right with the world. But that hopeful, wishful feeling left as quickly as it had come. I was numb, changed, constantly shaken, breathless, left hollow from a thousand fingers scraping me bare from the inside, and I was forced to stand there upright, out in the open, and answer, again, *How are you doing?*

105

sunday

he woke up
I saw him first
and I froze in the corner
where I'd been sitting all day
he moved his feet
then I saw his eyes open
when he heard the doctor
talk about him
like he couldn't hear
but of course he can
as I always knew he could
he woke up
and rolled his eyes
and sucked his teeth
he woke up
and was as sarcastic as ever
like he never left
he woke up, smiling
like I always knew he would
Then I woke up.

Why, why
am I left
with this now –
fucking hell
it's not the dream
it's the waking

Everyone wanted a miracle. Even just for the light to stay green. A miracle beyond some existential transcendence or enlightenment or whatever other philosophical woowoo was the latest and greatest viral craze. An ordinary extraordinary miracle. Other people get them, so why not Derek? That's what we'd been praying for. That's what everyone had been praying for. *A miracle.* Derek waking up. Derek recovering. Derek smiling. Derek coming home with us.

Instead, when we arrived to see him early this morning, Sunday morning, we're advised that the team would be ready for him around six tonight.

Ready for him.

I knew what that meant, and I didn't want to think about what that meant.

I just hugged him.

I just helped him get ready to go back to school.

I just hugged him. I just hugged him.

No visitors today except for us: Ken, Keyton, my mom, my dad, and me. How were we supposed to brave the hours until six o'clock while not wanting the hours to tick by at all? Time would be up in a blink and I couldn't face it. If I couldn't even read the Living Legacy papers I blindly signed, how was I going to –

Are we doing the right thing?

What if he – ? Maybe he'll – !

I couldn't stop thinking like this. And I was certain I always would doubt that we were doing the right thing by letting Derek go. Were we absolutely sure? *Were the doctors?* How can we ever know that what we were told was indeed the undeniable truth?

Six o'clock, six o'clock, they said. I ran my thumb and finger across the pink paper Shock Trauma ID bracelet I'd worn all week with Derek's room number next to the scrawled initials of the head of security. After Tuesday, we weren't given new ones – the woman with the sad eyes and gorgeous dark lipstick at the reception desk met our grim stares with her own as she pushed the sign-in clipboard toward us. I wondered how long the adhesive pink paper would stay on. Yet another link to the Before. The pink band silently came off in my hand one day months later as I was getting dressed. I tried not to cry as I slid it gently into the top drawer of my nightstand.

Nurse showed us Derek's handprints molded into white clay, a craft project children tended to do for their mothers on Mother's Day. I looked at the handprints of my 22-year-old son another adult made for me on the day he would die. I would take them home but not him. Don't touch, she said, they're not completely set up yet. Days later, I would display Derek's handprints on a narrow shelf behind a glass door in a desk that used to be my grandfather's. Derek had held onto my hand when he was little and was never embarrassed to hug me in public, never embarrassed period, except for a brief while when he was in third grade and stopped waving goodbye from the bus window as the school bus pulled away. After every high school football game I waited by the scoreboard to either congratulate him or share condolences on the outcome, and the big sweaty stinky hug I got from my tall, brilliant son was something I wanted the world to see, and he absolutely did not care who saw, just like when he challenged me to write, *Derek, you are so precious*, in chocolate icing on a chocolate cake. I hovered my hands above his molded in damp clay and thought again, again, and again about my little boy, the one smiling in the New Mexico sun with my arms wrapped around him, the one who loved dinosaurs and race cars and then soccer and football and then music and history and politics and girls, and yes my hands fit in his. They always would.

When we trimmed his hair yesterday, we made these for you, Nurse then said, and handed me a baggie full of tiny clear bags tied with short lengths of navy blue ribbon. I started to shake my head, uncomprehending, and I stammered, I don't know what – . She continued, These, she said, pressing her finger into the thin cellophane, are for you. They're locks of his hair, so let me know if you need more. Numb, I stood still and stared at her finger. I didn't know what to say. She sniffled and said, I'll make more keepsakes.

No one prepared me to receive keepsakes.

Keepsakes: items kept for the sake of the giver. Derek was the giver. I would keep everything. For his sake.

None of this was real.

This couldn't be happening.

This isn't my life.

♥ ♥ ♥

In the half-light, I conjured that old adage about bringing all of your troubles into a crowded room and dumping them onto the floor next to everyone else's dumped troubles, and by the end you'd gaze upon everyone else's problems, and if you had a choice you'd pick your shit back up and leave the crowded room with the same exact problems you came in with – you know that one? The point of it was to realize that your troubles weren't so bad compared to everyone else's, so carry your problems, quit complaining, because someone always has it worse than you do. Figure it out.

My problem was, *The team will be here at six o'clock.* I'd be out of my mind to pick this problem again.

I'd take up this problem again though: One bright winter afternoon when Derek was two-and-a half, just a few months after we'd returned to Maryland from our summer in New Mexico, Ken took him to a small nearby playground for a few hours while I baked cookies. When they came back, I was the one who started crying when I saw the blood. Derek's blue eyes stared at me as I peered at his chin. He'll be okay, right? Grab your coat; I think we should go to the hospital, Ken answered. He needs stitches. He does? It's not really bleeding much. Yeah, I know. It just looks like he needs stitches, he said, a little slower for emphasis. So off we went to the emergency room two days before Christmas. Derek had been climbing up the sliding board, then sliding back down while Ken watched him, over and over, until he lost his footing, slipped, and fell, hitting his chin on the top of the slide, where metal met wood. Once we arrived and were called back from triage, I think the nurse saw my whitish-greenish face as she readied the suture tray and said, Only one parent can be back here at a time, sorry. Whew, I thought, and fled to the waiting room. Derek got two tiny stitches to close

110

the very deep cut in his chin, a zebra-striped bandage, and a lot of extra attention that year when we visited relatives for the holiday.

I'd also pick up this problem again: Derek was in seventh grade and had stomach pain for a few days with a bit of a fever. Then the pain got much worse. Derek was so rarely sick and even more rarely missed school, and he asked, Should I still set my alarm for tomorrow? Sure, let's see how you feel in the morning. Meanwhile, I scoured webAlmostMD and realized that he probably had appendicitis. And yes, the pain was worse in the morning, so I called our family doctor, suggested it might be appendicitis, and he agreed, saying, That sounds just like appendicitis; go to the emergency room. Derek's appendix was removed before it burst, thank goodness, and he recovered nicely in the colorful pediatric wing. The nurses told us they were thrilled to have him as a patient. He was older and funnier and not as sick as most of whom they usually see. They treated him like a little prince, and I think he had more ice cream brought to him in 48 hours than he ever thought possible. There wasn't space for another bed in his room, so Ken spent the night in an uncomfortable chair next to Derek's bed so he wouldn't be alone. Keyton and I picked them up the next day. Derek lifted his shirt to show his grandparents his small set of sutures the next time they visited: These'll leave a nice scar, he smiled.

And I'd pick up this problem again: One night Derek called my cell phone to tell us he'd been in a fender bender on his way to meet us at a restaurant. I couldn't speak, so I just handed the phone to Ken. I'd always just done that to my husband, hadn't I? Here: take the phone, find the words, handle this, fix this, lift this, help me. For once, this particular fender bender turned out to be just that. A bump, no marks, no insurance exchanged, and somehow Derek convinced the other driver that she was the one at fault even though she was in the car in front of Derek at the intersection.

And I'd pick up this problem again, too: That time when I thought both of my children were missing. Not together – separately, years apart, and missing not for very long. Keyton, in middle school, and Derek, a freshman in college. Keyton rode the bus home from school every day, and the bus stop was on our corner, literally just feet from our front door. I heard the school bus arrive, idle for a few moments, and then pull away, and when she

111

didn't walk through the front door like she always did, I didn't panic for maybe 40 whole seconds. I looked out the living room window, the side window, the back window, Cinnamon following me from window to window, and I thought that maybe Keyton's walking a different way for an unknown reason. Did she go home with a friend? And forgot to tell me? No text, no call, because Keyton had no cell phone until high school, just like Derek. Maybe she stayed after school for extra help from one of her teachers – why would she do that – she never did that, my mind raced. Backing out of the garage, I glanced at the short note I'd left on the front porch, hoping she wouldn't panic if she got home before I did. I went to the school, rushed into the main office, and asked after her. My stomach churned and I knew what my panicked voice probably sounded like. An announcement was made immediately, calling Keyton to the office. I waited. And waited. Are you sure she didn't walk home with a friend, one of the secretaries asked me. No, she'd tell me. You know kids, she shrugged. I looked away and waited for what felt like forever in the office until I was finally told, Looks like she's not here; she's probably waiting at home, wondering where you are. I jogged to the back of the school just in case. No one was there. Not even an errant game of pick-up soccer. Frowning, I went back to my car and drove home. I saw her sitting on the front porch as I turned onto our street. Where were you? she asked. *Ohmygod ohmygod ohmygod she's here and she's okay.* I was just talking to so-and-so across the street from the bus stop behind those trees, see? Yes, I see, right where I couldn't see. What a strange and alarming fifteen minutes.

And Derek also went missing. We were at Penn State for the weekend and decided to meet him for breakfast in the morning on our way out of town. He set the time, and we went to pick him up in the alley behind his dorm. Always reliable, always early, but this time he wasn't waiting for us. We waited, and waited some more, and I called him. No answer. Give him five more minutes, I said. I called again. Nothing. He was in a dorm with a locked main entrance, and it was eight o'clock on a Sunday morning with no one up and about to let us in, so we thought he was just out late and had overslept. We figured he'd wake up in an hour or two, so we gave up and went to breakfast. I must have called six more times in the next hour. And again and again on the three-hour drive home. I was on the near-side of being apoplectic; why we headed home without connecting with him I have no idea, except perhaps I still thought the world was a safe one. When we finally got home, Ken called the Penn State campus police. Within minutes they called us back. He's fine – he'd been asleep and didn't hear his phone. When Derek called us a few minutes later, he was quiet and apologetic and admitted he was out late at a party. And more than sorry that he'd worried us and missed breakfast. We'd gone to his favorite place for blueberry waffles. It was the same restaurant we were at just before we got the phone call.

I would pick up the fearful few hours of not knowing where Ken was on 9/11. I'd pick up the frightening and stressful problem of the DC sniper, domestic terrorism inflicted on the DMV in 2002, when both my children learned to run zigzag into their schools for weeks to avoid getting shot. I'd pick up Snowmageddon, the monster blizzard in 2010 when 40-plus inches of snow from two back-to-back storms covered Germantown, and we were without power for days.

And I'd take back this problem again, too: Derek called me when he was 20 and asked for a ride to the hospital. Immediately, he asserted. It was a gorgeous day during spring break and he was with a bunch of friends at the field behind the elementary school playing touch. Ken was at work, so I had no one to hand my phone off to. Derek said one guy showed up straight from baseball practice. Wearing baseball cleats. He tackled Derek (I thought this was touch?), his cleats somehow met Derek's knee, and all the guys covered their mouths with their hands and looked away when they saw the blood. Fortunately, one friend kindly gave Derek his black shirt to stanch the bleeding. I didn't know how he was going bend his knee in order to get into my car (or out of it, for that matter), as low to the ground as my Infiniti was, but he managed. A quick evaluation at the nearby urgent care directed us to Shady Grove Hospital about 15 minutes away. We followed the ambulance with Derek inside to the same hospital where he'd had his appendectomy. Stitches again, inside his knee and out, after an MRI showed no ligament damage. He needed crutches and was given a strap to put around his ankle to lift it when he got into bed or to elevate it while he sat. This'll be a nice scar, he said. He hadn't changed a bit, and he was right. It would be impressive. He wound up getting two weeks off school to recover, and after the first week mostly in bed, he pulled out the tube that had been inserted to drain excess fluid. It was in my way, he said in a whiny voice, and I tried unsuccessfully not to laugh. I drove him to the orthopedist twice to have his wound checked. Not a fun ride for him whatsoever; I went as slow as I could, especially over the speed bumps, but his pain in his knee as he jostled around was tremendous. He said he saw white lights with every bounce. What bothered him more than the pain, though, was what to tell his college football coach. He injured himself playing football over spring break, and that was not only frowned upon by the coach, Derek feared his punishment would be punitive, even vengeful. And punitive was not at all hyperbole. The year before, in their last game of his freshman season and down 27-0, he'd caught a three-yard pass and ran it in for a TD with 6:40 left in the third quarter. In his excitement over his first-ever college touchdown, Derek spiked the ball. Furious about the inevitable penalty, the coach pulled him for the rest of the game to evidently teach him a lesson. The game ended in a loss, 55-14, and the team finished three-and-six for the season. The team had been instructed to avoid basketball, soccer, and any other active endeavors over spring break and to instead focus on golf or video games. So, Derek decided he'd tell his coach he slipped on some stairs. I rolled my eyes and shook my head. This injury came from some stairs? Unless you literally were pushed, no one would ever believe that. Just tell the truth. He actually wrestled with this for a few days, telling me he'd made a list of pros and cons (which I'd taught him to do when a tough decision had to be made) before admitting that it would be best to tell the truth.

I'd pick up all of these problems again in a heartbeat if I could.

♥ ♥ ♥

Sitting alone with Derek in his room on the corner, the baggie of locks of his hair on my lap, I jerked forward and straightened my posture with the sudden realization of hair and DNA. *Could we clone Derek? I'm 42 – I could get pregnant, and then – .* I felt my mouth go dry

114

just like it did when I imagined taking Derek home and caring for him. A hand on my shoulder startled me from my fantastical thinking. I looked up, my breathing fast, tears filling my eyes. Dad's getting food with Keyton, my mom whispered. Come with me for a minute and let's get some water. I'll be right back, I told Derek. As we leave, a nurse I'd never seen before breezed in and chirped, Good morning how are we today? I scanned the tray behind her filled with doses of propofol, fentanyl, and who-knows-what else, at the locks of hair in my hands, at my son. I was too stunned to speak. Jesus Christ, here we go again: how can people ask me something like this? Or ask me anything? I didn't know what to do, nothing made sense, so how could I possibly answer questions, especially the inane, *How are we today?*

♥ ♥ ♥

Derek was due to be born on April 2, but he chose to wait until April 14. Why did he wait 12 extra days to be born? And why was he being taken from me so terribly soon? Why was he being cheated? Why was I here to watch this? Why was there so much evil in the world and why was my good son and our entire family suffering this devastating tragedy? Was this karma? If so, then karma fucked up. Derek never hurt anyone; he never had a bad thing to say about anyone. He was young, strong, and incredibly smart. It's impossible to believe. This world needed him. And I felt helpless that I couldn't switch places with him. I wouldn't wish this on anyone, yet again I wondered, of all of the guys on the field that day, over a hundred, why Derek? Why did this happen to him? He was ready to go out into the world, ready to contribute, ready to share all he was with everyone. He would have made such a difference, maybe at the CIA, maybe as an attorney. He wanted to get married, to have children. What a wonderful father he would have been.

♥ ♥ ♥

Derek would work only a half-day on Fridays during football season of his senior year in high school, coming home around eleven-thirty

115

from his semester-long internship at the law office in Rockville. I'd be in the kitchen, with three or four other women, cooking for the football team. I'd ask him to eat now because I knew he wouldn't later when it was too close to game time. The other moms teased him, complimenting his shirt and tie and how fancy he looked. Who did you depose today? Did you try an important case, they would wink. No, no, not today; we just moved furniture and file boxes; that's pretty much what they have us interns do, he'd say, humoring them. Well, at least you get to miss school. Yeah, but then I get behind sometimes, he'd answer with a frown and a shake of his head. I'd make him a plate of pasta. Do you want salad? Sure, just a little. Hey, this is really good. We're making brownies too, I offered. Mmm…I don't know. That's a lot of sugar; I don't wanna get sick. I'll save you some, I would promise. Then, can you ride with me back to the school? Help me unload? Sure, he'd agree. And he'd make himself scarce for a couple of hours while we finished cooking and cleaning up and packing the cars.

I started to help make the game night dinners for the varsity football team when Derek was a sophomore; when he was a junior, I did half the shopping and half the cooking; and when he was a senior, I planned the meals and hosted the cooking at our house. It was a tradition, feeding the team before the game. Coach wanted to make sure all the players had access to a good meal, knowing as he did that some of the boys would eat who-knows-what and some wouldn't eat anything at all if left on their own after school before the game. We made pasta and marinara sauce (a bunch of times), chicken and broccoli, even meat loaf (I wasn't a vegetarian back then, but even so, cutting up chicken one week and another week making enough meat loaf for 60 boys was super-gross, what with squishing all of that meat and seasoning and onions and eggs and breadcrumbs together by hand) in mass quantities alongside salad and cookies and brownies, even crazy cake one time, with the peanut butter icing being a huge hit. It was difficult to calculate how much food to make, but somehow, we always had plenty. Maybe because the starters barely even took a plate, they were so full of nerves, so it was the younger players and the guys who didn't play at all who loaded their plates and then lined up for seconds.

Thank you, Sheely's mom, thank you, Mam, thank you, Miz Sheely, they'd mumble as I served a scoop of macaroni and cheese or green beans onto their waiting plates. Gratitude, always, and eye contact and smiles, sometimes, depending on who the opponent was. The other moms and I did what we could to foster that sense of family that Coach was trying to build. The team slogan that year was even *Embrace*.

Coach recited an inspirational poem and a Muhammed Ali quote to his players before every game, a poem that Derek loved and lived:

> This is the beginning of a new day
> You've been given this day to use as you will
> You can waste it or use it for good
> What you do today is important
> because you are exchanging a day of your life for it
> When tomorrow comes, this day will be gone forever
> In its place is what you have left behind
> Let it be something great
> Don't count the days…
> Make the days count.

The team assembled for study hall before school, was required to sit in the front row in their classes (if possible), gathered for study hall every day for an hour after their last classes, where I tutored writing and grammar a couple of times a week, practiced after school every day, wore shirts and ties on game days, had games on Friday nights, and lifted and watched game film Saturday mornings. During the winter, all the football players were required to be on the indoor track team to stay in shape, and in the spring, they made up a large portion of the outdoor track and field team. In summer, attending off-season conditioning also was required. Only Derek's tenure as a third grader in the powerhouse peewee league in York prepared him for this grueling schedule. And like those exhausting practices, Derek loved it all. He couldn't get enough of the practices or his teammates. This rekindled interest in football was surprising at the same time it wasn't: except for two seasons of flag in middle school, Derek hadn't played football since fourth grade, as he focused on soccer. But the summer before his freshman year, he asked to sign up for the junior varsity team at Northwest High School. Even though none of the high school coaches knew him from the feeder football leagues in Germantown, Derek's dedication and work ethic set him apart despite his smaller-than-average size at the time. During those long, hot, tiring daily summer conditioning sessions before his freshman year in high school, Derek's work ethic caught the attention of the varsity head coach, who told Derek if he continued at this pace he could get called up to the varsity as a freshman. Inspired by this potential, Derek worked even harder to prepare himself. When the season started Derek was on the JV team, but the coach was true to his word, because Derek was called up to the varsity team for the last game of the season and for the playoffs his freshman year.

All the hard work paid off, as the team won the state championship when Derek was a sophomore. Unfortunately, a heartbreaking loss came in Derek's senior year just one game away from the championship. Derek was elected captain when he was a senior, and won the Jaguar Award, an honor given to the senior with the highest grade point average for all four years. Don't be complacent, he warned his younger up-and-coming teammates at the end-of-the-season banquet, or you'll never find success.

It was perhaps, likely, really, that this feeling of family, of brothers, of making the days count, is why Derek wanted to transfer from Penn State.

And yes, we were completely in the dark when it came to the possibility that playing football in college could (would and did) lead to our son's death. It never entered our minds. We worried about a broken leg or arm, and not much else. We thought we were old hands at this. Both of our kids were involved in sports for years. In high school, Derek's teammate broke his collarbone, another pulled his hamstring, another rolled his ankle sprinting across uneven turf, and all of them missed several games until they were recovered enough to return to play. We knew that every football player had bumps and bruises from time to time. We thought Derek once had broken his leg in a high school game: the tackle from behind had been so egregious he bent backward at an improbable and gruesome angle, yet he'd needed only to be taped up about his ankle, missing barely a few plays before he trotted back in. He had ongoing hip flexor issues from playing sports year-round to "stay in shape," aches and pains here and there that ibuprofen quelled, and slept in most Sundays to recover from a physically grueling week. Sure, we signed waivers and permission forms and requested which hospital we preferred in case of emergency (the closest). But never, never in a million years, were we cognizant that he could die on the field of the game he loved.

We all cared about each other. Derek's teammates were like brothers to him. Jaguars forever, they said. Jags for life. And now they say, 40 forever. Sheely forever.

♥ ♥ ♥

They told us six o'clock and it's now past seven-thirty. We weren't told why, and I shuddered to think of reasons, but the team was delayed and we're waiting in Derek's room on the corner. The waiting made me anxious because it's terrible to wait like this for what we're waiting for. Nurse-I'd-Never-Seen-Before (a.k.a. Nurse-I-Didn't-Care-For) was still there; I wished her shift would've ended by now, but it was clear she was pulling a double. At this point in the day she'd made far too many jokes to try to lighten the mood. One joke was one too many. Whose mood was she trying to lighten, anyway?

And absorbing these not-funny jokes as I sat next to my son, forced me to imagine the kind of remarks that might have been said to Derek or around Derek when we weren't there in the room with him. All of the nurses, doctors, medical students, literally anyone passing in and out of his room, what was possibly uttered by them when they thought he couldn't hear them? What was possibly said during rounds when we weren't there to listen? I believed when people decided to enter the medical field, most did so because they wanted to help others, to give back in general. And that one of the first things you had to learn as a medical professional was to check your humanity at the door. On the surface, that made sense. This boundary would maintain sanity, for one, and prevent every case from coming home with you. Otherwise, you'd be blaming yourself for everything, whether it was your mistake or something not even remotely your fault.

Still, I hoped this wasn't an either/or situation: Either you saw my son as a fellow human being, or you didn't. Either you're compassionate and caring and always communicate that, no matter who's around, or, this poor kid's in a coma and going to die anyway, even labeling him as CTD, coarse code for *circling the drain*, so you told joke after joke. Yes, of course, you're overworked and had very little time to spend focusing on patients one at a time, but. Every patient had a story. Every patient was worthy.

♥ ♥ ♥

Nine o'clock now. They would be ready at nine. It was excruciating. They're giving us more time with our son before they took him off life support. How were we able to sit and wait in the first place?

Let's do what we did last night, Keyton said. Let's play music.

So we did.

Keyton asked to use the computer and Nurse-I-Didn't-Care-For was kind enough to open an internet browser for her so she could find songs. Derek's music: Pastor Troy, Three 6 Mafia, Rick Ross, Kid Cudi, Wale, Fort Minor. Even a few Elvis selections, including "In the Ghetto," which Derek always sang in his falsetto. Keyton also chose some she thought Derek would like, an eclectic mix she wasn't sure he knew. I asked her to find "1979." My parents knew practically none of these songs, as they sat next to each other and listened with us, likely processing the music in one collective ear and spitting it out the other side without comprehending, like one would a foreign language, since they had songs from the 50s and only the 50s permanently on replay in their car. What song was playing didn't matter: my dad's shoulders shook as he sat next to my mother, who took off her glasses every few minutes to wipe her eyes. So that I would never forget the songs we chose, I carefully typed every song we played into the flip phone I don't use anymore.

Nine o'clock came and went, and shortly before ten, we were told they were on their way.

Keyton leaned back against me, and we watched as they wheeled Derek ahead of us, and we followed down the hallway, a slow procession of dark silence. We crowded onto the elevator with him in the transport bed, his hands in ours, our heads bowed over him.

120

Pastor was there, close by us, with the assistant minister. When the elevator doors opened, we paused for a moment, and I watched Pastor give Derek the last sacrament, last rites, whatever it was that Lutherans did, and Derek went one way, and we went another.

Despite having a day full of waiting, now everything was happening too quickly, and I didn't have time to think. We were handed paper one-piece scrubs that zipped up the front and told to sit on folding chairs that were arranged in a circle. The scrubs were blue and crunchy and wrinkled everywhere. My head was bare, and I didn't receive a mask with my scrubs. I looked on the floor, thinking maybe I'd dropped it, but when I glanced around at my family, no one had a mask. My dad fussed about his scrubs, that they probably wouldn't fit and what would he do if they didn't. He was close to 300 pounds then. He's about 160 now, but that's a story for another page. He was the only one talking as we sat in the circle, and his fretting was getting to me. My mom was doing her best to calm him down. Just don't zip it all the way, she said, trying to be quiet yet getting visibly upset.

Jesus fucking christ shut up, Dad. Please.

We waited maybe five minutes or forty. We were instructed at least three times what we would be allowed to touch and what we weren't, and then we were left alone.

Wait a minute – Was it *Don't touch the white areas* or *Don't touch the blue areas?* What areas?

Was Derek going to be already disconnected from life support when we were allowed to enter the room?

Would we have only moments to say goodbye from that circle of metal chairs to wherever he was? I had no idea what we were going to see once we went through the doors I couldn't see from where we were sitting, and no one wearing real scrubs was nearby to give us any answers.

All we could do was wait until we were summoned, my parents seated across from me, Keyton and Ken to my left, and an empty chair to my right.

♥ ♥ ♥

Derek is in a dark room and there are bright lights, bright enough to see him lying there, but dark enough to shroud almost completely the strangers standing silently close by, watching as I move to be next to him on his right and Ken on his left, and I immediately lean down and put my face next to my son's, feeling his warm cheek next to mine, as close as I was to him just moments after he was born, and I whisper, Derek, I'm here, and tears fall and make me gasp and fight to breathe, and somehow I pull Keyton close to her brother, and she starts to cry, and my mom and dad are next to Ken, and they cry and whisper to Derek, and then they back away, and Keyton suddenly pulls back and puts her hands to her face and to the top of her head like she can't believe this is happening none of us can believe this is happening and I look at her but I can't move I don't know what to do I feel like I'm running out of time they told us we only had a few minutes too few and I can hear Ken saying goodbye goodbye why is he saying goodbye I can't say that I can't I say I'm here my sweet boy I'm here I'm right here please stay please stay I will see you later I try to believe this as I kiss his cheek you're my sweet boy I just hugged you and I'm hugging you now and then I back away and I hug Keyton and take her hands she's crying uncontrollably as if she can't breathe none of us can breathe and I turn back to look at my son and then we have to go they make us go and leave him in the dark room alone warm and alive and he is he still is and even though I keep watching him not looking where I'm going I don't know when he isn't anymore because we already backed out of the room doing what we were told.

Derek Thomson Sheely died at 10:32 p.m. on Sunday August 28, 2011. My son was twenty-two years old.

part
two

Please, crumple this up. Let me start over. Maybe I'll be able to rearrange the words in such a way that the ending turns out how it's supposed to.

after

Keyton started screaming. Her body shook as I wrapped my arms around her. I wanted to cover her completely and shield her from everything. To do the impossible, for no shield existed for this kind of protection.

Somehow, we returned to the Ronald McDonald House, where, after a dozen false starts and edits, Ken sent out an email:

It is with heavy hearts that Kristen, Keyton, and I must inform our family and friends that our beloved son and brother, Derek Thomson Sheely, has passed away this evening after a courageous fight. I want to thank all of you for your thoughts and prayers. They have meant a lot to Kristen, Keyton, me, and especially Derek.

We are incredibly proud of Derek. He is everything one could hope for and wish for in a son/brother and more. I want you to know that Derek has never run from a challenge and that he fought this with everything he had. Please, if you can, go onto Derek's Facebook page and put a note on his wall.

I would like to leave you with a few quotes that Derek posted and by which he lived his life:

"This is the beginning of a new day. You have been given this day to use as you will; you can waste it or use it for good. What you do today is important because you are exchanging a day of your life for it. When tomorrow comes, this day will be gone forever; in its place is something that you have left behind. Let it be something good; let it be something great."

"Trying is failing with honor."

"History will be kind to me for I intend to write it."

"We must move forwards, not backwards, upwards, not downwards, and always twirling, twirling, twirling towards freedom."

"Losing doesn't leave scars; it leaves open wounds."

"No one will just give you anything; you must earn everything worthwhile in life."

"It takes more effort for me to give up than to try."

"Courage is not doing something you're afraid to; it's doing something that everyone else is afraid to."

"Some men see things as they are and say 'Why?' I dream of things that never were and say, 'Why not?'"

"It's not a life unless you live it. One must focus on having a good life rather than a lengthy one. Never pray for an easy life, pray to be a stronger man."

♥ ♥ ♥

The terrible phone call started everything on Monday. We felt an earthquake on Tuesday. Wednesday started hopeful. We were even more desperate on Thursday. But complete silence gripped us on Friday. Friends braved a hurricane to visit on Saturday. And then Sunday.

Somehow it was Monday again – another week – would it always be like this? Remembering everything and reliving that week? Tallying reminders everywhere? Would we notice if we stop seeing the reminders? Was this what survival looked like?

I wanted to remember everything about our life Before. And I wanted to forget everything that happened After.

I wanted to remember Derek's voice, his smile, his laugh, his hugs. His face. The weight of his presence. I wanted to remember all the little ways Derek made everything better just because he was there.

I wanted to remember the person Keyton used to be. The person Ken used to be.

I wanted to remember everything. I wanted to know what Ken remembered that I didn't. And what Keyton remembered. It's all we had left, and if anything went missing, then a piece of Derek was missing and possibly lost forever. There must be a power in remembering and sharing Derek's story, right?

I wanted to forget nothing. If I forgot things about Derek, I'd lose him for good.

If you lose something, no matter how small, in a pitch-dark room, eventually you'll find it again. Maybe first you'd stumble into furniture, cracking both shins into a low table. Maybe then you'd bump your toe into the antique china cabinet you thought was a little to the left. Maybe then a knock to your shoulder against the doorjamb you thought was further away. No matter how slowly you move, crawling there in the dark room, feeling your way with your hands, what you're looking for is always out of reach. Is it under something? Is it tucked away in the corner, hidden? You know what you lost is there, somewhere. People have told you so. People have said to keep looking until you find it. People have said there's a reason – a plan, even – that explains where what you lost is. You're not one who gives up – you're no quitter – so you go on looking in the darkness for what you've lost.

For me, to be inside this darkness for days, weeks, months, and years was the kind of searching that never ended. In the dark room, the furniture, the doorjambs, the corners became so familiar to me I no longer feared the dark. I adapted until I felt safe there. And I'd never stop looking for what was lost.

♥ ♥ ♥

Once we returned to Germantown from Baltimore, we checked the mail and the answering machine, deleting message after message of thinking of yous, praying for yous, let me know if there's anything we can dos. We paused on one message that came in just a day before: a man from the Boston Brain Bank left his number and a request for a call back.

It had just grown dark that first night home when a local DC reporter knocked on our door for an interview. I had trouble processing his request, and his handsome face looked as if it were used to hearing, Yes, please come in; of course, we'll answer your questions. I couldn't imagine giving an interview, not now and not ever. Ken found the words to refuse, and when the reporter spotted Keyton, he asked, Would your daughter like to speak with me? No, sorry, we said, as she fled upstairs. Derek's story was in the news all last week. A few stories appeared in local papers and on the local television news, and one was picked up by the AP. Seeing his face, especially on television, and hearing the succinct summary of local tragedy, *our tragedy*, stunned us. But like most news stories, Derek's faded quickly from the headlines. For a while.

As we huddled with Pastor the next day, accepting his advice on planning a service, choosing songs and readings, selecting photos for a slide show, and then bowing our heads together, I looked up at the ceiling, a photo of Derek at his high school graduation in my periphery. No, I thought, when tears filled my eyes. I couldn't do this...I couldn't pray...why should I? I looked at smiling Derek in the photo. Prayer didn't work.

I kept these thoughts to myself even as we chose the design for prayer cards we'd have available at the service. As Lutherans, we stood still during hymns, even with the church band with their electric guitar and drums. We didn't raise our arms and press our hands into the air and shout, Hallelujah. We didn't cross ourselves. And we abhorred change. Maybe I didn't understand every nuance nor read every verse, but I'd always believed. Why didn't my belief, and all of the thousands – literally thousands – of prayers matter? Why didn't god save Derek?

Later that night, Pastor called to check on the progress of photo selection. And then he said that anyone who tells me that what happened to Derek is god's plan is bullshitting me. I thought about the thread of identical comments whispered into my ear last week at the hospital. You can't be grateful for all the goodness in your life and then surrender to the mystery when bad things happen, he stated. *Lay down, mere mortal, and yield to the almighty benevolent, omnipotent, omniscient one.* How good and loving was it to take a child from his family? And omnipotence – what, you're all-powerful but not powerful enough to save Derek? As for omniscience, really? All-knowing, yet you didn't know this would happen and would cause such pain? And then Pastor said, It'll take time. *Fuck, et tu, Pastor?* No amount of time was going to fix or ease the loss of Derek, my beloved son.

Ken chose six photos from our selection and a dear friend had them enlarged for us, three large and three smaller photographs made for display at Derek's service. They were affixed to foamboard and placed on heavy tabletop easels. On one of the larger photos, Derek's seventeen-year-old face smiles in his senior portrait, on another he is just two, shivering and smiling in the cool night air atop Sandia Peak at sunset, the lights of Albuquerque just out of frame. In both, his blue eyes are just like mine, his smile mine. His smile is the broadest and best in the third photo, the one taken just four years earlier in front of the scoreboard on the high school football field, with the five captains together holding the championship trophy aloft, the five captains covered in mud, and exuberant, ecstatic, elated beyond belief at their victory over their arch rival two miles down the road. Four of the captains visited the fifth three times last week. They cried over their friend and didn't care who saw.

Two days before my son's funeral, I answered a knock on our door while Ken was out speed-mowing our overgrown lawn. I recognized the man in the suit from somewhere, and let him in – we were getting visitors with flowers and plants and edible arrangements every few hours, it seemed, so maybe this man worked with Ken – and as he stepped into the foyer, he handed me a gift bag. He spoke quietly, saying words now forgotten, and I suddenly recognized that this man had sat with us at our dining room table only three days ago, this man reviewed the funeral home's itemized price list with us, this man had made gentle recommendations, agreed with our decisions, and took our credit card number; this man didn't work with Ken – he was instead from the funeral home, and as I looked down at the bag he had carefully yet casually handed me I realized I was holding a box with Derek's name on it, **DEREK THOMSON SHEELY** in typed black ink on a rectangle of white. How calmly and for how long did I stand there, frozen, holding my son's ashes, staring at the printed sticker that spelled his name, and as he left, I thanked the man – *I thanked him. Of course I did* – and I stood still and alone in the foyer and looked down at the bag – *the box* – and my mind flipped over on itself. We left Derek there, in that dark room in the hospital, and he was returned to us in a small black box.

Look at it. Pick it up. Hold it like I do: like a baby in the crook of your arm.

Ken told me later that this same man spoke softly to him upon arrival three days ago and showed him several photos. Again, to protect me, my husband had to confirm the tattoos in the photos were Derek's. Another gruesome box to check and initial.

Once Ken finished cutting the grass, he returned the call from the man who was connected with the Concussion Legacy Foundation and the Boston Brain Bank and its ongoing study of CTE, Chronic Traumatic Encephalopathy, the neurodegenerative disease that linked repetitive brain trauma to behavioral and cognitive problems. CTE sounded familiar, but I had only a vague understanding of what exactly it was.

Then we were asked, Would you consider donating Derek's brain to this study?

I sank to the floor.

Jesus fucking christ.

Somehow Ken kept his composure and said it was too late.

I wiped my eyes and looked at the small black box.

♥ ♥ ♥

Will it help if we come down? Do you want us to come down in the morning or the afternoon?

I didn't know how to answer my mom's simple questions. I didn't know the answer she wanted. Whatever's good for you, I said. *Yes, of course it would help. Why, why do you have to ask? You're my mom – why can't you just know?*

Once they'd arrived, my parents scurried from one task to the next. My dad cleaned the kitchen sink, vigorously scrubbing the slightly stained corian surface with some abrasive powder. My mom took Keyton shopping for "a suitable dress to wear." My dad picked up dinner. My mom dusted upstairs.

I scanned my closet: Did I have a suitable dress to wear? I touched each on its hanger, one at a time, pushing them to the left, beads on an abacus. Maybe a skirt? Which shoes? I thought of my hair and went into the bathroom. The mirror hid nothing. I shook the applicator bottle and squeezed the mixed medium brown 4A color onto my roots. *What was I doing?*

The next morning, we arrived at our church an hour before the service. A few other early arrivals milled around a large monitor set up in the narthex. Here was the slide show of photos I had chosen. I stared at the photo-fade-to-the-next loop of Derek as a baby, his smiling face framed within bars of his crib, Derek as a middle schooler, holding Cinnamon, Derek grown and strong and healthy. Derek alive.

Where was he?

He's not lost – there is no map for this.

134

I knew about the buses that arrived full of students and football players, Derek's friends and teammates, hundreds, really, so many that a monitor was rigged in fellowship hall where the overflow crowd gathered to broadcast to them what was happening in the sanctuary once the service began, but I didn't know until later that reporters had asked to enter the church. Ken told Pastor that it would be disruptive if the reporters were in the church but it was okay if they were across the street. So, they reported from across the street, *Funeral for a Football Player.*

Ken, Keyton, and I stood in a receiving line, the kind we would never stand in at Derek's wedding. Someone placed a chair behind me, in case I fainted, I supposed. We're so sorry…if there's anything we can do…Thank you for coming…Thank you. And when the line of coworkers and neighbors and friends and strangers morphed into a line of football players, I was glad for that chair. As the young men filed past me and introduced themselves in quiet voices, all Derek's size and shape and age, I found myself pressing my hand to their chests, just for a moment, as if I were adjusting their neckties. Or rather, was I in fact confirming they were alive?

Folks wanted to write something to you, Ken, and Keyton, someone whispered in my ear, so we taped sheets of paper to the wall in the church hallway for you to read later. Don't worry, someone else whispered, there'll be plenty of food for everyone afterward. I shook my head, I can't do this, I said. I can't do this anymore. I sat down.

♥ ♥ ♥

I kept my head down and avoided eye contact, as if to keep Derek to myself. I pushed grief down and made it small, compressing, conjugating, and compartmentalizing it into perfectly aligned bottles all filled to the top. And I decided once I left the church today to carry these bottles wherever I went, even though they'd often arrive ready to pour before I did. Anyone nearby could peer closely – *please look* – and see neatly printed labels like
guilty and angry notes,
full-bodied sorrow,
dark depressed pinot.

You should know that they all tasted the same. The cork would slide out because it wanted to be released, a soft pop and it breathed finally, and I poured until both glasses filled.

cheers

Perhaps one day, though I doubted it, I would toss the bottles into the bin for recycling, one at a time, watching each smash into thousands of glinting slivers only because they appeared to be empty finally. But then I thought: Why would I rid myself of even one?

There was no possible transformation here. There were no possible possibilities. There would be no lesson to be learned amongst the shards.

Know that these shards of glass found in dirt are gorgeous winks of light in darkness.

I am a grieving mother who knows that always the bottles are full. And over time I will watch as their contents shifted and changed. There'd be more of one thing and less of another, and I would never know exactly what the bottles held. So for sure I would save the bottles, nesting them in a line neck to stern to save space for more. They moved with me wherever I would go, their gentle perpetual clinking the reminder of the beautiful family I used to have.

And I looked across the room to the slide show, the frozen-in-time images that didn't seem real anymore. It's almost like they never happened. The posed people, and the ones in the candid shots, they weren't *there* anymore. My family. I almost didn't recognize myself in those photos. Me: Before. *Who is that? Is she still me?* The sharp realization was brutal and foreign. She was gone. My son was gone. If I was that unrecognizable now, was I then not Derek's mother anymore?

Was I ever his mother if I'm a different person now?

That's the saddest thing I think I've ever written.

♥ ♥ ♥

When it was time to move into the sanctuary, Derek's senior portrait was propped on an easel on a table. We sat right in front of it for an hour. And I stared at it while Pastor spoke, while Derek's friends spoke, while one of Derek's professors spoke. He described Derek as a remarkable leader who understood that leaders acquire influence as a result of the quality of their relationships and the respect they give to others. Never complacent, he strove for excellence, and he understood that influence was much more enduring than power.

Derek's professor then went on to paint a portrait of Derek so eloquent, so genuine, that the entire sanctuary was silent so not a word was missed:

"Derek was a guy who normally sat at the back of the classroom, which was where most sat to avoid discussion or duck attention. So in our first semester together, I called on Derek, who didn't miss a beat, returning fire and leaving me a bit dusted but thrilled that at least one of my students seemed to have a grip on the course. He told me, 'You didn't think I was paying attention back here, did you?' That was the last time I ever underestimated Derek Sheely. He combined his sly facial expressions with his keen intellect, and that's how he lit up a room. His comments ranged between incredibly profound to savage humor, and always with a disarming half smile. He understood public policy, frequently with a viewpoint well beyond the norm, and frankly, his views surprised me. He's this tough, macho-looking young man who stood up for the little guy, and always made the case for a better society that was compassionate and looked after the most vulnerable. I was used to hearing shallow and limited views of what our political community could achieve, and Derek sounded different, refreshing, and welcomed. When he spoke, we were all better for it. He was a student, but also a leader, a teacher, and he hid behind no one. He also never shirked his responsibilities, balancing a rigorous academic schedule with a competitive football schedule, never complaining or seeking an easier path. Even when it was time for advising, I just sat and listened, as he had already planned his entire academic career in his double major of History and Political Science. He didn't need directions, as he knew where he was going and how he was going to get there. It's hard for us to understand that someone so strong and capable is gone. He seemed such an unstoppable force and someone whom I thought could never be slowed down. He was a force on the football field and in the classroom, gracefully combining a tough athletic and physical schedule with a demanding academic courseload. He did this so gracefully that for the first semester, I did not realize he was the starting fullback for the football team. We are now left to wonder where he would have gone and what he would have achieved. We know only that we are all diminished because Derek is gone. We should learn from him, to strive for excellence, meet each challenge, and make the most of every moment, hopefully like Derek, with a half smile and a bit of humor."

Through tears, Ken then gave the eulogy, describing Derek through the years, from setting up the plastic chairs in the backyard after peewee practice to standing up to the bullies on the school bus to becoming a football captain. He reminded us of the silly side of Derek, the side that teased his new teammate with the roundabout way to get to the weight room, the side that practiced celebrity impersonations, the side that made all of us laugh. And Ken spoke of Derek's integrity, his authenticity, as Derek was the same person day or night, at home or at school, with lots of people around him or alone – Derek never pretended. Derek was smart and witty, silly and sarcastic, caring and passionate, teasing and comforting, leading and driven. Ken spoke of Derek's big heart, warrior willpower, beautiful smile, strong hug, sharp wit, and amazingly warm blue eyes. Ken said Derek was looking to the future to serve his country as he applied to the CIA, and he described Derek's belief that life was not about how many touchdowns you score, but it's about that block, that assist, no matter how small, that you throw, and while you're there on the ground laying on your belly you look up and see your buddy running in for the TD. As Ken said those words, Keyton leaned into me, and I tilted my head toward hers. Last week we prayed for a miracle, Ken said, when we realized that Derek was the miracle – he so truly enriched so many lives and we are grateful for him.

The next thing I knew, the president of the university presented Derek's diploma to us, mispronouncing his middle name and hovering over me, apparently expecting me to be able to stand and thank him. I didn't and couldn't. Keyton's head was on my shoulder, just like it was at my grandfather's funeral six months earlier. Derek had rested his head on my other shoulder. My grandpa was 95 when he died, and six months later my 22-year-old son was dead.

What was happening?

And then it was over. And the hundreds of people who very kindly came to show their care and love and support for us all lined up again to hug us and they said they were praying for us and some said everything happened for a reason and some said there was a plan for all of us that we couldn't understand and some said it got easier.

It gets easier?

Narrator: It does not get easier.

Another certainty was that there were a lot of people at the church I'd never hear from again. Though they'd hugged us and brought flowers and sent cards, they're on the Before side of the line, the side we knew. And we were on the After side of the line. This line was already starting to blur into something unrecognizable, the line that was drawn where one side was the Before and one side as the After and the line never moved and Derek was here and then he wasn't, and that damn line never moved, and all at once it was as if my son just disappeared. And so many of the caring people disappeared, too. I couldn't pinpoint exactly when it happened, but it did. Like the line of Before/After, there's the line of caring people saying that you could be sad now and now and now and – *Stop!* Enough time has passed, so get over it.

I didn't like thinking about that line. I wanted to think instead about Derek and his boring life as he called me in the middle of the week or texted me late at night after watching a movie I recommended or stopped by just to chat and said, Oh by the way I brought some dirty laundry can I do it while I'm here? and I replied, Let me, and he asked, Didn't you say you made brownies? and then he shared a few funny stories and swear words and a glass of wine and a hug and I never tired of any of it because he was him and he was alive.

♥ ♥ ♥

The next day, we left. We left behind some of the larger flower arrangements (one was a wreath on a wire stand straight out of *The Departed*), some miscellaneous food in the fridge, and we went to our house at Penn State. We had to get away. Now I know it doesn't matter where you go, but we didn't know that then.

And maybe it was that night that Ken turned to me and said, We need to be together. I've never forgotten how he said that. And I just cried in the bed with my husband, crying over my son and everything we'd lost and feeling so tired and sad and hopeless, we both couldn't stop crying and saying, *I'm sorry, I'm sorry,* my words and my tears mixing with his.

then

We weren't back to normal, not at all, but barely days later we did a fairly normal thing even though we both still wore our pink paper Shock Trauma bracelets and I wanted to be anywhere else.

We sat in row S, seats five and seven, seats my parents used to sit in, seats Derek should sit in, seats merely 19 rows up, seats so close to the team I could see their white teeth and the light in their eyes. Alone in the crowd of fans, I saw Derek everywhere.

Some might wonder how I could sit there and watch a game that killed my son, and I admit I wondered that too. But to think about how much Derek loved this game – in a short video filmed by his best friend he declared that football was the greatest game ever invented – it made me feel closer to something he loved, thus closer to him. In a way I tried to honor him by going, and so I looked for those wearing a 40 jersey, like the one I wore on this hot September afternoon, and when tears came, as they did as I watched a queue of recruits file in, their beautiful young faces shattering me, and the sharp blue and white sky, and – and – and I stared at the field, and imagined Derek's sure step on that soft grass, what that would sound like. I knew he should be here; I knew he should be sitting in my seat, and I would change places with him now if I could. I would've given anything to save him: my blood, my marrow, my bones, my liver, my lungs, my life…anything…and they wound up taking my heart. Despite the noise of the cheering crowd, this was what I thought about in this place, and this was what I thought about every day, wherever I was. What was Derek doing? Running outside, walking Cinnamon, hearing a 40 mentioned on television, or sitting on a narrow bench in a football stadium, wherever I was, I teared up, and I listened for what he's trying to tell me. Even though he couldn't. I tried to listen and let thoughts like those take me wherever they wanted.

♥ ♥ ♥

We went to Derek's apartment a few weeks later to pack his things. My parents came along, just in case we needed their car's extra space, which we did. I didn't know why I opened the freezer, but there were Derek's bottles of vodka and rum we'd bought together in the duty-free shop on Keyton's graduation cruise barely three months ago. He'd been saving them and never had a chance to drink any of it. His unopened bottles now waited downstairs in our cabinet. When was the right time to drink my son's liquor? What's more, Derek ordered a pair of sneakers with custom embroidered touches, like **40** and his initials, **DTS**, and when their shipping was delayed, they arrived after he was dead. He never had a chance to try them on. His unworn sneakers now were downstairs in our closet. Ken wore them once, but it was too much for him to walk in his son's shoes. Derek's college diploma was displayed in our hallway; he never had a chance to walk at graduation. He wouldn't see his sister graduate college. He wouldn't get married, have children. So many things…so many terrible things.

The absolute worst thing of all, and I couldn't stop it – I couldn't save him. My love couldn't save him.

This shaking anger was palpable, as I thought about Derek's lost future, his lost hopes. But could all of this be a huge mistake? And we're only now discovering that he's embedded deep within an official state secret, so secret not even we know. He's in the CIA like he'd planned, deep, deep undercover, and too far away to come home. That's why we couldn't see him. Just play pretend. I slid into imagining this, and I wondered what else he would be doing.

Even steam casts a shadow.

As I wondered, I remembered him. And filling in possible answers kept him close. The Derek I knew sketched just a part of who he was. He's unfinished. I had to retreat into the imaginary answers and let them paint a current portrait of my son, a portrait that would shift and evolve as time passed.

I shook my head.

How was my son dead? Where was he? Where did my hopes and dreams for him go? *Nothing made sense.* Grief like this was stark, laid bare, and nothing existed that could save me from it. Anger collided with sorrow and forced me to look into a very dark place. I hated to look, yet I couldn't look away. It was like staring into the sun, like that day of the eclipse twenty years ago in New Mexico. It burned, it blinded, but I was paralyzed, trapped, caught there, staring, stunned and numb.

I packed his soap, his razor, his toothbrush and toothpaste, his shampoo. His clothes were strewn on his bed just as he'd left them; he'd run out of hangers (he left behind a huge bundle at home, forgotten). His football jerseys from high school pinned to the wall above a couple of photos. A spiral notebook on the bedside table, **Financial Climate**, written on its cover in his handwriting. I paged through it: it outlined his budget, some notes and to-do lists, a re-copied list of all of the Super Bowl match-ups and scores, and his fantasy football draft picks he'd discussed with Ken the night before we got the phone call. On the back of each notebook page, he'd left pen impressions, runes left behind for me to decipher.

A few of the pages contained a detailed listing of IOUs, payments, and dates. Ken and I had worried that because of The Contract, Derek might have very little money left after paying his tuition and rent, and even that he might skip important bills to buy an Xbox game or two. As it turned out, Derek was loaning his roommate money to help him pay his share of the monthly bills. This kid, who was working around the clock all summer to pay for his tuition and improve his strength and stamina, was loaning the few extra dollars he had to his best friend and roommate. This kid, whom we worried whether he was ready for the real world – was. We should have known better than to doubt Derek.

His roommate pointed to the notebook and told us he owed Derek a few hundred dollars from the spring for the cable and electric, and we just shook our heads, Forget about it, we told him, and he hugged us. A couple of years later, he texted me to let me know that he'd just bought a house, an accomplishment, he said, that would have been impossible had it not been for Derek loaning him a few bucks here and there to help with his bills, help that elevated his credit rating to the point where it was solid enough to purchase his first house.

He was quiet as he followed us through the apartment back to the front door. I wanted to say something, *anything*, to him, and maybe he wanted to do the same, as we stood together at the balcony, but we instead said nothing; after a moment, something caught my eye: a **40** scratched into the brand-new railing. With this, he forever left his mark, my son.

From the apartment we went to the athletic director's office to sign papers. Insurance forms, claim forms, instructions on what to do with bills we'd received that our health insurance denied. No matter how I tried not to listen, all the words said churned in a loop in my head. A service for the students and faculty was held last week, the athletic director said as he handed us a poster signed by the team, a football signed by the team. I held the football with shaking hands, and, in a moment of clarity, I asked about Derek's helmet. I had purchased his high school helmet for him when his senior season ended, and it was a mainstay in his bedroom, dorm, and most recently, his apartment. We have to hold onto that for a while; we're expecting an investigation, we were told. I nodded, feeling my legs starting to shake. I can offer you a token helmet, he added, grabbing one from his desk drawer. This token helmet (an actual phrase said to us by this school official: a token helmet, like something you can set on a desk next to a spherical metronomic desk toy or a tiny Zen garden with a mini rake and bonsai tree) was about one-tenth the size of an actual helmet. It'll even have a 40 on the side, he offered. I shook my head; I didn't want a toy – I wanted his real helmet. Ken then asked whether Derek's jersey number could be retired. That's easy, we were assured. There would never be another 40 on that team. Ever.

♥ ♥ ♥

We returned to the school the following Saturday for a dedication ceremony. Derek's name had been inscribed onto a plaque that was installed onto a sizable rock that the team purportedly touched before every practice and game. On this plaque, my son was called a warrior and quoted, If you're not going to give 100%, then keep your hands off the rock. This quote was said by Derek a year earlier on a video for a school project filmed by his best friend, the same video where he said football was the greatest game ever invented. And this was the same field where he collapsed just a month ago.

Why would we want a marker there? Was this really an honor, or was this ghoulish? I found out later that for the rest of the season the team carried Derek's jersey out onto the field with them, elevated above their heads on sticks. When I saw photos my heart sank and I wanted to vomit. Those images sickened me. The team rallying around my son's empty jersey like that. Could not one of them done something to save him? Could they not then pool their energy and tell us everything that happened that day on the field? Why was their strength and vigor used instead for, to my eyes, a gruesome display like this?

How are you coping? Ken's sister asked Keyton after the dedication.

I'm not, Keyton said. Her laugh was harsh.

Her words chilled me. She'd be back at school next week, and I thought she'd been getting back into a routine, but now I wasn't sure about anything. Should we keep her home from school longer? Before I could react fully, Derek's girlfriend touched my arm. There's a blanket, she started to say. His initials are on it? May I have that? I let out a breath. *Why was she asking this? Why now?* It's dark blue, she finished. Part of me pictured the blanket, and then pictured Derek, and I remembered no special connection; this wasn't his favorite blanket. The other part of me screamed, What the actual fuck? I'd run my fingers over his pen impressions on a piece of notebook paper to touch everything he had, and now I'm asked to *give away* something of his? Like this? Like now?

Every caustic thought roiled inside me as I tried to stay standing.

Let me think about this, okay? I can't give anything of his away. Yet. *Yet, I thought. Why did I say that?*

The next thing I knew, a queue had formed behind Derek's girlfriend. Parents of Derek's teammates walked over and arranged themselves where we stood after the dedication.

You're so strong, was murmured into my ear. And then someone I didn't know said, It will get easier. Then a warm hug, followed by, Hopefully some good will come out of all this. The hug that put new distance between us. Thanks for that: There was no such thing as a good anything when you lose a child.

Hold on to your memories, a tiny elderly lady whispered, my hand pressed between both of hers, for in them will I find comfort.

I should be used to this: I'd heard this before, first in the hospital, then in the days leading up to the funeral, and every day since. Those whose lives seemed unbroken looked me in the eyes and told me these certainties. To hold on to my memories. That's like trying to hold love. Or hold hope. Or hold truth. *Or hold possibilities.* Who were you to tell me what to hold? How to grieve? How to feel?

Telling me it would get easier? How could losing my son ever get easier? Telling me he'd be in a better place? The better place for him was here with us! And telling me god needed another angel? I needed him a lot more than god ever could – I thought god had loads of angels, anyway. Multitudes.

I wanted to hold my son. Not my memories of him. And how exactly would memories of Derek comfort me? As if it would be just that easy: substitute a memory of my dead son, and poof, grief would be forever soothed. Photos, stories, memories were all the more painful to hold on to when they're all you had left.

But I should be used to this.

My son was dead. Nothing comforted me.

What would comfort you?

♥ ♥ ♥

About a week later, on her first day back to class, Keyton asked me to walk with her. I clipped the leash to Cinnamon's collar and we walked up the street to campus.

I don't know if I can do this, she said.

I know, I said. *I didn't know anything.*

Keyton had dropped one class, which maintained her full-time student status. Almost a month into the semester, she had a lot of catching up to do. All of her professors had answered her email that described what had happened, and one even offered support in the form of a former student who'd also experienced a profound loss. *He'd know exactly how you feel,* the email promised. They emailed twice and then stopped.

I'm going to throw some of the flowers away, I said when we reached the corner and waited to cross the street. Do you want me to save some flowers for you? I asked. Press them in a book? The flower arrangements we'd brought with us from Maryland were days past beautiful, drooping and dropping petals onto every table.

She scoffed, No. All of that is bullshit anyway.

I raised my eyebrows at her swearing, but said nothing. We weren't a cussing-out-loud family. Then.

Where were all those flowers before?

What do you mean?

Just. At the hospital. All those people, all those flowers. She shook her head. Give me flowers now; tell me I'm awesome now; tell me you love me now; don't wait till I'm dead because I'll never know how you felt about me, and that fucking sucks!

She looked both ways and crossed the street. I'll call you later, she yelled.

♥ ♥ ♥

Derek and I got our first tattoos together the summer before his senior year in high school. I did my research, learning that one of the places on the human body that usually didn't sag and wrinkle with age was the lower back, so I opted for a dragonfly there, naïve to the fact that a tattoo on that particular location was called a tramp stamp. Academic me missed that key detail. Derek chose to have his last name stenciled onto his arm, a choice I found curious, until a few tattoos later, when he revealed the rest of his design to me (not to Ken at first – he didn't approve of tattoos, only for how expensive they were), which showed our last name flanked by two sleek raptors, the Maryland flag in the background, and the entire design outlined to look like a shield. This tattoo took many visits and was completed just weeks before the phone call.

And now Derek was on my arm. His signature was etched above my left wrist, and Keyton asked for the same. We went to a shop downtown on the one-month anniversary... remembrance... milestone... and I watched the needle bring dots of blood to the surface of my skin. *This pain was nothing.*

♥ ♥ ♥

Before my tattoo had healed completely, Ken and I drafted an outline of what to do next. Well, Ken did. I sat off to the side, my hands in my lap, my right clenching the top of my left. What kind of outline would be thorough enough to capture a life interrupted?

DEREK THOMSON SHEELY at the top of the page, Ken then wrote FOUNDATION next to it also in all caps. Underlined. Then, Scholarship in its own bullet. Followed by, Fundraiser (Race?). And, Concussion Awareness.

What were we doing?

Emails arrived, one after the other. Ken knew people who knew people who wanted to help. Suddenly, we were incorporated. An attorney volunteered her time to review paperwork for the IRS, so we needed to submit a draft of bylaws and a draft of Form 1023, necessary submissions to become a nonprofit. We had a call to begin discussing a scholarship, an award that Ken wanted larger than any other offered. Students should want this, really want this, he said. The Derek Sheely Leadership Award, he wrote on the paper. Underlined.

Derek would hate this, Keyton sighed when we told her our plan.

We have to do something, I said.

Well, he'd hate a race. He hates running, she said, shrugging and shaking her head.

I hated all of it.

I didn't want to learn QuickBooks or how to run a website.

I didn't want to respond to emails.

I didn't want to write a pamphlet called Concussion Awareness, my son's smiling face centered above a description of his life. And death.

I didn't want any of it. And I felt impossibly tired.

The next morning, all I wanted was to be sad. No foundation, no race, no scholarship. Derek deserved my sadness. Jarring was the disconnect I felt between life as I knew it stopping and life continuing on as if nothing had happened. That disconnect made no sense. Nothing made sense. Nothing.

What was there to say when just taking a breath in the morning was a transaction – what did I have to give up to take in oxygen? What Derek looked like that one day at that one place? How instead of humoring me and chuckling when I tried to make a joke, he made cricket sounds? And when I asked, Are you mocking me? He'd say with a half-smile, Are you mocking me? What he said under his breath that made me laugh in the silent auditorium? Or that short video shot just a few weeks ago and shared on effbook of Derek smiling and playing beer pong and rapping along to "Cookies n' Apple Juice?" The tradeoff wasn't fair: How badly did I need to breathe, anyway, if that meant I had to surrender yet another slice of memory? Missing that smile of his had taken over my life. I weighed the breath, this air I supposedly needed, its heaviness; how important was this air to me, really? I moved my head as slowly as possible toward the window, to the slant of light that woke me up every morning, a quiet reminder that I had lived through another night, so that if nothing else I could hug Keyton and tell her that she was loved. Next to Ken, I closed my eyes for just another minute and tried to ignore the growing day, the hours that would press without being asked onto every one of my breaths, and when I felt my pulse beneath my eyelids I imagined my thoughts of Derek to be aligned that exact magical way that would finally allow me to conjure his existence out of nothing but the light that slanted through the window.

next

Dead stars lit the sky just enough for me to see where to place the bin on trash night, and it seemed as if all at once the days began to grow shorter. Everywhere I looked I saw Derek. Morning light hit the trees, leaves red in November. Bare branches, their outline sharp against a bright blue sky. Frost on grass, blurry as fur.

A few weeks ago, Ken returned to our house in Maryland and went back to work in DC, Keyton went to class and lived in her dorm, and I was alone.

I'd tried, at first. I went home with Ken, and the first day drawn endless ahead of me, and before I knew it I was lost in Derek's room, opening and closing his closet, sifting through his dresser drawers, pacing in circles and lamenting, *Why did we straighten up his room why didn't we leave it the way he'd left it why why why?*

And as the rabbit hole widened, deepened, I stretched my arms in the space. I tried to get as comfortable as I could, since I knew I'd be there for a while. I nested there, circling and circling like Cinnamon did when she looked for a comfortable spot on the sofa. I had saved Derek's papers, his bank statements, whatever had his name printed on it. Anything he had held, I held now, something solid that connected us across time. And anything with his handwriting was a loose thread I pulled and pulled, trying to follow, letting it take me where it wanted to go. His notebooks from high school and college: I traced the figures, the patterned back of each page, trying to feel the weight of the ink he used, trying to feel something in the embossed symbols he left behind. His To Do list on a small pad of lined paper, each bulleted item crossed through: The list was dated August 7 – 14, and this date sent me reeling. Take comfort in your memories, echoed in my head. As if I could cherry-pick. One minute I was lost in the middle of a pile of paper on the floor of my dead child's room, and the next I was abruptly confronted with remembering him waving me in for a hug the morning he left for school, then to have the horrible and crystal-clear memories wash over me of what happened eight days – *eight fucking days* – after my beloved son completed that To Do list. And I was supposed to – no, *expected to* – push that particular horrific memory aside and find comfort in a replacement memory of my smiling curly-haired boy?

I screamed into the empty room, Our memories are ruined! All our memories do is remind us of what happened!

There was no comfort in our memories. There was comfort in nothing. I had lived almost two of my son's lifetimes. Survivor's guilt was real.

Laying on Derek's bed, I stared at the ceiling he used to stare at. I turned my head toward the mirror, the mirror that would never hold his reflection again, would never again catch the light of his smile. The walkingincircles feeling came over me when I saw the books he'd never read. His Xbox games he'd never play again. I got up and touched his shirts hanging in his closet, shirts he'd never wear again. His glasses, his wallet. His fan, the fan I turned off to wake him up the morning he left for school when I told him to have fun and be careful. This empty room, empty because he wasn't in it, was full of all his things. And I looked everywhere to see what was left. One of my top Clifton Strengths was *input*, and input compelled me to look everywhere. Everywhere was not enough and I kept looking at the same places again and again – this compulsion forced me to grasp something, anything, to keep from going under. I even combed through the pages of his books – *keep looking keep looking* – until a scrap of paper slipped from his copy of *Watership Down* (my copy [my mom's copy {my grandpa's copy}]). I gasped, excited to see this newfound treasure. A piece of him. What was it?

But input was bottomless and yearned to be fed. I held Derek's driver's license (with its small beautiful photo) in my hand. It would expire in two years. By now I knew this without looking. His black wallet was zipped into a side pocket of my handbag and I'd opened it again&again sifting through the contents over&over hoping to find something new. A snippet of paper, maybe, with his handwriting. I did this all the time, hunting for something – anything – that might lead me to him. *Input*. His wallet had just $105 plus the two-dollar bills (a gift from his great-grandpa when he turned 12: six $2 bills; I got the same gift from the same man when I turned 12); credit and cash machine cards; student ID; business cards from three tattoo shops; two paper DC metro cards, one for $1.05 and one for $2.60; his late Pap's credit card. Derek traveled light, leaving few clues, but I kept looking because I just never knew. I checked every drawer and every pocket of his. Input was insatiable.

I studied his driver's license with its small red organ donor heart next to his signature. Too small for what it symbolized, the red heart pulsed a reminder to open the letter downstairs from Living Legacy, a one-pager that would spell out gratitude for my son's corneas so that someone could see, a kidney so that someone got off the transplant list, and his ACL so that someone could run. Derek hadn't been able to be as generous as he probably would have liked when he had checked the organ donor box (What will I need them for anyway, he'd said) because of reasons I didn't fully understand or wanted to think about, like the various vials of medicines he'd been given in the ICU.

I fell to my knees in the dining room when I read that letter later that afternoon.

I felt lost, so lost I didn't know who I was anymore. On our next trip up to Penn State, when it was time to go back to Maryland, I decided to stay at the house.

And so it was to this house that I found myself living, alone, isolated and in retreat. Here was where I was close by Keyton, in case she needed me, always available, we reasoned, but was I really? In the harsh light of early grief, I didn't have much of anything to give anyone, even to my own daughter. And here was where I could look backward, back and further back, and tumble down the rabbit hole, so comforting and a perfect fit. I nestled in and wondered what I could have done differently. Lost in the sorrowful what-ifs of guilt.

Was feeling guilty even a choice? Or feeling sad? It sure seemed like it – the effbook memes I quickly scrolled past proved it. Just like choosing positivity, or choosing to see the glass as half-full, again and again the toxic feel-good-or-else tropes flooded social media. As if my thoughts could control anything, good or otherwise. *My thoughts didn't control what happened to Derek, so how would my thoughts now control my guilt or my sadness?* How long would it take for me to hold a photo and stare into the eyes of my dead child before I would say that now, *Now*, was the time for me to choose to sparkle, to choose happiness, positivity, life? How long would it take to *choose* fucking anything besides guilt and sadness? That new age aphorism: Everything is energy, so *choose* what you let fill you. Choose? For me, inasmuch as I can choose, my choice is Derek. Every time.

♥ ♥ ♥

I hid in the house during the day. I tried to read a book here and there, heavy hardbacks with gauzy covers that had been offered in gift bags with a hand pat and a murmured, You should read this; I think it would help you a lot. Yeah – nah. I doubted it. I'd combed through the stacks. One glance, and nope: Books exhorting me to think good thoughts and trust the timing would not bring my son back. Positive vibes would not bring my son back. The constant silver-lining-no-matter-what positivity lurking around every corner was not helpful in the least.

I didn't want help. I wanted to be sad.

Derek deserved my sadness.

And as for feeling guilty, the guilt that filled me was sharp. And almost all I could see anymore were edges. Jagged edges, razor thin, that sliced clean through whatever was in the way. But the blade had to barely penetrate, barely draw a thin line of blood, before the pain of loss leaked out. It's just below the surface, no digging, no scraping needed.

Hey, good girl, I said to Cinnamon. She sighed and settled deeper into the couch cushions. I asked her, Where's Derek?

She opened her eyes and pricked up her ears.

I know, I said, petting her head. Where is he? I scratched her ears, and mused that maybe Derek *were* in fact here, the same as he ever was, but just not as orderly. I sniffed and wiped my eyes. Don't they say only a veil separates us? I walked to the bathroom and stood in front of the mirror. I squinted and searched the corners of the frame, where the mirror curved, trying to see through to the other side, hoping to catch a glimpse of my son reflected back. Just a glimpse, just a moment. *How I wanted to believe things like this.* If I looked hard enough – one more time, next time, next time, he'd be there the next time. There you are, I would think, here finally to take what should be yours – my life for his, gladly given. But he's never there. He's gone, and now, so was I.

Feeling a cold nose nudge my leg, I took a breath and looked down at Cinnamon. I asked, Are you ready for a walk?

We took several walks a day, but only after I learned the rough schedule of the other dogs in the neighborhood. I didn't want to see anyone, and most days I spoke to no one, unless Keyton called me, and then my singular evening phone call from Ken. Some nights it seemed like Ken talked more openly with me on the phone than he did in person, both of us in tears as we sipped drinks 190 miles away from each other.

And late at night I walked by myself. Usually around midnight, I left Cinnamon warm and curled under a blanket on the couch and out I went, bundled against the cold in my parka and twothreefour glasses of wine. I didn't give a thought about safety – the worst had already happened to me. Tears ran down my cold face as I looked in the dark for my son. I spied into the windows of houses, sometimes glimpsing normal people in their normal lives in the lit rooms. I'd never felt this way before, feeling jealous when I saw happy families, whole families. I crossed the street onto campus and suddenly saw dark figures his exact size and shape. Derek was everywhere. But he couldn't be – could he?

♥ ♥ ♥

Marcel Proust says that, "People do not die...but remain bathed in a sort of aura of life which bears no relation to true immortality but through which they continue to occupy our thoughts in the same way as when they were alive. It is as though they were traveling abroad."

Thinking Derek was traveling abroad, both literally and existing in another plane, cocooned me in layers of denial. And yet. Was it really denial when I couldn't believe what had happened in the first place?

The fact that I saw Derek not only on my night walks, but at the football games and the grocery store, everywhere, and when I didn't, believing instead that he was traveling and couldn't come home right now, wasn't only rooted in literature – it's proved by scientific research. Thanks to forward-thinking scientists like Dr. Mary-Frances O'Connor, research into a new understanding of grief and its effect on the brain compelled my attention. When it came to our loved ones, the brain learned over time what it could expect through predictable behavior. I could think about Ken, who might not be in the room with me right now, and my brain shuffled through possibilities: at work, at the store, at the gym – likely options based on Ken's previous known behaviors. One of the options would never seriously be *Ken isn't here, so he must be dead*. If it were, I'd be going mad with fear and panic constantly whenever my husband left my sight. But these thousands of instances of predictable outcomes have a cost: When we do lose someone very close to us, our brain cannot predict that, cannot compute that, and cannot accept that, for a long, long time. It explained why I saw Derek during my night walks, or in a crowd, or thought he was in the next room, and why I rightfully and predictably believed that my son couldn't come home just now. So, my seeing Derek every-where was my brain, used to always knowing approximately where Derek was, protecting me from sheer and utter panic. Like when each of my kids went missing for those short periods of time, my brain didn't immediately send me into hysterics because it knew – predictably – that my kids would turn up. And they did. But the problem now was with reality not aligning with predictable behavior. My brain predicted Derek would turn up, like he always did. But when he didn't appear, not only did I keep looking for him everywhere, I also kept seeing him everywhere.

Reminders were everywhere, too. Driving for groceries for food I didn't really want, just a mile or so up the road, I sat in silence on the way. I kept the radio off, a deliberate decision that prevented singing along followed by the inevitable guilt the singing wrought. I parked away from other cars, and I heard Derek's voice in my head, You parked so far away from the store you should've parked at home. I wiped my eyes and walked to the entrance.

I saw him everywhere, like the college student with his same haircut looking at frozen pizzas, so I kept my head down as I shopped and pretended that I had a whole family instead of a hole in my family. His favorite cereal was on the middle shelf. Next I picked up root beer for him. And then realized what I'd done. I put the cereal and root beer back and somehow found my way to the cashier, where my items totaled to something-dollars and 40-cents. When I got home, I carried the groceries into the house in one trip because that was what Derek would do when I would get home from the grocery store, trunk laden with multi-packs of energy drinks and bags of snacks and veggies and apples and protein powder and chocolate syrup and chicken and fish, and ask him for help bringing everything in. He'd slip on slides and amble out to the car, moving slowly as he pulled up his pants (he was always pulling up his pants upon our constant requests to do so since the early 2000s, his pants pulled down on purpose to show off his boxers like every other boy his age did) and quiet, likely thinking of a sarcastic one-liner to toss my way just to see whether I'd catch it and what I might toss back. He'd string the handles of the plastic bags neatly over his fingers, one after another, a ridiculous number, really, enough to weigh the skin of his fingers down until they turned a gruesome white, so starved for blood they were, and I'd gasp and say, Let me get the rest. Nah, he'd say, one trip.

Everything, absolutely everything, reminded me of him.

♥ ♥ ♥

We had extensive landscaping done soon after we purchased the house at Penn State. Leveling of the desperately uneven lawn, stone walls and steps done by a local landscape design company. Seventeen trees were taken out, random adolescents growing haphazardly and some older, larger, lumbering and very overgrown trees had branches that swooped and brushed against the house, providing convenient entrances and egresses into the attic for raccoons and skunks and who-knows-what other nocturnal critters. When the landscape designer we worked with learned about our loss, she immediately sent a card and offered to plant a tree in our yard in memory of Derek: I kept the flowing scripted card of Kahil

Gibran's words: *When you are sorrowful, look into your heart, and you shall see that you are weeping for that which has been your delight.* It rained the day they planted the tree, like even the earth was grieving. The young tree was a Persian Ironwood, destined to be strong and beautiful. I wept from the window while the three men carefully put it in the ground, balancing it, making sure it stood tall and straight. Perhaps it wouldn't right away because it'd just been planted, but it's supposed to flower in the dead of winter. A show of promise. Life. It's just off the deck; I glimpsed it from the bedroom window, from the car when I turned in the driveway. I already saw Derek everywhere, so there should be symbols for him that others could see. Ironwood. A strong tree should be the perfect symbol. But I could barely look at it. A tree could not replace Derek.

♥ ♥ ♥

Happiness felt by one person isn't a closed system – there's a ripple effect more times than not. Good news is shared and even though you might have absolutely nothing to do with it, you're happy for your friend and her joy courses through you and bounces back to her. Mutual happiness. And this feeling of inner joy is so wanted, so craved, that we freely steal it from anywhere, even pilfered like this from someone else's experience. The happiness ripple effect is magical.

The problem was that the ripple effect – the magic – failed miserably when it came to grief. Most people wanted to help me feel better, because feeling better solved most anything: You felt better, I felt better, we all felt better. This was good, and it made sense; the ripple effect worked. But. When it came to grief, *feeling better* didn't fix this. Grief just *was*. Grief complicated the whole feeling better narrative. Grief must be listened to, held, carried, even shared. Not fixed.

But, grief, sorrow, and hopelessness weren't the kind of shared experience wanted nor craved, ever, and everything possible was tried to stop the ripples before they came too close. Rugged individualism suddenly made an appearance, and just like that, I was on my own. Ripples of grief relentlessly swirled and lapped, never-ending, never able to be shared.

I was alone, in the kitchen, sorting through just-delivered Concussion Awareness pamphlets and folding information sheets from the Centers for Disease Control into thirds, when I realized with a gasp that Thanksgiving was next week. And then December. Derek should be graduating from college. Then it would be Christmas. *What were we going to do?*

The holidays aren't a wonderful time of year for everyone. Those warm joyous ripples stopped cold with me. And when my mom called and suggested we have dinner together at a restaurant next Thursday, I told her I'd have to ask Ken and Keyton. Let me know where you'd like to go, she said. It's important for all of us to be together.

But we weren't going to be all together...Derek wasn't here.

This was nice, my mom remarked after Thanksgiving dinner, trying to normalize the abnormal. After hours of going through the motions, including watching Keyton not eating nor smiling, *nice* wasn't on my mind. Today was so hard, I said. I know, Mom agreed as she hugged me. I felt my shoulders relax as my eyes started to prick with tears. But maybe someday it'll get easier, she whispered into my ear.

There it was. I stiffened as the ripples of my grief were met with yet another blockade. My face got hot, and I bit the inside of my cheek as my chest filled with heat. *Maybe someday* meant that the pain I was feeling right now was being dismissed; *maybe someday* meant that I shouldn't feel the way I felt; and *maybe someday* meant that everyone, even my own mother, was definitely not okay with me the way I was now.

Maybe someday my mom would understand that some things were just unacceptable. I know what happened, yet I wasn't going to accept that it happened, because it wasn't fair, it wasn't normal, it wasn't okay that it happened. That was what losing a child felt like. Utter unacceptable-ness. So my mom's hand resting on my arm with good intentions and her serious eyes looking at me with good intentions in an effort to make me feel better, and even adding a hopeful *maybe someday,* was like she was forcing me to accept what I did not accept just so that she could process what had happened for herself. Not for me. No. Forget the breathe-out-negativity-breathe in-positivity magical-meme fuckery. No, thank you. Maybe it's my stubborn Taurus-ness or maybe it's something else, like that trapped feeling I had when I was small and was admonished to *Get that look off your face.*

I wanted to run up the stairs and slam my door.

♥ ♥ ♥

On to the next obstacle: Christmas.

Derek and Keyton always were so excited to wake us up on Christmas morning. They'd spent weeks waiting patiently since the tree was decorated, the cookies baked, the stockings hung, well ahead of the big day. And even when they grew older, their enthusiasm was real. They watched the same television specials I remembered, *The Year without a Santa Claus*, and *The Grinch that Stole Christmas*, and *Santa Claus is Coming to Town*. Joking around with each other, singing the Heat Miser/Snow Miser song and asking to watch *Christmas Vacation* for the third time even though it was only the first week of December. Even when she reached high school, Keyton would remind Derek to put out a carrot for Rudolph. In the morning we played CDs of Christmas music, Johnny Mathis and Elvis and Bruce and Run DMC and sometimes Alvin and the Chipmunks blasted through the speakers. After ripping open their presents, they'd both help me in the kitchen. We made "Christmas Braid," a sweet dough filled with cinnamon and pecans and shaped into a braid, then topped with icing and red and green sugar when baked. My mom made this one time when I was a kid, and I made it a tradition in my own house.

But now I didn't want to make it ever again.

All I wanted to do was burrow under a blanket.

I hated everything, especially those damn Christmas songs. And at the same time, I recognized that homes still got decorated, presents were given, and smiles were real. Great. It's fine, more than fine. Do it. Light the lights, drink the nog, shelf the damn elf. It's cool. Really. I would not try to take all of that from you. Likewise, meet me where I am. In other words, *Beannacht* me. Be the earth that moved to balance me. Because the ribbon, the tinsel, the merry fucking music all grabbed my heart and twisted it until I wanted to scream. A magical time of year for so many, but for me it was a time that magnified our loss: Derek's empty chair at the not-decorated table was all I saw.

The first Thanksgiving, the first Christmas, the first-everything without Derek gripped me and wouldn't let go. I stood stock-still as the world continued to spin without him. Numb as I was, I wanted my grief to ripple outward in a giant wave and soak everyone I knew. I wanted the velveteen to fall away and reveal what it's really like for us during the holidays. Look at me as I navigated the store up the road for toilet cleaner, dog treats, and eye liner and I'm accosted by decorations, music, and so much fucking festiveness it was all I could do to stand up straight at the check-out line. Thoughts flooded my head: Derek wouldn't be home for Christmas. Derek wouldn't be home, ever.

But Keyton would be. So I pulled a tiny artificial tree with lights attached out of the closet the day before her winter break began and arranged it in front of the fireplace. I unfolded her stocking. Derek's. Cinnamon's. Hung them with care.

Do you want to make the braid? I asked Keyton.

If you want to, she shrugged.

Ken's mother called. Were we coming down? Ken told her no and explained how difficult it was for us since all we saw was an empty chair and the holidays would never be the same for us, and she said that *maybe someday* it would be different.

After hearing this so many times I started to wonder if this *maybe someday* thing was an attempt to bribe us out of feeling sad.

What if I wanted to be sad?

And my sadness wasn't only about the holidays. It was every day. The ordinary days and the ordinary ways when my beloved child was missing from my life from the moment I opened my eyes in the morning until I lay sleepless in bed at night. It was those ordinary everydays that I missed most. The simple days. The ones we forgot about. The everydays of grief.

♥ ♥ ♥

On the last night of the year it was cold and white clouds filled the black sky. I waited for Cinnamon to return from her last loop around the backyard, and I looked up and cried and tried to believe that Derek was close, that I just had to keep looking for him.

He had to be nearby. He's college age, and so were all the students I saw walking to and from class, and so many of them had his height, his build, his walk. He's still here; he had to be here; so I had to keep looking.

Still was what I said when I thought about Derek. I still missed him, and the pain still hurt, and I still couldn't believe it, and I still kept remembering back when he was very little and a smile lit his entire face when all I had to do was give him time for a story or for coloring books or for a walk or for lining up race cars or fire trucks or for any and all dinosaurs, and there was that same smile when I tossed him the car keys or made him his favorite dinner or poured him a glass of wine to drink together out on the deck when it got dark, and now I (still) missed that smile of his and (still) missed his hugs, like the one he gave me that last morning, and this missing had taken over my life and folding this loss into the everyday (still) was a complicated scattered mess I neatly pleated into a small square for daily use, a square so very quiet and ordinary that eventually no one even noticed it anymore.

Still, when that slant of light woke me this morning (or the morning of the funeral or the morning we cleaned out his apartment or yesterday morning or maybe tomorrow morning), I closed my eyes and tried to (still) ignore for just a few more moments the growing minutes of yet another day without Derek. I felt my pulse beneath my eyes, and I imagined that I was (still) trying to conjure my son's existence from that slanted light. Still was a word that caught my breath; still was perhaps an apology for why I (still) felt this way; still, if only Derek would come home, then we'd still have dinners together and laugh together and celebrate Christmas and the silence would end and we would still be a family.

wtf

Winter ebbed and flowed up at Penn State, unseasonably warm and bright one week and then harsh and bitter the next. Keyton was back at school, Ken was in DC, and I was alone again on this quiet grey of a morning, breaking blue, for the first real snow of the new year. The new year? I didn't want anything about this new year. I wanted the old one, the one that still had Derek in it.

I shivered as sudden wind gusts shook paw-sized clumps of snow from branches. Why did they have to fall where I just shovel-ed? Why didn't I have warmer gloves? Thoughts like these popped into my head and were nearly loud enough to drown out the drone of the snowblower two houses up but not the operator's incessant whistling. A student walking by offered to help shovel. I thanked him and said, I got it – who cared if he was just being kind – the simple gesture spoke volumes.

Then, out of nowhere, a borough employee zipped down our street in his small front loader, stopped at my plowed-in driveway, and in seconds pushed all of the heavy snow away. He gave me a thumbs up and I thanked him, thanks he couldn't hear for the noise, tears running down my cold face, tears he didn't see because he was gone already.

Shoveling snow into piles you would dig in for a fort with your sister, tiny pellets of snow clinging to your pants your mittens you two would stay outside until you were nearly frozen, and when you finally came inside shivering you toed off your boots and socks and we lined them up along the bottom edge of the refrigerator to dry just like I did when I was little, the magical heat that blew from beneath the fridge to dry our wet snowy gear. I remember all of this, and I want to hide there in the snow fort with you, Derek.

And then, it happened like it always did, first I leaned on my shovel as overwhelm overtook me, then thoughts of Derek made my heart heavy and my breathing shallow as a tear ran down my cheek, me staring at the sharp blue sky with the snow a handful of glitter in the sun, then the two nice guys – I had to keep my head down and focus on the snow. I needed to get out of here before anyone saw how much this random-act-of-kindness effect affected me. Shovel, shovel, toss, don't have a heart attack, shovel, shovel, toss, I thought. Don't be a display for the neighbors; be careful not to let them track my tears. Finally, after an hour I was back inside, warm tea in hand, warm dog leaning close, overwhelmed by emotions, and I thought about those two nice guys again only to feel the familiar sting behind my eyes. So shines a good deed in a weary world, I thought – indeed, how weary and how I had to hold all good deeds close. I closed my palm around each one.

♥ ♥ ♥

Another sleepless night. I felt like I never slept at all – the fits and starts made it seem like I was eternally restless, lying there for what felt like hours, wide awake, and I would wonder, *Am I dreaming? Am I thinking?* I did seek sleep, the cool side of my pillow, trying contoured memory foam for better sleep guaranteed, my spoonk, a mat covered with hard plastic geometric prickles for acupressure that was, yes, just like a bed of nails, melatonin, valarian root, ibuprofen pm, cbd oil, magnesium, you-name-it tablets, sound machine, but really: What was the point of trying to sleep? It would happen, eventually – when I was completely exhausted. Later I would find out that no matter how little sleep I managed to get, my brain would acquire a little rest here and there, some from REM, some from deep sleep, some from light sleep, until I would feel rested *just enough*. Just enough to function, just enough to relive every moment of the week in the hospital, just enough to lie sleepless the next night. Even when I managed to close my eyes, I still saw Derek right in front of me, so more tightly shut they went until I saw Derek young, strong, helpless, afraid, handsome, alive, dead, my son, my son, my only son, and that was all I would see when I opened my eyes. Disbelief in a loop. An endless do loop of grief, repeating itself in a self-sustaining chain reaction of very dark places. All I could do was try to push away these relentless thoughts until I became numb to everything. I was flat to the racket in my head – adrift, lost, no soft place to land.

Because in my mind sometimes, everything was the way it used to be. Everyone was precisely where they belonged. Everything was the way it used to be, and everything was perfect. And this was me the day before the week in the hospital. I thought of those first flashing few seconds upon waking when I had no memory of anything – not even realizing I was an actual person waking up, when you think about it – numb to the world – dumb to grief. Nothing. There. Relief? Maybe. But it's swift, disappearing into the ether like it was never there, and suddenly – BOOM – waking up, being wide awake…and I remembered the worst thing, the absolute worst thing, like someone grabbed the back of my head and turned it *hard* to face reality, and all my obliviousness was obliterated. *One of my children is dead. How could I have forgotten?*

Now I couldn't tell when the automatic counting stopped, when I automatically knew, minute by minute, day by day, how long it had been since the worst *worst* day, but I definitely didn't have stretches of time go by only to be shaken by my shoulders with the realization, *Oh shit my son is dead I had forgotten.* Maybe these counting rituals were like a sort of scaffolding, to keep me going in whatever this life was now. Maybe when I started to lose track of minutes-hours-days-weeks-months was when I focused more on the enormity of my loss. Counting seemed to be a distraction, like running or staring at screens or drinking. Even in the dark as I tried to sleep, I looked for patterns, or I counted backwards by eights or fours – anything to lull myself away from what was right in front of me. But with sleep, when it did happen for me, upon waking, was the forgetting. And the forgetting became my goal for a while. Waking up was waking to that dumb oblivion, maybe just for eight to ten seconds. And then came a heavy pressure of feeling guilty for forgetting, and this pressure I embraced. Powerless in its crushing clutch, this choke I craved, for without air I breathed easier – I learned how.

Looking away from Derek, even for a moment, compounded my grief with guilt. How could I even be capable of looking away, to go out for a run or to lose myself in episode after episode of *Outlander* or *The Last Kingdom* or *Better Call Saul?* What did that make me? I couldn't love my son any more – but did my being able to look away for three hours to watch a movie like *RRR* somehow mean that I *did* have space available to love him just a little bit more? The wonder of compartmentalization. Who decided that just because I could get out of bed, run four miles, paint my nails, walk my dog, and on and on, that I wasn't doing all of that in grief? Who decided that the only way to do these things I must put my grief aside, neatly in a drawer? Or worse, that I was over it? That I was better? Emptiness filled me, and pain filled me until I was empty. Time blurred. Time meant nothing. And nothing made sense.

♥ ♥ ♥

Despite the lack of sleep, I tried to surrender to some sort of structure to get through the hours of each day. After coffee, I went for a run. A phone call from Keyton usually came as she walked from her class at one end of campus to her next class at the other. I walked Cinnamon through the neighborhood to the arboretum and followed the paths across frozen ground, broken brown stalks of long-gone sunflowers, asters, and dahlias sprinkled here and there. Sometimes we spotted deer, sometimes only tracks in the snow. And every afternoon I tried to sit at my desk.

The wall to my right was a distraction larger than life. The three photographs of Derek we'd had made for his service adorned the corner of the room. I tried using poster putty to make the photos stay put, but time pushed the foamboard into a gentle curve, inhibiting a strong connection. Yet another unfortunate detail in grief world I discovered one afternoon as I made my way to my desk to work on the Foundation's website, and each of the three had fallen and now rested cockeyed on the floor against the baseboard. Some days I didn't make it up the stairs to my desk, so I didn't know for sure when they fell or how long they waited on the carpet. Their descent had been silent. I felt ashamed and sick looking at them, and sicker yet when I pressed them back onto the wall, one corner at a time, knowing they were obviously too heavy and convex for the physics of the poster putty, but pressing harder just the same, because *this time* they will stick. They did not. I finally tried pushpins and so far so good – the photos stayed tacked to the wall. No matter how many times I looked at those photos, the result was the same: Derek was frozen in time, and I wanted to be frozen with him, back in time, to the time Before.

Nothing made sense.

It didn't matter that nothing made sense. Some days I couldn't even look at the photos. I didn't even make it to my desk. Grief itself was a blur of shadow. Yet function we must, we grievers, we walking dead. Or function as best we could, whatever that meant. Have you heard of Spoon Theory? People have a limited number of spoons at their disposal every morning, where spoons equal energy, not actual spoons, unless you had a spoon collection, which my sister had when she was a kid, spoons collected in states we'd traveled to, spoons labeled California and Florida and New Jersey nestled in an ornate wooden rack hung on the dining room wall, a rack that was knocked into by accident many times for different reasons, the most common of which was when the phone cord from the kitchen phone was stretched to its limit, stretched alongside the narrow rack, sending the spoons clattering upon a sudden retraction of the cord followed by hanging up. I brought a spoon back from New Mexico for my sister, but only then found out she didn't collect spoons anymore, her collection dormant and dusty and still on our parents' dining room wall, left behind on purpose when she got married. Anyway, Spoon Theory called for imagining having only so many spoons in your pocket, or a very limited amount of energy, and every time during the day you had to struggle – like really struggle – to complete a task, no matter what it was, you had to surrender a spoon. Maybe taking a shower, and then having to get dressed, and then there was a knock on the door, and after talking to a stranger, having to pay bills, feeding the dog, and then having to eat something – with all of the steps involved in each task, each step requiring a spoon or two, you might be out of spoons by 9:00 in the morning on a truly terrible day. Out of spoons meant out of energy. On days like these it was a challenge to do what looked like the smallest action, like eating, as if the slightest movement would vibrate outward and inflict damage onto others. Other days it was possible to tackle big things, like making phone calls or sending emails or writing thank-you notes to Foundation donors or driving to an errand I'd put off for weeks.

Visualizing these spoons in my pockets where I could spend them like currency on whatever I liked was freeing. It's also validating. I wasn't lazy or forgetful or unfocused because all I was able to do this morning was get out of bed, have coffee, and put my contacts in; I had but one spoon left, and I needed that one for the afternoon when I had to finally respond to an email I'd been dreading, so I'd stay in bed under the covers for another hour or three. I was grieving. Like a traumatic brain injury, grief is mostly invisible, misunderstood, and typically lost sympathy all too quickly.

So when I forced myself to venture out on an especially uncomfortable errand, in anticipation I banked some spoons. Standing still as if pressed between two panes of glass, I barely could breathe, the act of mailing the letter to the National Collegiate Athletic Association paralyzing me in the line at the post office. I'd put off this errand long enough, and though I calculated how many spoons this task would cost me, I doubted I had enough in reserve.

Before I sealed the envelope, I scanned the three-page letter one more time:

Mark Emmert
NCAA
700 West Washington Street
PO Box 6222
Indianapolis, IN 46206-6222

Dear President Emmert,

As you know there is a growing concern about concussions in sports. What you may not know is that there are an estimated four million sports-related concussions each year. **This is one concussion every 8 seconds!** All concussions are serious because they are traumatic brain injuries and most occur without the person being knocked unconscious. Concussions happen in every sport, with young children playing hockey, football, soccer, basketball, wrestling, baseball, and cycling at the highest risk. There are far too many concussions but far too few programs educating parents, athletes, and coaches to the dangers, signs, symptoms, and prevention of these traumatic brain injuries. There is even less attention being paid to critical research that could minimize, diagnose, and treat brain injuries.

THE DEREK SHEELY FOUNDATION was created to increase awareness and research of concussions and traumatic brain injuries, with a focus on youth sports. The Foundation is named in honor of my beloved son, Derek Thomson Sheely, a strong and healthy 22-year-old honor student who played fullback for ten years. Derek was a two-time academic all-conference selection in college and **never had a documented concussion**. On August 22, 2011, during practice for his senior season at ----- (an NCAA Division III school), Derek suffered a brain injury and died one week later on August 28. It is believed that Derek died from Second Impact Syndrome, which occurs when a second concussion is sustained before the brain can recover from a first concussion. As Derek's mother and the Executive Director of The Derek Sheely Foundation, I am dedicated to preventing other children and families from suffering through the devastating effects of concussions and brain injuries.

THE DEREK SHEELY FOUNDATION is committed to "Leading the Way" towards concussion and brain injury awareness and research. We often think about the level of medical support available to NCAA Division I football players and professional athletes during games, however, the vast majority of the nearly 4 million concussions that occur each year happen at youth sporting events where there are no medical professionals available, where the athletes are young children and the coaches are parents. In these cases, education aimed at young children and their parents could prevent hundreds of thousands of concussions per year from becoming more severe.

As you know, sports-related concussions and brain injuries are not something that can be solved quickly with a simple fix; rather, they are a national epidemic, requiring years of educating athletes while they are young to the signs, symptoms, and precautions. While helmet and protective gear technology is important, there never will be a concussion-proof helmet because they can never prevent the brain from hitting the skull. Therefore, The Derek Sheely Foundation has a unique goal as compared to other concussion organizations. That goal is to lead an initiative to educate young children, with a focus on ages 7-14, to what a concussion feels like, what you should do when you think you have a concussion, why reporting a concussion ASAP is important, and what can you do to avoid/minimize getting/giving a concussion. If we can break the stigma about athletes self-reporting concussions in these 7-14-year-olds now, then within a decade when these kids go on to play in high school and college, the concussion epidemic we are facing now could be greatly reduced. I know you are concerned about concussions and I know you have taken steps to help NCAA athletes, but I am asking for your help to use your power and resources to help me and The Derek Sheely Foundation extend concussion awareness and prevention to the millions of young athletes (sons, daughters, grandchildren, and great-grandchildren) playing and enjoying sports every day.

My son Derek was passionate about football and we are not looking to change the game. Derek may not have had the skills to play in NCAA Division I, but he did have the heart and dedication of an NCAA Division I athlete. One of Derek's favorite sayings listed on his Facebook page is, "Some men see things as they are and say 'Why?' I dream of things that never were and say, 'Why Not?'" It is with this spirit that The Derek Sheely Foundation has begun a campaign to raise $40 million to increase awareness and research of concussions and brain injuries (Derek wore number 40). We need the NCAA to partner with us to achieve this dream.

THE DEREK SHEELY FOUNDATION is open to many different partnering arrangements with the NCAA. I have listed several ideas below, but please feel free to edit or add to them. We could start small with one and build on our successes, or choose two or three that are most practical. Potential partnering arrangements:

Awareness Campaigns

Case Study on Derek's Accident: The Derek Sheely Foundation is conducting a Case Study of Derek's accident to determine lessons to help other children in the future. It was surprising to learn that the NCAA was not funding this Case Study, since Derek died from an injury caused during an NCAA sanctioned football practice. The NCAA can support and help fund our Case Study.

Concussion Prevention Hero: We can break the negative stigma with reporting concussions by rewarding young athletes who report a concussion in themselves or with a teammate. Prizes could be jerseys, tickets to see their favorite NCAA team, etc. Maybe NCAA Conferences/Schools could nominate one hero a year from their area for a special national heroes event at a conference football championship game or a BCS Bowl game. Much like the success with reducing breast cancer deaths over the past 40 years, the first key is education and self-reporting, and so we need to publicly break the stigma. No one can achieve this goal as well as the NCAA and its schools.

Public Service Announcements: Short 15-60 second You Tube, Facebook, Twitter style announcements given by famous NCAA coaches or players in a format today's youth can absorb.

NCAA Sponsors: Many NCAA sponsors (e.g., Nike, Under Armour, ESPN, Coke, Pepsi, computer companies, phones, etc.) target the same 7-14-year-old audience. The NCAA could reach out to these sponsors to get the message out and provide awards for the Heroes or funds for the awareness campaign.

Fundraising for The Derek Sheely Foundation

NCAA donations, whether checks or donated merchandise like BCS Tickets can help raise funds for awareness kits

NCAA Schools having coin boxes at games for donations – Make a Change with Your Change

NCAA press release noting support for The Derek Sheely Foundation and adding links to the Foundation on your websites, Facebook pages, and Twitter would greatly help

Thank you so much for taking the time to consider The Derek Sheely Foundation. I hope you can help us prevent concussion and traumatic brain injuries from affecting children, and your generous and tax-deductible donation can help us achieve our shared mission. Checks payable to "The Derek Sheely Foundation" can be sent to -----. Online donations can be made at our website, www.TheDerekSheelyFoundation.org. You can reach me directly at info@TheDerekSheelyFoundation.org.

Kristen L. Sheely
Executive Director

By the time I read the last line, I was out of spoons.

♥ ♥ ♥

What if what happened to Derek never really happened? I thought back to the phone call, to the time in the waiting room, to the time in the car with Ken on the way to Baltimore, to the rest of that terrible week, hour by hour, day by day: None of this seemed real. I ruminated about every angle of that week over and over again, all 156 hours 52 minutes, so often that I was now sure none of this happened; in fact, all of this must have happened to someone else, somewhere else. That's the only way any of this made sense. I grasped those thoughts as they came and tried to secret them away. I had to hold onto something.

Any memory we had was a memory of how we last remembered it. Not the actual event itself, but the *version* of it that we remembered. So, over time, that initial event I thought I remembered as a static, unchanging, carved-in-stone, I'd-never-forget-the-thing-that-happened-that-time actually morphed and changed in zillions of iterations every time I called it from my subconscious. So it followed that something I remembered, like Derek dying, because I'd called it forth so often, potentially never really happened. And what a glorious rabbit hole that was.

In fact, according to Dr. Mary-Frances O'Connor, in her stellar book, *The Grieving Brain*, the brain replays as memory "the neural activity that was generated during the original event," so merely a perception of the event is what is created as a lasting memory, which is then what is recalled in the present.

Therefore, perceptions could be wrong. Reality could be wrong.

Regardless, I wanted to remember everything, no matter how slanted, mutated, or blurred. Every scrap I found was a piece of Derek. He's slipping away, further away from me, with each passing second, so why wouldn't I want to search and reach for every bit and hold onto every piece I could forever? Including the horrible hours in the hospital. But Ken and Keyton were the opposite: they tried not to think about or relive that week because it was so painful, so sad; they didn't want to think about it if they could help it. I didn't want to think about it either, but if I blocked it out, kept it quiet behind a heavy door, then I would have to make every effort to keep that door shut no matter what. If all my strength were engaged in keeping the door shut, then nothing else could happen, not grief and not happiness, either. I couldn't choose to ignore and forget only the difficult and unpleasant things behind the heavy door and embrace only the joyous and wonderful things in front of it – I feared that avoiding my feelings would lead me to become even more numb to everything eventually, both the good and the terrible. And I didn't want to use up all my strength, all my spoons, to forget, because then I'd open myself to losing more of Derek. I'd lost enough already.

♥ ♥ ♥

Very dark places crowded together in my mind, a tenement of memories of the week in the hospital held fast with string and dust and sometimes they cascaded forward and tumbled out, splintering fast into tiny pools of silver mercury that bent and receded and then returned to form behind my heartbroken eyes.

Why wasn't my love for him enough?

Where am I supposed to go from here?

And there I was, standing at the kitchen island assembling concussion awareness kits for the foundation, rereading the pamphlet I'd written days ago that described symptoms and facts about concussions, that loss of consciousness didn't always happen, that a headache or blurred vision or slurred speech or nausea didn't always appear immediately, and some or all of these symptoms could occur hours or days later, that recovery could take weeks or even months. I tried to look for typos, but all I saw was Derek's photo on the back, with the last line, IF THIS CAN HAPPEN TO DEREK, IT CAN HAPPEN TO ANYONE, in all caps.

I kept shaking my head. *What was I doing?*

Why did I have to hold onto this calm, rational understanding, this going through the motions of normalcy? None of this was normal. Was this my punishment: I must go on living like Before – I must act normal and nice amid all circumstances no matter what, even though everything was changed and I was forever brokenhearted.

But it was impossible to be normal and nice as I retraced my steps back to Shock Trauma, thinking about those hours, remembering things I knew I'd forgotten and dreading the details I found, but desperate to find more and more because every lost bit found was another piece of Derek to save and keep close. My mind kept going to places I didn't want it to go, and then I felt incredibly guilty for making myself stop and come out of it, like I had to shake my head to free myself from the snare around my neck. Mindful, somewhat, of the growing gap between Ken and me, of the heavy door he held shut, and I knew that he didn't want to let that door open, not even a crack, and go back to that week in August. Reliving that time was painful and difficult for me, too, but anything I could forget was a part of Derek, and I couldn't keep losing him over and over again, a little bit at a time. There was no middle ground for us on this. I was alone, Ken was in Maryland for weeks at a time, and when we talked on the phone at night, I wanted to talk about it, but he didn't. So we didn't, because I didn't want to make him sadder. But I tried to go deeper in my own thoughts anyway, maybe even blurring what I remembered, because the more I went to very dark places, the more I dreaded them, and the more I dreaded them, the more I wanted to go to very dark places.

VERY DARK PLACES

♥ ♥ ♥

For weeks, months, I'd been writing to Derek, texting him, writing him a note every night asking him to come home. But one night I picked up my phone to text him, to tell him Keyton saw Wale perform at Penn State, and in a flash as I pressed *send* recognized that I was texting a phone that was downstairs in my handbag. Until that moment, texting him was from me to him, not from me to just his phone. Unbidden, time drew yet another indelible line. Maybe it was this line that drew me to cancel Derek's cell phone.

Are you sure you want to give up the phone number you know you can never get it back, the woman on the line at the cell phone company we no longer use and would never recommend said as I tried to cancel. I knew by her flat tone she didn't give a shit about what I'd just told her, the actual reason we had to cancel, yet still I tried not to cry. I'd made numerous calls to other places earlier that week, finding spoons I didn't know I had, and this woman wasn't as kind as the lady on the other end of the call at Derek's student loan place. Nor the guy at Xbox magazine. Nor the woman at Derek's bank. Nor the man at Derek's credit card company. I hated this cell phone woman in that moment in the middle of the big box store, the way she casually annihilated me with her indifference and lack of true customer service, and I tried to keep it together for the sake of the young 20-something guy who was seated quietly at his register, head down, trying to help me change my family phone plan of four down to three. I hated her, I hated I had to do this instead of meeting a friend for coffee or meeting Derek for a tattoo appointment like we did the year before he graduated high school, my design a dragonfly to honor my dearly departed grandma, his the start of an upper arm sleeve, a sleeve finally completed barely a month before he left for pre-season camp, a camp he didn't survive. I hated everything having to do with the foundation, the fun run we were planning, the scholarship we were funding, the goddamn thank-you notes with Derek's face on them, these notes I wrote and sent, wrote and sent. And I wanted the anger to fill me, fill me enough to replace the empty pain I felt with something else, something red and hot and fist clenching. I screamed and pounded the steering wheel as soon as I got back into my car.

Soon after I cancelled, I texted Derek like I usually did, and I got an unexpected response, *Sorry, this isn't Derek.* I stared at the screen for what felt like hours before I replied my last reply to my son's phone. Yet another connection I had with Derek was gone.

♥ ♥ ♥

I sipped my wine. Why not? I asked.

Just don't read it, Ken said.

We'd been on the phone for close to two hours even though he'd be on his way to Penn State in the morning. The fun run fundraiser we were planning was approaching fast, and there remained a lot to do. I didn't want to do any of it. When Ken mentioned an email had come in to the foundation's website, and I shouldn't read it, I was interested.

It's upsetting. Just don't read it. Please.

Fine.

We can look at it together tomorrow, he relented.

♥ ♥ ♥

There was an enormous fir tree in our yard surrounded by a stone wall constructed of flat blue stone. Another gigantic fir lived closer to our Penn State house, just off the corner of the front porch, so close its lower branches used to brush the roof. I liked to think that the two of them were connected underground, their roots stretching toward each other and intertwining, silent support from below. Every time there's a fierce wind, pine cones dropped and rolled, striking our roof with loud staccato thunks before they tumbled onto the yard, where they lay akimbo like abstract art until squirrels arrived and feasted, leaving behind neatly shredded pine cone cobs.

One afternoon, the fir tree just feet from our house was struck by lightning. The sound was like a bomb went off. Wood splintered and pieces shot in every direction. Fortunately, the tree suffered only minor damage that an experienced arborist pruned back to health a few days later, and there was no fire nor significant property damage, except for the total loss of our flat screen television, computer printer, and garage door opener, which were destroyed because they were all plugged into the same electrical circuit on the lightning side of the house.

We'd had numerous storms, many with substantial lightning, many resulting in blown transformers and downed wires, and our tree was one of countless similar ones over 100 feet tall and probably more than 100 years old in our neighborhood. But never had it ever been struck in an electrical storm. *Why our tree?* It was a fluke, an exceptional occurrence. Rare, even.

Thinking then about Derek's involvement in sports over the years, not only football, but soccer, track, lacrosse, and all of the teammates he'd had, the opponents, likely hundreds, even thousands of young athletes practicing and competing, and all I could do was wonder, *Why him?*

Since that Monday morning in August after we'd listened to the voicemail left by one of the athletic trainers, we'd been in a chronic state of disbelief. We'd played and replayed what we were told and tried to piece together the bits of information we were given by his teammates and the coaches who visited Derek in the hospital. What we learned was very little. What happened? Over and over, by different people, We don't know what happened, was repeated in the hallways, in the conference room, at the funeral. Derek was so young, so strong, and so healthy. Why did we have to, Call me back as soon as you get this message – *What happened on that field, exactly?*

We were told, This was a freak accident. We were told, We watched film from practice, and there was no unusually violent hit or anything like that. We were told, We don't know what happened; he was fine and then he collapsed. We were told all of this within days, within hours really, of getting the phone call, back in the waiting room in the hospital in western Maryland while Derek was alone in the white room. We believed what they were telling us, that it was some sort of unforeseeable, unpreventable accident, a lightning strike-type super-rare happening. We had no reason to doubt anyone. These were people who knew Derek, people whom he trusted.

And then exactly seven months later on Thursday March 22, 2012, we received an anonymous email (lightly edited below for brevity). It was from John Doe, and the subject line read, **Information Behind the Death of Derek Sheely**.

Hello,

I would like to start off by saying that I am very sorry for the loss of a great spirited man like Derek. I had only known Derek since the Spring of 2011, and I am proud to say he was a friend and teammate of mine.

I have struggled with revealing to the family some information that was either "forgotten" to be told to the family or that was simply left out. But I can say after reading many interviews from the family and seeing the different news reports, important information was left out about what happened that day and the days preceding his death.

The reason I have been so conflicted with telling the information with it being so vital is that I did not want to cause more hurt and pain and confusion to the family after losing their son and brother...But now I feel that the family must know that it was not just an "ordinary concussion," but also negligence on the part of some football coaches.

Playing fullback Derek was a lot of the time in the thick of the grime and the violence involved with football. During our position periods, the fullbacks often were working on blocking and violent collisions, which is normal for the game. However, the coach made it way more dangerous than what it should have been.

One drill the running backs and fullbacks would do is run through our plays so we can correct mistakes. The fullbacks who were not in the current offensive position had to go and play defense to give a visual to the offensive players. These players giving the visual look COULD NOT DEFEND THEMSELVES. When the fullback would go to block, the coach would often say, "KNOCK THE SHIT OUT OF HIM" (keep in mind this is a defenseless player), and when players would try to make their own contact to defend themselves, they were often met by the coach's fury for "not following the drill."

I say all of this to give background on what happened with Derek. Derek happened to be one of the defenseless players just because he was caught off guard. I am not 100% sure if a helmet to helmet occurred but after the contact, to me it looked as if Derek had gone woozy for a second or two. But he shook it off like we often did and he went through the next periods of practice.

178

Later in that practice, during the team period which is full contact, Derek had come back to the huddle and told the coach that he had a headache. I kind of felt like something had to be wrong because Derek NEVER showed pain.

The coach's response was, "Stop your bitching and moaning and quit acting like a pussy and get back out there Sheely!"

A second coach standing right next to him heard Derek's complaint, heard the first coach's response and said nothing. Derek did as he was instructed and continued to practice for a few more minutes.

Later a formation was finally called that Derek was not involved in and he got to get behind the drill where all the rest of the players were and he quickly took a knee, then knelt on all fours, kind of gasping for air. A few players yelled for the coaches, "Coach, look at Sheely!" and the two coaches scoffed and yelled at him to get up. When he tried, and they realized he could not, they waited a few minutes then walked over to him and talked to him. I do not know what was said, but then they called the trainers over and they went back to practice. That's when I went back to practice and the next thing I saw, were the trainers trying to help him off the field, when suddenly he collapsed.

I am not completely sure what was told to you as far as him telling a coach that he had a headache, but quite simply two coaches were aware that he did have a headache and took NO precautions to ensure his safety.

My thoughts are still with the Sheely family, as they have been since August 2011.

♥ ♥ ♥

Were it not for the courage of this young man, Derek's friend and teammate and the author of the anonymous email, we never would have learned what happened to our son. We still do not know everything that happened, but we know for sure it wasn't an accident nor a lightning strike. We've never gotten an apology. We've never even gotten a full explanation. All we've ever gotten were shrugged shoulders and *we don't know what happened.*

In just nine days at pre-season football practice, my son suffered so much brain trauma that he died. My beautiful, smart, 22-year-old son, in the best shape of his life. He died.

All of the coaches knew him – Derek was a senior, a seasoned member of the team, with a valiant work ethic on and off the field. After I read the email, I had countless questions. Was his blood not red enough? His complaints of being injured not dire enough? This was no accident. This was no lightning strike. This was preventable. I will forever believe that he should have been saved. Why wasn't he?

What happened, Derek? All I see now are layers of nightmarish secrecy, and then you're called a warrior, your name inscribed onto a stone. Like you died on the battlefield wrapped in a flag. This wasn't a field of war – this was a game – not even a game – this was practice! Taken together, everything we know now could be called torture. What else happened that we never knew about? Preseason camp should be about bonding with your teammates, building strength, learning plays and strategy. All of this can't be normal, these brutal drills, the vicious verbal abuse; this can't be a common occurrence in the life of a college student athlete. Can it?

This was no accident.

This was preventable.

This was preventable.

What the fuck, this was preventable!

empty set

half of me remembers everything
and the other half forgets nothing
half in full color, half in greyscale
my hands are full
I have to hold everything
leave nothing behind
as half of me is missing
Derek is missing
It's still your birthday
yet you're not here
you stay 22 every year
the math fails me –
Such thoughts cascade and multiply,
overwhelm and divide
The math of grief:
take away one, add one, keep one, carry one

I struggled with high school trigonometry and then college algebra and calculus. I whined daily, I'll never use any of this! But that turned out not to be true: all of it, from the exponents to factorials, from sines to cosines, I use all of the math now.

Even on days like today, Derek's birthday, there's math and grief, and I doubted anyone could begin to calculate the sum of my suffering, no matter what advanced degree you might have. In the bent geometry of grief, there were too many variables, imaginary numbers, real numbers – I couldn't solve for x because I didn't know all of the numbers that belonged in that particular equation. And no one knew all the numbers that I studied every day, the numbers I shuffled around, the numbers I transposed, enough numbers that became fractions and multiples and decimal places to the point oh-oh-oh-oh-nth place. To ultimately an empty set as the answer.

Take the Fibonacci sequence, where each number built upon the one before it. Perfection: 1, 1, 2, 3, 5, 8, 13, 21, 34, 55, 89, and so on. The pattern spiraled onto a pine cone, a pineapple, in sunflowers, in artichokes. Trees and their leaves thrived upon this spiral sequence, as did honeybees. The sequence grew and grew and nothing lessened, not ever. It fit right in with grief math, didn't it, the never-ending sequence spilling onto reams of graph paper, this golden ratio of sorrow.

The math of grief: time passing by, yet Derek stayed 22 always. How to define this mathematical proof that I must defend with theorems and postulates, numbered and written in complete sentences. Period at the end. QED. Why did my math have to make sense to anyone else? No one needed to question the math. No one needed to question the answer. No one needed to tell me that unless I could learn something from all of this and thus become a bigger and better person and have songbirds singing a song of positivity around me, then I'd be a failure and my math was wrong. My math *must* be wrong. No one needed to challenge my mathematical proofs, my theorems, my calculations that spooled and spooled into my cupped palms. I couldn't possibly miss Derek this much; there was just no way. I *couldn't possibly* be in this much pain yet still be standing upright? It was not only possible, but it is. *It is.* A Fibonacci spiral never reversed, never lessened, and neither did my grief.

Maybe there was a baseline now, a baseline of sorrow, developed over time. The x-axis of time was ever increasing, but the y-axis of grief was reasonably stable, as I'd gotten used to the daily unbelievable-ness and constant unacceptable-ness. Random spikes of profound sorrow dot the graph on days like any holiday or Derek's birthday, the kind of spikes that not only are exponentially sharp but also enduring. Anticipatory stabs add to the peaks until the resulting graph looks like a reading from the earthquake while Derek was in the hospital. The erratic-looking graph proved it was taking a long time to adjust. To know – *really know* – that Derek was gone. I had only just gotten used to his presence, and now I had to face his absence? I didn't know how to do that, and even science told me that my brain didn't know how to do that.

I tried my best on his birthday. I'd put out a plea on effbook for everyone to post photos of 40 that they might find. I scrolled and scrolled, 40s as mile markers, house numbers, dollars and cents on a receipt.

It's still Derek's birthday, even if people forgot.

Another year older, yet he's really 22 every year from now on. For me, all I did was lose years: as my son stayed 22 forever, I turned 43, 56, 74, 90-something-dead.

Happy Birthday, Derek! I must love you hard, and love you well still in the missing. Where should I go to let you know I hadn't forgotten?

Especially on his birthday I woke to life only about one-half of the way because I had to be ready, vigilant. I'd dreamed that Derek could be back, and I had to give him my full attention. I would tilt my head toward what might be him. A memory, his presence, his anything. His return. Jesus emerging from behind the stones, if I believed in that sort of thing anymore. Perhaps I should start believing in ghosts, or pretend that I had all along, just so I could imagine Derek with the strength to travel, to say Hello. The hum of reality dimmed for me on days like these, and stepping over and around the familiar-unfamiliar was convoluted and strange. Everything was muted when I was only half-there, half-listening, half-alive. So easy to trip over the truth when I couldn't bear to look at it every day. That's the special sad logic of grief for you.

Here's a beer, a dinner. A cake, a card, a check. Work tomorrow, so I'll be home by eleven, you say. (Because of course you still live with us.) My breathing pauses hours later, waiting to hear the garage door go up, signaling you're safely home. The soft click of the door, your slow trying-to-be-quiet footsteps on the stairs. Tap on the door. I'm home, you whisper.

Why couldn't it be like this?

Why did I instead have to be still completely exhausted, still totally overwhelmed, still consumed with guilt, still numb in disbelief?

I was defined by what I was missing: my son. Love in negative space.

Why was I the one feeling left? When he's the one who left?

183

♥ ♥ ♥

While Ken had told me not to read the anonymous email because it was too disturbing, he nevertheless thought initially that it was from a disgruntled teammate. This can't be real, Ken said over and over. For some time, we didn't even tell anyone about the email; it was too unimaginable. Our utter disbelief paralyzed us, numbed us as we awarded the first Derek Thomson Sheely Leadership Award and Scholarship at the same school where the email said Derek was on the ground while coaches stood over him berating, ridiculing, and mocking him, coaches who sat at the next table at the scholarship ceremony, coaches who smiled and laughed over dinner as Ken and I sat there in silence.

According to the facts of the case, Derek asked for help for his hurt and bleeding head four times. According to the facts of the case, Derek collapsed on the field of the game that he loved. Now Derek is kept in a box next to my pillow as I try to sleep – how is this my son – how did I let this happen? How small and dark the box, how hot the flames, how violent the people.

All of our emotions, the anger, confusion, sorrow, helplessness, blurred together and combined into something we couldn't recognize or name.

All along we'd been assured that time would help, that it would get easier, that peace and healing would arrive. I didn't believe any of that when I first heard these platitudes from the mouths of people I knew and trusted, and I certainly didn't believe any of it now. Peace? Healing? *Easier?* What the actual fuck? My son's death appeared to have been preventable; what part of that sentence could possibly become easier?

♥ ♥ ♥

And where was the NCAA investigation?

Though school officials had predicted there'd be an investigation, which was why we weren't allowed to have Derek's helmet, an investigation had never even been initiated. I did finally receive a reply to the letter I'd sent months ago, though, a terse one-page response that assured me the NCAA was doing everything it could to ensure athlete safety, and I was directed to their web site.

March 20, 2012

Ms. Kristen Sheely
Executive Director
The Derek Sheely Foundation
14001 Falconcrest Road
Germantown, Maryland 20874

P.O. Box 6222
Indianapolis, Indiana 46206
Telephone: 317/917-6222

Shipping/Overnight Address:
1802 Alonzo Watford Sr. Drive
Indianapolis, Indiana 46202

www.ncaa.org

Dear Ms. Sheely:

When your letter arrived, President Emmert shared it with members of the NCAA national office staff who work on student-athlete health and safety issues and asked that I reply on his behalf. Your son Derek's death indeed was tragic, and I send my heartfelt condolences to you and your family on behalf of the NCAA. I applaud the courage and character it takes to make a positive impact out of Derek's death.

Part of the NCAA's core mission is to provide student-athletes with a competitive environment that is safe and ensures fair play. While each school is responsible for the welfare of its student-athletes, the NCAA provides leadership by establishing safety guidelines, playing rules, equipment standards, and supporting research into the cause of injuries. Unfortunately, neither the NCAA nor any other organization can take the risk completely out of contact sports, but we will continue to devote our attention to health and safety issues and do what we can to study the causes of injury. This will include educating student-athletes, coaches, trainers, and administrators about recognizing health and safety issues, developing and distributing guidelines to best deal with them, and to enact change to our rules and standards when the medical evidence indicates it is appropriate to do so. The NCAA consults with a number of knowledgeable experts in the field, including those who serve on the NCAA's Committee on Safeguards and Medical Aspects of sports, to guide us.

I encourage you to visit the NCAA's health and safety landing page at www.NCAA.org/url/healthsafety if you have not done so already. There may be resources there that will be helpful for your foundation's awareness campaigns, including encouraging student-athletes and those who work with student-athletes to understand the symptoms of a concussion and to report those symptoms as soon as they can.

The NCAA will continue its efforts to try to prevent the tragedies that can arise during participation in athletics. Again, we are so very sorry for your loss.

Sincerely,

David Klossner, PhD, ATC
Directory of Health and Safety

DK/tmm

cc: President Mark Emmert

National Collegiate Athletic Association
An association of over 1,200 members serving the student-athlete
Equal Opportunity/Affirmative Action Employer

We're sorry for your loss.

There never was an investigation. An actual one probably would have shed more light onto what happened to Derek and prevented it from happening again more than anything else could have. We were so lost in the numbness of grief that we probably would have continued to believe whatever we were told.

♥ ♥ ♥

When I woke up, it was still dark. Was it still raining, I grumbled as I pulled myself out of bed. I peered out the bathroom window and saw color, the pink, orange, and blue hues that promised the sun.

The first annual Derek Sheely Lead the Way 4.0 Run/Walk was today, and I was anxious and sweaty as I anticipated hours of the unknown. Ken was in charge of nearly all of the moving parts that went into directing a race, so what was my role today?

I applied for all the permits, and I met with officials from the high school. I designed the postcards advertising the run/walk, and Ken and I littered the neighborhoods around the school, tucking a card under a welcome mat or in a storm door. I designed a banner that announced the race and recognized our sponsors. I ordered medals and race shirts. I flooded social media with race reminders, and I applied for freebies, like protein bars, fruit bars, and water, fast food coupons, bagels, and bananas. For the past week, I'd been stuffing goodie bags with t-shirts, bibs, and the swag items for the runners and walkers.

And I had no idea what to do today.

Run the registration table, Ken suggested.

Okay. Good. That I could do.

Keyton was close by my side until her cousins arrived, and then they wandered off. My parents mingled with Derek's friends, and my dad pilfered a couple of bagels for them.

Everyone wanted to hug me. I smiled into the sun and murmured and nodded my head, holding my breath from one encounter to the next, my teeth on edge, the fingernails of my right hand scratching the back of my left, as I tried to act as normal as I could.

From the beginning, I knew I was going to run, so when the song came over the loudspeakers that was second to last in the playlist curated by Keyton, I started walking around the track to the far side, where the starting line was. "Remember the Name" blared into the morning air, and the tension I'd been feeling melted into tears. The next thing I heard was Ken's voice, announcing the race and talking about Derek and then thanking everyone for being here.

Suddenly he shouted, Ready, Set, Go!

And we went. Around the track and out the gate to the street, keeping to the right of the cones, the hundreds of cones we'd rented and loaded into the Escalade, the cones my three brothers-in-law had placed on the street, past our house, to the turnaround about two miles away. Police kept us safe at the two intersections we had to navigate, officers who'd volunteered to help us on race day, thanks to a friend in the department.

Ken's mom and her partner were at the water station set up almost in front of our house, and I heard them yell and cheer as I went by. When I reached the turnaround, Ken's brother clapped and shouted, You're halfway there!

By the time I returned to the stadium, so had my tears. I'd been running faster than my usual pace, and I wanted more than anything to veer left and sit down in the stands. But I had to stay to the right and run around the track to get to the finish line. I had to get my medal. So whatever kick I had left pushed me into a sprint.

And here comes Derek's mom!

Shit, shit, shit, I'm really crying now, I thought when I heard Ken.

The last turn, and there was Ken and I saw the finish line. I pulled up and hugged my husband, sobbing into his chest, almost unable to breathe. Go finish, he whispered.

So I did. A very small girl I didn't know tried to hand me a medal, but I bowed my head. Please put it on me, I asked, and crouched low into a squat. Thank you, I said, as she looped the medal around my neck. I stood and turned and saw Keyton running around the back side of the track.

Keyton! I screamed. I watched her duck her head for a moment, so I stayed at the finish line. I hugged her hard a few seconds later.

I don't want to do this I don't want to do this I don't want to do this, she cried.

I know, I know, honey, I said. *She's out of spoons.* Let's get some water. I kept my arm around her shoulders as we walked to the bleachers. Let's watch people finish, I said.

All told, over 400 people came out for Derek's race that first year. An amazing turnout, and a successful fundraiser for our fledgling efforts at concussion awareness. Unfortunately, the numbers began to slowly dwindle from this June to the next June and onward, and so a few years later we decided to simplify the whole operation. Instead of needing extra permits and cones and police and almost 40 volunteers for a 4-mile out and back race, we kept the race to the track, where we ran or walked for 40 minutes. Running in circles instead of hairpin turns and dead-end curves to nowhere.

♥ ♥ ♥

Once the flurry of the race was over, I contacted an attorney and began to learn what a lawsuit would entail should we choose to pursue one. We were desperate to get to the truth of what happened to Derek, *because we don't know what happened*. At its core, the lawsuit wasn't about money, and it certainly wasn't going to bring Derek back. It wasn't about healing, either. Healing comes from the Old English word, *hǽlan*, for cure, to save, to make whole, sound, and well, and there'd be none of that derived from a lawsuit. Not for us. And honestly, the lawsuit wasn't even really about justice. What justice could be had? It was pretty much a last resort effort to share Derek's story to try and save other kids from meeting a similar tragedy.

Healing was also nonexistent when August arrived, despite my willing it not to.

One year.

And with this milestone was the horrible truth that I would have to carry with me from now on: This week defined me.

Monday –

Tuesday –

Wednesday –

Thursday –

Friday –

Saturday –

Sunday.

Everything that happened that August week haunted me. Was it more real, one year later? Or was it more unbelievable?

It could be both. It should be both.

One year was not a lot of time, and yet it was more time than could be measured in grief world. And there were truths to be found in those 365 days, truths I'd rather not know. For me, there was no understanding to be found in this. No lesson, no reason, nor newfound possibilities, either. There I was, caught in the narrow between of what I remembered and what really happened, and I couldn't actually believe any of it.

It's head-shakingly and mind-numbingly sad: *There* and *then* was where I existed, landed, and moved; never was I just *here* and *now*.

And this was grief's stranglehold.

Sure, I could absolutely remind myself not to think about Derek's last week of life, to try to step around it to see if I could avoid falling in over my head. But since that week continued to affect me more than any other time in my life had, I must look directly at it. I had to see it, for all its pain, its horror, its darkness. Everything stopped then; there was no forward, no back, no other way to look but at that week, and what I wished should have been done to save my son. And it's there, exactly there, where I wanted to be.

♥ ♥ ♥

It's disconcerting the way the calendar never stopped. My heart managed to crack and break a little more every day – the pieces were almost too small to see and impossible to fit back together.

May came around again, and we awarded another scholarship to a rising senior at the school where Derek transferred. I was glad we did this in Derek's name, but I didn't want to be doing this. Grief made it difficult to read the essays written by students who were nominated for the award, painful to read about their hopes and dreams, difficult when they mentioned Derek, and more difficult when they didn't. This whole concept of a young person getting something – honored for their hard work with a scholarship – only because my son was dead, like how he was an organ donor and it's only useful to someone else when he's dead. Such a sick idea, these kinds of benevolent gestures, gestures that had fallout that's rarely considered in polite company.

189

The scholarship then made me think of the recent fundraisers held in Derek's name, his picture and story used to raise money for concussion awareness. His face on a t-shirt sold to raise funds for his foundation. Could I be grateful yet also awkwardly question: Why weren't we asked first? Why didn't people ask us what we needed? These raisers-of-funds, why didn't they ask me what I needed instead of stepping in and trying to save me with their idea of what would? Here, look what we did, we had a 50-50 drawing, look at our poster we made, that the sorority made, look what the booster club put together for you, and we raised xxx dollars and xx cents, here's a check let me press it into your hand and wasn't this so wonderful what we did and please thank us and now *doesn't this make you feel happy and grateful and better?*

Was Derek there to be shared by the public? Was my family? Were all the other families grieving their children's deaths because of traumatic brain injuries also there to be publicly shared? Were we all just images on poster, clip art free for the taking, in a way? When was enough *enough?* Was it okay for a journalist to write a story about yet another dead kid from playing sports and refer to Derek's story and his picture as a vetted secondary source without asking us first? Was I too sensitive about this? It's a mindfuck to have the "on this day" notifications out of the blue chime first thing in the morning *(please notify me before the notification),* let alone scroll along on the bird app and unexpectedly see my son's face and then plummet into shock for half a day. Yes – of course we wanted his story shared. Yes! But to use him like this – when did he become just another example? Didn't this treatment of him flatten him? What about his life and how he lived?

Was I also guilty of flattening him?

My grief had a thousand questions. And I had to ask them.

♥ ♥ ♥

The complaint was filed on August 22, 2013, two years to the day of Derek's fatal injury. And right out of the gate, the defense tried to dismiss our case, claiming that the NCAA had no legal duty to protect student-athletes. Words, that when questioned by a congressional committee, the then-NCAA president admitted were a "terrible choice of words."

No shit!

After the filing, discovery moved forward, interrupted here and there with more paperwork, hearing delays, weather delays, motions to this, motions to that, motions to dismiss. I started to feel like Derek must have, all those years ago on the bus, when those big kids put their coats over his head and started punching him from all sides when he wouldn't give up his seat.

I don't see your name on it.

Derek had suffered, as his coaches, who, according to the facts of the case, berated him, didn't care one whit about his condition, and forced him to continue to play to the point of collapse. And then we suffered, as the truth was kept from us, that no one knew what happened.

What would Derek do?

He would stand up for himself and for others. He would keep going.

So we kept going, too. We didn't back down, deciding to provide pages and pages of complete answers to the interrogatories, and share photos, whatever videos we had, even Derek's high school football helmet. One of the tasks I had to do was scan page after single page of Derek's medical record to send to our attorneys. From both hospitals. Trying to do this without looking was a feat beyond impossible, like sitting in Montgomery County's Register of Wills office asking for copies of Derek's death certificate without saying the actual words. I had to look; I had to ask.

We also put out a public appeal for the anonymous writer of the email to come forward. I could feel myself holding my breath as we waited, our plea adrift in the electronic ether of the internet; what if the email wasn't even real? That it was from an angry, vengeful teammate, like Ken had wondered. It was too terrible to be true – if it was, then Derek's death really was preventable. Was he really screamed at, cursed at, berated, dehumanized to get up when he was down on all fours? Called disgusting names? Ridiculed though he'd collapsed? It was so horrific in its detail, how could it possibly be true? But it was – our attorney went on a tireless search to find the anonymous teammate. After more than a year, he was able to identify the IP address where the email originated, a gym in Maryland. He then subpoenaed the gym for a list of its employees, and one of whom was a former teammate of Derek's. Since the anonymous email writer had left the area and moved to North Dakota, our attorney did not give up. He was able to confirm the former teammate had indeed written the email, and all of it was true. I promise to meet this brave teammate one day to hug him and thank him for his courage.

We also decided to give interviews. *Good Morning America* called first. Our attorneys were elated with this significant exposure. We were at Penn State and our interviewer was in New York: Our first national platform and we looked at a camera, talked to a phone, and I shook with nerves and fretted about how my hair looked. But our interview was heavily edited for time: It aired over Labor Day weekend in 2013, and the big story at that time was someone swimming the English Channel. We were relegated to fewer than three minutes on air to describe Derek, our grief, and his preventable death.

But sharing Derek's story was the point. So we took every opportunity we could. I remember talking to the *Baltimore Sun*, and then another newspaper, and then another, and it was someone else at yet another paper who asked near the end of the conversation how Derek was doing now. Upon hearing my answer, a cringey apologetic murmur stuttered into the phone: You're so strong; I don't know how you do it.

We talked about Derek whenever we could. For weeks, you could search Derek's name and find a new article published about him. We talked to *CBS Sports* and *Fox Sports* and *SBNation*. We talked to *CNN* and *HBO Real Sports*. It was bewildering, this attention, this being in the spotlight for terrible reasons, our grief on public display, and yet we knew that once the trial was over – if we even went to trial, which our attorneys had suggested was unlikely – the attention to Derek would wither and fade as the news cycle churned to something else, so we took advantage of the spotlight for Derek while we had it: we talked and talked and talked. Derek's story mattered to us as much as it ever did, and we did what we could to make it matter to everyone.

Well, Ken talked. He was very well-spoken as he tried to keep his emotions controlled. He had points and he methodically and calmly made them. Full-contact practice limits. Awareness of signs and symptoms of traumatic brain injuries. Teammates looking out for each other's well-being. Our attorneys talked about the lawsuit. And I barely spoke. All I could manage to do was cry and say, Derek was [redacted]. And every time I said it, I meant it more than the time before. Exponential growth. More math for the grief workbook that cannot be calculated because there's no correct answer. Grief was algebraically impossible to quantify – no solving for x here – yet we're always forced to show the work, weren't we? As if to prove our understanding of the impossible.

Though Ken spoke eloquently and I prepared as best I could, giving television interviews was challenging and awkward. They took much longer than I'd ever thought. We also sat under more hot lights than I'd imagined. Choosing what to wear was simple for Ken: shirt, tie, suit jacket; but it was a nightmare for me: why I put so much stupid effort into choosing what to wear I had no idea, because no matter the color or style, I wound up wearing an uncomfortable costume that didn't fit right and made me itch all over. I also didn't know why I wore something different for each interview; that was dumb. No one cared or remembered what I wore except me. My husband and I then were powdered and mic-ed, the sound guy handing me the small mic with a shaking hand and asking me to run it up my shirt and clip it to my neckline and then he'd make sure the wire coiled as smoothly as possible back down. Our furniture was shifted around for the best look, our seats chosen with care, with our straight-backed oak dining room chairs looking the most photogenic, and the best background had curtains opened or closed, books and pictures moved, positioned *just so* as if any of it made a fucking difference as we described what we knew about the sudden, traumatic, and preventable death of our son. Ready, quiet, action, and then our central air conditioner powered on during one interview and was so loud we had to stop. Another time Cinnamon decided to walk behind us as we sat, her nails click-clicking on the hardwood floor. How embarrassing. We also had to create a B reel sometimes, and so we walked with the interviewer outside as if casually engaged in light conversation. Smile a little, I was directed. I walked on shaking legs in new heels on the sidewalk in front of our home alongside my husband and the guy from HBO in between talking about what happened to Derek and what we think should have been done to save him, and answering that dreaded question, What do you miss most about him? and yeah, no, I'm not going to smile. Could you?

I gave a few interviews over the phone by myself. In one, a few phrases after the dreaded, How are you, I gave a leaden response to a question that prompted the interviewer to gently say, I hope I didn't upset you.

No, dude, I was completely fine until you reminded me about my dead child. I had forgotten all about that. How could you?

I took a breath to temper my caustic thoughts. No, you didn't upset me, I replied. *I'm always upset.* I wanted to tell him so many things that he didn't know and turn this interview upside down. I wanted to tell him the truth: Sometimes I just wanted to stop and sit in a dark room, because every day without Derek *was* my dark room. And that I looked for the bleak; in the dark was where I could see my son most clearly. I wanted to tell him I yearned for the very dark places, because there's safety there. Derek must be there, so why would I ever try to leave the dark?

It was never the questions. I needed only to wake up in the morning. I didn't need to look for the darkness. It's always there. A glimpse, a glance out of the corner of my eye, was all it took. No need to conjure the very dark place. It's right next to me on this couch at this very moment. It's the photo of Derek on the mantel, it's his hoodie folded away in a drawer upstairs, it's me sitting outside in the sun yesterday. I would close my eyes and see Derek's face. I'd imagine him asking me, I thought you'd help me, Mommy; where were you? Shoes on, and I ran out of the house, but of course the darkness followed me. The horses stood in the rain eating breakfast as I passed by. My shoes got wet, but I didn't mind. Who could care about rain when all I wanted was my son back? I'd run for hours. Perhaps then I'd find Derek somewhere in the woods, in the wet. Perhaps I'd find myself. I didn't know what to look for because I was lost. I knew I was lost. And I had to keep looking, always looking, for what I'd lost. Whom I'd lost.

Print interviews, however, were very different from talking on the phone or being on camera. It was a conversation, not a production. Our attorneys weren't even there. When we shared photos, we didn't have to position our faces a certain way for proper lighting. When I cried, I didn't try to compose myself after three-four-five seconds for the camera. Ken and I were able to go on tangents, clarify, interrupt each other. It was just as difficult, and I still worried about what to wear, but I wasn't as afraid to speak. I was more focused. I also wasn't as afraid to pause and take a breath after a question or inference that sounded presumptuous or coarse or obtuse like, Starting a foundation to honor your son was a wonderful way to turn your tragedy into something positive. *Oh is it really well what is swirling in my head right now are not thoughts of rainbows and sunshine plus there's no silver lining no bright side because none of that works for us not even trying to consider our wonderful memories no nothing brings us comfort so please fuck all of the way off because there's nothing positive that comes from losing a child.* I said only the last nine words out loud, but had I been on camera I would have said nothing and just looked down at the twisted tissue caught in my fists.

For months, in every interview I did, from *Good Morning America* to *HBO* to *CNN* to print journalism, I insisted that Derek was [redacted]. It's next to impossible in a two-minute 40-second interview to relay what Derek meant to us and that what happened to him was preventable. We tried our best to repeat that the decisions that were made to force him to continue to play and subsequently to viciously mock and bully him caused his death. But speaking the truth, that the last words Derek likely ever heard were ones that cruelly berated him, words shouted by people who knew him well, people who took more care to protect themselves after the fact than to protect their players before, was heartbreaking to articulate.

♥ ♥ ♥

Justice ran on slow wheels, and it was more than a year after our complaint was filed until Ken was deposed for eight hours. When I was deposed the next day, which our attorney found incredible – no one wants the mother on the stand, he said – I was questioned about teaching Derek to read, and that since I did – *I knew it was my fault* – shouldn't Derek have been able to read the warning on the back of his football helmet that football was dangerous? And that what happened wasn't intentional nor malicious nor neglectful nor planned – it was something terrible that sometimes happened during dangerous activities, and there was nothing anyone could do about it. So, according to the facts of the case, his being pressured to return to play despite asking for medical attention four separate times turned into it was my fault for teaching him to read, and it was his fault for reading and doing something dangerous anyway? I remembered the first doctor we spoke with at Shock Trauma, the one who clicked his pen like punctuation, had asked us whether Derek had been in a car accident. Then, Wasn't he wearing a helmet? No reading of a warning label that measured an inch by less than two inches would have made a difference. No reading of a warning label would have helped someone whose thinking was impaired because of a brain injury, someone who wanted to keep going no matter what. Especially not paired with the facts recounted in the anonymous email.

♥ ♥ ♥

It is important to note that athletes, children, or adults with concussions have a brain injury. Concussions alter brain functions, so the person may not even know they are injured. A concussed person may not have the cognitive skills to understand the seriousness of their injury or when it's safe for them to return to play. Concussions are not physically obvious, and brain swelling can continue for days, and symptoms may not appear immediately. Therefore, concussed players, brain-injured players, should not be, cannot be, should never be made responsible for their return to play decisions. It is true that sports (and life in general) are dangerous, but they shouldn't be made more dangerous with gladiatorial practice drills. And coaches, teammates, parents, trainers, and friends need to step in and protect concussed players from further injury.

VERY DARK PLACES

♥ ♥ ♥

Sunset then sunrise played on repeat, and in my mind all I thought about was the lawsuit and why we were in it in the first place. I didn't really deserve to be here or anywhere; in fact, it would be best if I were nowhere. How could I continue to bear this thing I was in, this afterlife: *the life each of us entered after the life of someone we loved had ended.* Maybe I should just voluntarily lock myself in a room, a very dark place, like a sort of reverse *The Yellow Wallpaper* situation. Willingly give up, give in, my hands thrown up in despair and tears permanently stained on my cheeks and just like that I would stay, like that childhood warning, Don't make that face or your face will stay like that! Watch out, I thought, or this would be the day when it happened, when I'd cry so much I'd snap into something unrecognizable, like a bent-over crone or a cobwebbed goblin or a pierced horn-implanted tongue-split lizard-eyed old hag *and then they'd take me seriously* the next time someone said, You're so strong or I can't imagine or You've turned this tragedy into something positive. There was no telling what might push me over the edge when these bitter feelings cloaked me like this.

And then one morning, two new emails waited in my inbox to be read.

I hesitated, unsure of my spoons in reserve, considering I'd received a handful of emails that denounced Derek for playing college ball in the first place, that since he hadn't been good enough to be a DI player, it was no surprise that....

I took a breath and clicked on the first one. A trauma fellow from Shock Trauma in Baltimore took the time to fill out the contact form of the foundation's website to send a kind note to tell me she remembered Derek, the significance of 40, and that she thought of "Derek and my beautiful family often."

In the other, a second trauma fellow also mentioned the importance of 40, and all that we had had to endure. That Derek was in the corner room on the end. And she remembered climbing onto a makeshift milk crate ladder so that she could reach him, affixing EEG sensors to him, so tall on the tilt table and she so short. And we'd been in her thoughts ever since.

In tears, I remembered two of the ICU nurses who came to Derek's funeral, and I sobbed at the impact Derek had had on so many people, even the health professionals who I'd assumed had checked their humanity at the door.

How was it possible that these near-strangers had been thinking about Derek and us with such kindness and warmth all this time? And all the while we never knew. It's overwhelming and humbling to think about, these strangers connecting with me in meaningful ways. Contrast that with my oldest friends, the JKLMs, who had been pretty much inexplicably absent. Why weren't these women who knew me, whom I thought loved me and cared about me, there for me when I needed them the most? Same with some friends, family, and Derek's friends. Was I a reminder of what could happen to them? That they're better off staying away, clicking or commenting on two-dimensional me on social media and avoiding the full-color truth of me? Maybe. And maybe I was ashamed to admit that I focused too much on negative things like these. It's hard not to. Healing, time, better, peace – hollow words, deceptive, ridiculous, meaningless – sure, time passed, healing happened in some aspects (i.e., pain was not as sharp nor as long-lasting), peace even came in a way albeit ironically as friends and family and their platitudes and interest splintered and fell away.

Peace was the quiet that appeared, but it wasn't real peace nor was it real quiet. To know anyone was thinking about Derek at any given moment was unbelievably meaningful. Even if the note was a brief, *I thought about Derek today.* This feeling of appreciation righted me, the way a proper wind could right a listing sail, even though I wasn't looking to be righted, even though I didn't care or was aware that I was even in danger of capsizing. Was this yearning for connection, a confirmation, a sign (!), that I was getting better at putting my grief to the side, for safekeeping, to save it for later? Did I have to do this to make room for kindness? A question like that tipped me into unevenness, an unevenness I needed the ground to rise up and meet, to steady me. Urgently.

Beannacht, the blessing of ease, that the clay should rise up to balance me.

♥ ♥ ♥

Based on everything we were told, we thought what happened to Derek was like a lightning strike, a tragic and rare accident, and that no one was to blame – we even told reporters this at first in early interviews we gave – but all that changed in the light of the anonymous email and compounded by troubling insights shared by some of his teammates when they were interviewed by our attorneys. I have effbook messages from teammates who shouldered blame *to this day* because they believed they should have done more to help Derek. Not a single message from an adult in charge, however. White-hot waves of rage coursed through me, unexpectedly expected, and I wanted to spit at them, strike them with missiles, pummel them with fists. We now had to shift to grieving the *preventable* death of our son, as if our grief couldn't get any worse. This grief shift felt as if Derek died all over again.

It's awesome you're suing, a neighbor of ours called from across the way, a seemingly encouraging comment instead sounding to my ears like, sickening, disgusting, terrible, horrible that we're having to do this in the first place.

As day after day went by, even more anger gripped us, coupled by bitter thoughts like *fire them fire everyone now* especially when we found out that a coach or two did leave only to keep on coaching at other colleges, and the head coach himself continued on as before for three more years until he retired.

All of the depositions were transcribed into two neat columns on countless pages, lines numbered. The complaint and all the associated legal memos and emails sent back and forth surrounding our case filled file folders, stick drives, stapled papers stacked inches thick. And once all the documents were filed, the depositions sat for, the pretrial hearings completed, we waited. This waiting felt endless, one hearing after the next, postponed or delayed, and finally a date came in June 2016 for trial.

According to the facts of the case, though Derek was on school property, the school wasn't liable, its employees weren't liable, since by the time we'd received and read the anonymous email, too much time had passed to pursue litigation. And, though the NCAA was the governing body of collegiate athletics (it's in its name), it wasn't liable, either, since it obdurately maintained it lacked the authority to enforce its own rules, like forbidding dangerous drills and the accompanying accountability. Or to rephrase: It insisted it didn't have the authority to enforce *certain* of its own rules. When questioned by congress, the then-head of the NCAA, the same one whom I wrote to pleading for help, stated that the organization had a "clear, moral obligation" to protect and support student-athletes; however, the NCAA's official position, declared in a legal filing, was that they had no legal duty to protect student-athletes, especially with regard to Derek's case. Despite the walk back in his congressional testimony, calling the legal filing a "terrible choice of words," the then-head of the NCAA was subjected to significant public scrutiny and political pressure.

Created in 1906 at the insistence of President Theodore Roosevelt, the NCAA's mission was to curtail severe and mortal injuries among football players. Fast-forward to 2011 when this nonprofit organization raked in $871.6 million in revenue the year Derek died, and tens of billions of dollars in the years since. How did such an influential entity appear to be in a chronic state of powerlessness when it came to enforcing rules that would actually protect student-athletes? Rules they did care about, however, seemed to be ones that might affect their bottom line, like recruiting and eligibility violations and (until recently) name and likeness rights. It's perplexing and infuriating. They also seemed to be quite arbitrary in what punitive action they did take, for example, the sanctions levied against Penn State for the horrific decades-long Sandusky child sexual abuse, but no sanctions levied against Michigan State for the horrific decades-long Nasser child sexual abuse, no sanctions levied against Ohio State for the horrific decades-long Strauss sexual abuse, and no sanctions levied against Frostburg State University for the wrongful death of my son, Derek Thomson Sheely.

♥ ♥ ♥

Then, one week before the trial was slated to begin, we received word of a proposed settlement.

Ken and I went back and forth on this. At first a sense of relief rushed over us: No trial. Nearly five years had passed since the week in the hospital. Living with the stress of a looming trial with the grief of losing Derek was an exhausting balance on a narrow highwire that kept swinging and threatening to throw us to the ground. We'd been warned that just one Montgomery County juror could blame Derek/put him at fault (like for playing football in the first place), and we would lose. The $2 million damages cap in Maryland was also low compared to other states, and a verdict in our favor would certainly go to appeal. Not to mention we wanted to protect Keyton, who, even though she hadn't been deposed, had to be prepared to be called as a witness and describe her close relationship with her brother and how living without him devastated her. We didn't want to put her through that.

But then again we thought, *What would Derek say?* Would he be pragmatic and settle? Or would he steel himself and continue fighting? Derek's voice was in my head: *Fuck this! Fuck everything! They want to settle because they're afraid of a trial. They're the scared ones — they tried numerous times for summary judgments to have the case dismissed. No one was investigated, no one was arrested, no one was held to account in the stockade in the public square; not even a single meeting was convened as far as we knew.* And in my head I agreed, Let's fucking go! Let's never give up!

It seemed like a no-win situation. A literal dilemma: two terrible choices. An empty set.

We had to decide what we really wanted the outcome to be. Not an easy conversation to be had to hash out this question posed by our attorneys. And when we took our emotions out of it (or made the attempt), a settlement gave us the most of what we wanted more than a victory at trial ever would.

Sheely v. NCAA was a landmark settlement that marked the first time the NCAA had ever settled with an individual plaintiff in a brain injury case.

We would like to think Derek's case helped spark and lead the way for the transformation seen in player safety and well-being. In 2014, Northwestern University football players, backed by the College Athletes Players Association (CAPA), sought to unionize to gain better health benefits, concussion treatment, and other protections. These efforts accelerated the national debate about the status of college athletes and what they are owed by universities and the NCAA. Unfortunately, it too often takes traumatic events and litigation to challenge the status quo and change rules not only regarding player health and safety but also compensation for the use of their names, images, and likenesses. The NCAA denying its legal duty to protect athletes in *Sheely v. NCAA* was their moral and financial undoing, according to a story in the *Washington Times*.

In the end, the scholarship in Derek's name was increased to full tuition and funded for ten years. A critical research project on traumatic brain injuries was funded. A conference on traumatic brain injuries was funded.

And The Derek Sheely Foundation received a $1.2M donation to help spread awareness.

affect / effect

Expired Vicodin from when I had my wisdom teeth taken out. Expired Tylenol with codeine from when Derek hurt his knee. Expired Percocet from Ken's kidney stones. All years old now but still looking pristine in their small bottles in the back of my dresser drawer, the edges of the white pills sharp and stamped cleanly with their appropriate identifiers. I'd tried one here and there, but nothing I took to try to feel nothing worked. I didn't know what feeling I was yearning for – I already felt numb. Was I now like the pills? Expired? Testing out these meds, secretly, what did that make me? It's a bitter truth: The way I felt, I doubted very many would come looking for me if some combination of those pills worked and I then covered my head and lay down in the dark. Nothing could hurt me anymore if I could hide forever.

It wasn't a good place to be, this wondering about one's own death. And I wasn't ever planning anything, not really; nevertheless, this visceral feeling filled me, of wanting not to be alive without killing myself. But sometimes that long stretch of time that lasted from the bottom of the final glass of wine to the top of the first one the next day, was just that: a long stretch of time and nothing else. Minute after minute, hour after hour of rumination and calculation. Not suicidal, yet preferring not to be living in this world anymore.

Despite time, despite space and distance, grief stayed close. And I could relate anything to my grief with very little effort. I had lots of practice. It was like the word association game, or, better, six degrees of separation. Give me a topic and I could connect it to my grief in the fewest possible steps. Well, maybe not the *fewest*.

What's something difficult to relate to grief? Something obviously objective, like science and mathematics. Not *The Imitation Game* nor *Hidden Figures*, not even close to cryptology, permutations, or statistics, and not even grief math, but maybe just a number? Five. And in a flash, I pictured Derek when he was five. Going back in time, to his curls, his missing-toothed smile, his starting kindergarten, his Halloween costume he wore that year (a firefighter), jolted me to see what's coming. That he's just a memory too, now. A memory that braided itself around me, squeezing tighter and tighter until I had no breath left. How could this be? Uncountable variables in grief math, but here also were absolutes, the always, the nevers, the answers. More math was 365 days times the years equaling thousands of days and nights filled with hours and minutes and seconds and the dreaded spaces between. The addition of suffering, the subtraction of Derek from my life – how could I live with this? From five I sifted through other numbers, from Derek's birthday (4/14) to his jersey number (40) to his age (22) and on and on, and I found them as numbers on a clock, or as miles to run, or as heard on television – just everywhere. But the times I thought of Derek? There's no math that worked.

♥ ♥ ♥

In our post-lawsuit, post-settlement world, August brought significance, and that month was like it always was now, silent and ready to be relived with dread. I walked early, before the heat closed in: Violet petals, so thin they were see-through, and Cinnamon's paws were silent in the early morning grass, wet furred toes, ears alert to signs of bunny, and a chipmunk hopped nearly into me under a painfully blue sky above swaying branches full with leaves. Was that a woodpecker, so small against the six-story locust? And then dusk: Press play for beloved movies on warm random evenings, like *Pretty in Pink* one night, and when I heard "Bring On the Dancing Horses" I cried until the next scene. Maybe I recalled my Echo & the Bunnymen cassette was stored up in one of the plastic storage bins we stacked in the room at the top of the stairs, blue plastic bins that held treasures like Derek's peewee football championship jacket and his high school yearbooks and his Super Nintendo, his favorite boxers, the ones made out of the Thomson family Scottish tartan, his pencils with his teethmarks pocking the soft wood, and his Xbox. Another bin filled with all the legal papers from the lawsuit, next to the bin with all of the medical bills and insurance claims, both clearly marked so I wouldn't open them by accident. Like the bin with the bag his practice clothes were put in upon arrival at the first hospital (*Wait — he always wore tape on his wrists for practice and for games; on one wrist he always wrote,* **Mom***; what did he write on his other wrist? Who cut the tape off? Where is that tape now?*) and are inside another bag I recognized and never opened, and slipped down the side of this bin were those photos my sister-in-law took of Derek standing in his room on the corner, unconscious in a medical coma, those photos in an envelope, clearly marked in her handwriting, Do Not Open, Kris. Or maybe the cabernet patted my shoulder in encouragement to just let the tears go, but the real reason was that the "Bring On the Dancing Horses" song took me back to 1986. Not that my tears weren't ever that far away, but when I let myself go back, I could feel, however fleet, like everything was fine. And everything was, for me, in 1986. I was still in high school, I had Michael Jackson posters on my walls, and I'd just met Ken. For a moment I had a memory without seeing the future. This almost never happened. I actually was able to watch the story of Andie and Duckie and Steff and Blane. Until that song came on. And reminded me, like a time machine, as songs do, of what would happen in this world, in my world. That everything was fine until it wasn't.

Memories like *Pretty in Pink* and "Bring On the Dancing Horses" and 1986 added to my loss. And off to the side, sometimes easily ignored, was what I remembered, so sharp and fresh still that I felt so off balance I stumbled under the weight of remembering. But instead of trying and failing to steady myself inside, the outside shifted to steady me now (graceful *beannacht*), and I paused in the space between breaths and wondered, Was there enough room for Derek here?

He takes up so much space —
he fills the room; he fills my thoughts

Willingly then, I pushed 1986 down and away and made myself smaller in the hope that more of Derek would stay with me, because surely my love for him had to be enough.

But it wasn't. We know this.

And that's a very dark place to go.

♥ ♥ ♥

My earliest memory of grief was when my dad came home from work with the news that Elvis had passed away in August 1977 at age 42 (the same age I was when Derek died – more grief math to note). I knew who Elvis was. We played his albums on my dad's stereo system, the speakers three feet tall, booming bass behind Elvis' voice; Elvis was a pretty big deal in our house. My dad went to college – nine years of night school while married with two kids and working full time that ended in a 1978 graduation with a B.S. in Accounting from Penn State – and he skipped class only one time, in 1973, the night of the *Aloha from Hawaii* concert, the concert that Elvis broadcast around the world via satellite, the first of its kind.

This news from my dad that Elvis had passed away carved its way into my eight-year-old mind and stayed there. I went to bed that night in August and cried into my pillow.

My parents didn't say anything else about it.

"The King is Dead," trumpeted the newspaper headline the following morning. My mom watched the story broadcast on the local news and then later reported by David Brinkley with footage of stunned tearful fans making the pilgrimage to Graceland, leaving offerings of flowers and teddy bears and candles at the gates. Photos of Elvis through the years were left behind.

A younger Elvis reminded me of my dad. Handsome, confident, strong, I called him *my hero*, my mom always said. I would run to the front door when I heard his car, My hero's home! I would yell, excited to see him when he finally got home from work. Anxious to be picked up and swung around, to play together in the backyard, to swim in our neighbor's pool in the summer, to have my dad smiling and laughing with me. To make him happy after his long day at work.

Stop crying, or I'll give you something to cry about.
Get that look off your face.
Because I said so, that's why.
Don't talk to me like that.
Don't be so selfish.

I learned to be quiet and pleasant, always, and I learned to doubt everything about myself. *Who do you think you are?* I learned to hide my questions, my confusion, and my anger, especially my anger. I learned to put everyone's needs ahead of my own. I learned how to be perfect.

Narrator: There's no such thing as perfect.

♥ ♥ ♥

A drink from the hose – a bikini top with the left strap loose along a thin bicep – bottoms of feet brown with dirt – run and hide between the scratchy yew bushes next to the carport – run back to base – pretend to be Wonder Woman – pretend to be Princess Leia – cry when your best friend moves away – a puppy but couldn't keep her – slam the bedroom door – Jimmy Carter runs for president – splash in puddles at the end of the driveway – a Barbie without a head – run in bare feet in the grass – play 45s – lick the cookie batter from the beaters – ride in the backest of the station wagon to the Jersey Shore to Colorado to Niagara Falls – build a fort out of sheets in the basement – paint fingernails – read a book about horses – roller skate to the end of the block and back – Dad smokes Salems till a cough makes him quit – pretend a popsicle is like a lipstick – stop fighting with your sister – listen to your mother – wait till your father gets home – scribble black crayon on the bedroom wall – lock the diary.

♥ ♥ ♥

My dad didn't share much about his childhood, but when he did, he often got choked up, and my mom would put her hand over his.

Five kids, three boys and two girls, so my grandfather worked two jobs, at the post office during the day and then as a short-order cook at night. When he got home at midnight or later, my grandmother told him how miserable her day had been because all five kids were bad. Especially the boys. So they were woken up and punished. An old vacuum cleaner cord wrapped around my grandfather's wrist snaked out over and over, snapping at the backs of the boys' legs until his arm got tired.

My grandmother stood and watched.

I knew about certain other things: A note was sent home with my dad when he was in first grade: *Please take your son to the dentist.* I knew that when my dad and his brothers got into minor scrapes, like skipping school or shoplifting, police drove them home from time to time, dropping them a block away. They knew the house, they knew the family, they knew the boys would get into bigger trouble. And that meant beatings, which made my dad cry, which made my grandfather call him a crybaby. *Should have drowned the lot of you,* my dad remembered hearing his father say as he cried.

But I knew none of this when I was small. And maybe I should call myself fortunate that low self-esteem and perfectionism were my only bruises. Considering.

But maybe not.

My parents lived one town over from the one where they'd grown up, so we visited my grandparents regularly. I didn't notice when I was small that their house reeked of cigarettes nor that the orange walls of the kitchen were so greasy you could scrape your fingernails down them and leave claw marks. I didn't notice they never asked us to stay for dinner nor that one Easter we couldn't visit because my sister was sick, so my grandmother ate all the chocolate rabbits she'd bought us. I knew they had cable, and that was it.

My dad didn't talk about his childhood until right before I got married, when he and my mom had been separated during my freshman year of college. Going to AA made him open up, about some things. But not everything.

There were some things we just didn't talk about. Ever.

Like death and grief.

♥ ♥ ♥

From the way my parents coped with my cleft lip (no baby photos of me until my cleft repair surgery) to the way they handled my unexpected pregnancy (had they not planned my wedding, I bet we would have never, ever, talked about my growing belly) to the way they each avoided talking about the pain of grieving Derek, even admonishing me to *calm down* and *don't be so hysterical* and *the phone works both ways* when I tearfully begged to talk to them more about it, avoiding the difficult seemed to be genetic and inevitable. Like so many women of a certain age, I was raised a certain way, is my excuse: Show me a Gen Xer who didn't grow up similar to how I did. Wanting to ask questions but instead holding back, wanting to express anger but instead screaming into my pillow after slamming my bedroom door, I folded almost to nothingness, to be as small as possible. I should have rubbed sandpaper onto my elbows and knees and got on with it rather than internalizing every single thing from the time I could remember. I never outgrew trying to make myself small.

And my grief was no different.

Though they abruptly ended their vacation and flew to Baltimore as soon as they could, how I was feeling didn't matter to my parents. But what they felt mattered to me. And that's how it was.

I love my parents, but I gave up asking them for help.

I called this *risk mitigation*, and I worked at not looking nor acting sad in front of my parents, and almost everyone else, because then not only would I not be subjected to hearing incredibly unhelpful platitudes from people trying to fix me, but also keeping my chin up prevented me from sharing the burden of my pain. And with my parents, this was a burden they were incapable of lifting off me anyway. It worked: my mom admitted once that because she knew I got out of bed and got dressed, she didn't worry about me. Little did she know that to do those things meant I was close to being out of spoons those days.

Except for visiting each other about twice a month, we stayed in touch mainly over the phone because they lived nearly two hours away, so because of this it was easier for me to affect an *I'm fine* attitude when I could keep my face and my tears hidden, my finger on the Mute button just in case. Ironically, their voices often broke and they succumbed to tears during our conversations, and it was so unfair that they put me in that position: as usual, I was the one to comfort them, their grief on full display, not mine. When I was sullen and despairing, I could practically feel a seismic shift over the phone – my dad would disengage immediately and hand the phone to my mom because he couldn't cope with the sound of my grief.

And my poor mother, already in the early days of Alzheimer's, wanted to soothe my sorrow or calm my molten hot anger with hopeful wishing that *I'm sure everyone feels bad and is sorry.* A nicety like that coldly disregarded my feelings, and confirmed that whatever I was feeling was wrong.

♥ ♥ ♥

When a mama orca cradled her dead baby for days and days, her grief was on public display, and I couldn't scroll very far on effbook when it happened without seeing that story shared and shared again. I would've done the same as she if I could have. Keeping her baby always with her, protecting it as a mother should, her sadness a slow wake behind, her pod encircled her, taking turns cradling the baby, no matter how long it took. This mama was wrapped in the love of her pod's companionship, and they swam and grieved together for seventeen days, sadness and sorrow for all the world to see.

Brokenness.

And of course, her profound grief displayed on social media was extraordinary, sweet, compelling, and incomprehensible. *An animal acted this way?*

Yes – animal after animal did this: studies of chimpanzees, giraffes, and elephants all documented that they exhibit behavior that resembled mourning, such as caring for the dead body, carrying it for a period of time, protecting it from predators, and gathering together around the body, as if for a funeral. Elephants were observed standing close around their dead without touching it, sometimes for months, in mourning, even as the dead elephant disappeared into bones. Chimpanzees isolated themselves, refrained from eating and sleeping, and rocked rhythmically when one of their group died. Even more compelling was the sight of a mama chimp carrying her dead baby for days, months, sometimes until the body became bones. There's even an account of a tower of 27 adult giraffes gathered around a dead baby giraffe, a sorrowful vigil of grieving giants. Deer grieved, as they'd been seen revisiting the site alongside the road where the death of one of their herd-mates occurred. Wolves, too, mourned for weeks the loss of a pack-mate, as they walked slowly with their heads down and tails low, and, most strikingly, instead of howling as a pack, they howl and cry individually as they grieved for their friend. These types of animals existed with intelligent social bonds that only now were beginning to be understood, social bonds as a group or a herd, so it's thought that that's why they appeared to be bereaved after a loss of one of their own. Our beloved dogs, too, grieved when their person or favorite canine friend suddenly went missing. Dogs usually slept more, ate less, and paced, panted, and whined as they sniffed and searched for their missing companion. Not every animal appeared to grieve, however. Crows, while they called to each other and then gathered together around a dead corvid, seemed more to be assessing immediate danger as related to the death, instead of mourning their dead. Crows fascinated me – a crow was tattooed on my shoulder – *one crow was for mourning* – a group was a murder of crows – I could go on and on about how they could learn to use objects as tools, they could learn to solve a puzzle, they could recognize and remember human faces and bring gifts to friendly ones, but grievers they indeed were not.

What was this? My own parents didn't have the capacity to meet me where I was in my grief, yet animals circled together in mutual comfort and mourned for days and days, month after month? How could this be, that a mother elephant or whale grieved for her baby for this long? Out in the open? And a dog that seemed depressed after its owner died? A dog? This could not be grief; this was beyond grief.

Beyond grief?

Human beings, the only animals aware and pretty much terrified of our own mortality, were shushed when we grieved "for too long" and were usually then slapped with a label, called *prolonged* or *complicated* grief. Why? Grief was in everything; grief ruled the world! But maybe if you violated the grief code (whatever that was), then you're beyond hope, beyond all reason. It morphed into being complicated, a disorder, a syndrome, or even a mental illness. It must be labeled; it must be overcome (I was overcome with grief = I must overcome this problem). It's so much more acceptable to focus instead on healing, moving on, and finding joy. And it's so much more comfortable for everyone else, too. But healing comes from the word for wholeness, so if I couldn't ever be made whole again because I fundamentally were missing a piece of myself – my son, my heart – how could I ever truly heal?

Some brokenness could not be fixed.

Which reminded me of this story: "I'm just a broken guy." They were some of the last words heard by air traffic controllers as a 29-year-old man flew directionless in an Air Alaska jet out of SeaTac. He had been motivated to steal a jet and fly, just like that, but nothing urged him to stay here on earth for one more day.

Brokenness.

I had no idea why I felt drawn to this story, except that the aimless flying mirrored my grief. But the weight of my brokenness was too heavy to put me on a plane and fly into nothingness. Why wasn't my brokenness enough to kill me? It sure felt like it was sometimes. Not all of the time. But sometimes.

So perhaps it's the not-all-of-the-time that kept me on the ground. It's the not-all-of-the-time that compelled me to stay for Keyton and Ken. It's the not-all-of-the-time that saved me. And nothing would have saved that plane thief. He'd saved his spoons, cheeking them for that particular day. That's incomprehensible to most, for sure. What was he so sad about – he was young, he had family, people who would miss him – but the dark corners of his mind seemed too closed off to anything that smacked of love, of hope, that nothing at all good would ever find its way in.

What motivated this young man, a member of the ground crew on the tarmac, to steal this plane in the first place? What happened? I listened to the recordings of the air traffic controller talking to him, trying to help him find a safe place to land, trying to be a life raft of sorts as he tossed about on the perilous waves. A tether. What we all needed when we felt down and lost. That unexpected smile from a stranger, and it's that smile that buoyed your heart for hours in your lonely darkness. The acknowledgment that you existed, that you're seen, you're heard, and, most importantly, that you belonged. But for this man, he didn't seem to want the raft. And I doubted he even noticed it was within reach. He'd already made his decision. He even sort of laughed it off, saying, I wasn't really planning on landing.

Just a coda: The investigation conducted by the FAA, the NTSB, and the FBI revealed that this man's friends and family were not aware he was suicidal. But they wondered in hindsight whether multiple concussions from his years of high school football could have contributed to brain damage, leading to chronic traumatic encephalopathy, or CTE, the insidious neurodegenerative disease that linked repetitive brain trauma to behavioral and cognitive problems, making one do things out of the ordinary, like suddenly stealing a plane and crash-landing it.

♥ ♥ ♥

Despite my brokenness, my brain was trying everything it could to relearn reality. It had no choice. It thrived on accurate predictions, so when something very unusual happened, like the death of a close loved one, its learned predictions weren't accurate anymore. This took time, as my brain struggled to learn invisible information that couldn't be ignored, like Derek's sudden and prolonged absence. How long this would take was dependent on the closeness of the loss.

The mother-child relationship was particularly close. Not only was our DNA shared, our cells swirling over, under, around, and through each other during pregnancy (called fetal-maternal microchimerism), new studies pointed to fetal cells remaining behind in the mother's body. For decades. They're found in the brain, bones, and even in the heart. *Derek is my heart.* Mother and child forever separated, forever together.

There's another level to this everlasting cellular bond: the cerebral one. Dr. Mary-Frances O'Connor described how neurons fired a certain way in the brain when you see, talk, and interact with a close loved one. This certain way of firing was a permanent wiring: All I had to do was think about Derek, or Keyton, or Ken, or anyone close to me, and *poof*, there they were in my head, in my thoughts. Simply because Derek existed in the first place, and we talked and laughed together, and we loved each other, that permanent wiring ensured he will always, *always* exist. There's never any interruption, not even when he died. The wiring was the same. But, knowing that he was in these two very different worlds, that he's in my head, existing, but he's not here, with me, existing, was confounding and overwhelming. My grieving brain let me carry

213

Derek with me forever. This continuation of his presence was like the tide or even like breathing – never ending rising and falling and wave after wave. Never stopping and everlasting. Derek was gone, and yet.

♥ ♥ ♥

My sister had "Another One Bites the Dust" and I had "Funkytown" on 45s, and we played them over and over until we learned all the words, but I didn't recall hearing either one when I went roller skating at a place called Hagy's Fountainbleu when I was ten, but only on Saturday or Sunday afternoons, with my group of girlfriends, the JKLMs. We'd try to skate backwards or crouch down, one skated foot raised up, both arms outstretched as if we were flying low to the ground, but the best was skating as fast as we could, half-bent, our arms seesawing side to side, propelling us faster and faster around the huge wooden oval, "Dancing Queen" or "I Will Survive" or "Rubberband Man" wailing from the speakers.

I was never allowed to go on Friday nights, however. Too many big kids, my mom cautioned, adding, And you're so small.

But everyone is going! I shouted, stomping down the short hallway to my room. Furious, I slammed my door, not caring in the least that my dad had told me if he heard me slam that door one more time, he'd take it off its hinges. He wasn't home to hear.

One of the JKLMs told me the next day that she'd never go back skating on a Friday night ever again. You're so lucky you weren't allowed to go, she confided. There were so many big kids we couldn't skate anywhere.

I didn't tell my mom that she'd been right.

Yet, had I been allowed to go, maybe I could have learned how to stand up for myself and fight for space in that roller rink.

Earlier that same year, I was placed in the gifted program, which met at the middle school one morning a week. On my first day, I walked to the entrance at the same time dozens of seventh and eighth graders zipped and crossed the pavement in front of me from every direction, elbowing me from great heights and calling fourth grade me a "midget kid." I told my mom at drop-off time the next week, and she persuaded me to wait in the car with her until all the big kids exited the buses and were inside the building.

Had she persuaded me instead to keep my chin up and head for the doors like I belonged there, maybe I could have learned how to stand up for myself and fight for space in the schoolyard.

My mom raised me how she'd been raised: to be a good girl. And that meant quiet, polite, meek, and small. In contrast to my dad's family of five kids, my mom was an only child, her parents aged 30 when she was born, quite unusual for the time. Her parents were the same people who'd driven for hours every weekend to take me to see Ken at Penn State when I was a student at Bloomsburg, the same people whom my dad described as doting, that the mold had been broken after my grandparents were made.

My mom quit her secretarial job a few months before I was born, and she stayed home with me and my sister. She went back to work when I was in fifth grade, my sister in third, which my sister rebelled against, falling ill at least once every two weeks so Mom would stay home with her. I didn't mind Mom working; I felt important and responsible carrying my own house key, and I enjoyed the hour or so of freedom after school. One of my favorite activities was rearranging my bedroom, pushing my twin bed into a corner, and then shifting my desk under the window, my bookshelf my dad had made fitting along the opposite wall. And then a couple of months later, I did it all over again. My mom was always impressed with the new design, even suggesting slight alterations to achieve symmetry.

I used to rearrange my room when I was your age, she'd smile. It's like a whole new life, isn't it?

Mom cooked dinner every night, and we sat together at the table, all four of us, unless my dad had to work late due to month-end or quarter-end or year-end. An accountant, he was at the mercy of others as he waited for the numbers he needed to balance the books and report the reports. Thinking back, the meals we had were comforting yet quite unexotic: beef stroganoff, chicken a la king, miscellaneous crock pot concoctions served over rice, spaghetti, S.O.S., and tacos (but not until I reached high school, and they were not spicy whatsoever). On nights Dad worked late, she made fettucine alfredo with powdered parmesan, which the three of us liked, but Dad did not.

Mom worked, she cooked dinner, she painted my nails and put my wet hair in plastic curlers whenever I asked her to, and she even sewed. One year, Mom stitched a Snoopy costume for me for Halloween. My sister would be Snoopy the following year, while I was a fortune teller. Mom had wrapped a plastic pumpkin in tin foil to be my crystal ball, and I wore a bandanna on my hair like Rhoda did on the Mary Tyler Moore Show, which I found by accident one day. I loved Rhoda. But this year I had other plans.

Stand still for a sec, Mom said, as she pulled at the sheet I was wrapped in.

I'm trying, I complained.

It just needs to be straight, she said. There! Okay, you can go.

I jumped off the chair and went to my room. Even though my hair was still a little too short, I tried to coil my pigtails into donuts so I would look more like Princess Leia. Mom was working on my costume, but my hair was key. It had to be right.

I went back out to the living room. Can you help me with my hair?

Mom had a needle in her mouth as she peered at her stitches. Sure, she mumbled, glancing at me. You can't wear those for trick-or-treat, though.

I looked down at my feet and laughed. Mom's size 5 ½ Candie's slingbacks were fancy and beautiful and I loved them, their four-inch heels clicking as I walked on our hardwood floors, my not-quite Princess Leia hair bouncing with each step. I know, I said. I just like wearing these sometimes.

Mom helped my sister and me make Shrinky-dinks in the oven and blanket forts over the clothesline. She took us to the humane society one Saturday, and we came home with a precious black and white mutt I named Heidi. She came to my softball games, though it was Dad who threw catch with me in the backyard. And she fostered my love of reading, taking me to the library where I discovered Stephen King years before I probably should have. Reading *Cujo* in elementary school elicited more than one comment from my teacher.

You know you taught yourself to read when you were about Derek's age, she informed me once. Derek was barely four at the time. It was definitely before you went to kindergarten, she added, certain.

There was a pause as I pictured myself alone in my room, illiterate, yet somehow deciphering letters, guessing sounds and meanings.

I'm sure you taught me, Mom, I sighed.

She shrugged.

My mom did this a lot. She was no dummy, yet she put herself down so that it fell to someone else, in this case, me, to boost her back up. She remarked after we started the foundation and began planning the first race, that she wouldn't even know where to begin. Sure you would, I soothed her as I described how easy it was to find information on the internet.

After Derek died, my mom told me she had asked god to take her instead, that she survived breast cancer and heart failure and that she'd gladly trade her life for her grandson. I couldn't speak. What was there to say? Her plea had been ignored, of course, and I wondered if any guilt stayed with her until she died eight years after Derek. An offered bargain like this: Would we have gotten the phone call if my mom had indeed died soon after she was diagnosed with breast cancer? Again with the grief math, take away my mom, carry my son.

But when it came to Derek and grief and me, my mom missed it. She leaned into her faith and away from me. She couldn't bear to see me in pain, yet wouldn't talk to me about it. And when I tried to talk to her, our words would remain on the surface or she'd *maybe someday* me or she'd change the subject.

Our relationship thinned further thanks to Alzheimer's, so much so I started to wonder whether she'd forgotten Derek ever existed. She hadn't forgotten; but, like my dad, facing this loss overwhelmed her. Around that time I wrote in my journal, *Mom told me I've changed, that I've pulled away. Why does she think I've changed when she doesn't even know me?*

For sure, I didn't give my mom the grief she deserved when she died. How could I? I'd already experienced unimaginable loss; all the grief I had was for Derek – what was left for my mother? Everything recalibrated. Numbness took over at her funeral, where my hands were clasped, my cheek kissed, and I was hugged by her friends who seemed to know my mom better than I ever did.

My dad sat stunned in an arm chair and didn't get up once.

And my sister never stopped moving.

♥ ♥ ♥

Our kitchen was in the basement, separated from the washer and dryer by a frame of 2x4x8s. All of our appliances were olive green metal and only about three feet tall, but my sister and I pretended they were real. We had a tea set, white with blue coneflowers just like Mom's casserole dishes, and we had forks, knives, and spoons, miniature pots and pans we stirred dry macaroni in and then fed to my Baby Alive doll, whom I didn't ask for and didn't really like – I had wanted a Big Wheel but didn't get one the year my sister asked for a Sit 'n Spin. It was in this kitchen with the smell of Fab laundry detergent hanging in the air, where my sister and I played restaurant, then beauty parlor when I got a Barbie head one year for my birthday even though I had asked for a Big Wheel again, and then we played grocery store with a makeshift unfolded box from Korvette's, and then we built blanket forts, the tiny olive green fridge and oven draped in flowered sheets, a sign written in my newly-learned cursive taped crookedly, *Do Not Enter NO MATTER WHAT!*

We moved to a larger house when I was 11, and our kitchen was given away to our younger cousins. I never saw it again. The smell of laundry detergent sometimes reminds me of the basement and the kitchen, and I asked my sister about it.

Don't you wish Mom and Dad had asked us before they just gave our kitchen away?

Good one, she scoffed.

♥ ♥ ♥

Every year, a reminder of Elvis made its way around social media, his groundbreaking look, culturally-appropriated music and dancing, and his passing away.

VERY DARK PLACES

Was Elvis dead or had he passed away? I didn't remember being confused about this when I was eight, but I wondered now why we're so afraid to talk about grief and death and why we refused to use real words. Was it something to do with our being aware of our own mortality, our own fear of death, that we veered away from being direct? We actually knew the words to use, and we refused to use them. Why? Thinking again about elephants, orcas, and giraffes who ritualized death and gathered together to grieve even though they're apparently unaware of their own mortality, why were we humans, we who were absolutely aware of our own mortality and completely aware that our own death was always inside us, crouched and waiting to spring, so unevolved when it came to death and grief?

We didn't want to say dying or dead; instead, we wanted to say passed away or passed on or slipped away. We wanted to say we lost our person. I said that, as if Derek were a lost book or misplaced cellphone. He's not, and I should stop echoing that ridiculous notion. She kicked the bucket, he met his maker, they bought the farm, she bit the dust, he's pushing up daisies, they're sleeping with the fishes, she gave up the ghost, he shuffled off this mortal coil, and the brief, R.I.P. Obituaries read like bizarre fantasy stories: Returned home – what, returned like a library book? Why not use the word? A word was something solid, a foundation onto which to rest your burden, your grief. A word was scaffolding to build upon, and thus to hold you up. Why use these euphemisms for death? Grief was what needed the euphemism. Death didn't. Death just *was*. Death was death. Dead people didn't even know they're dead.

Derek is my son. Derek is my heart. He died. He didn't pass away. He died. He died yesterday and the day before that. He'll die tomorrow and the day after that. He dies today. Now. And now. And now. Over and over and over again. He's still dead no matter what I do.

He dies when my eyes open every morning. He dies when I drink water. He dies when I walk my dog. He dies at lunch. He dies when I try to read, and when the words blur he dies again. He dies when I go running, and when I get home, he dies when I walk through the door. I clean the house, or not, he dies. I write, or not, he dies.

219

Whether I wear black or not, he dies. Whether I'm silent or not, he dies. He dies during dinner. He dies when I talk to my husband, and he dies again when my husband talks to me. He dies when we drink wine, when we watch tv, when we look at our phones. When we go to bed, he dies, and he is still dead when we wake up. He dies all of the time. What we look like or what we do, nothing matters. Nothing matters. He is still dead. My son died. And he dies again every fucking day. I know this, because I am the one watching him die every time.

My son dies. Over and over and over again. There is no euphemism for this. And for me, there is no, *maybe someday* I won't feel this way. There is no, *at least* I'll always have my memories. No. Not for me. The loss of my child brings no comfort with my sorrow. There is no gift to be found in my suffering. No inspiration, no strength, no signs, no bright sides.

Just grief. That's it.

I miss Derek. Every day.

inseparable

Derek's grey Penn State hoodie (his winter coat, his friends said, for when he wore it you knew shit was serious outside) was draped neatly atop his bed pillows on an ottoman in our bedroom. I'd worn it, many times, its xl heaviness enveloping me on my late-night walks. His green t-shirt – Penn State Intermural Champion in white collegiate letters – was folded over the back of a wooden chair across the room. Through washings, this shirt used to smell like him, he wore it so often. It's dusty now at certain spots along the fold. His clothes were a part of the room. Apart from the room. They were him; he was them. And they were too much to look at sometimes, which was why they're now folded neatly in the chest of drawers in the spare bedroom. Kept. Saved. Keyton has his green t-shirt now. I knew of other grieving parents who donated or even tossed away their child's clothes, and this difference baffled me and made me wonder whether they were the normal ones, or were we?

Framed photos of Derek stood on the counter in the kitchen, on my dresser, on the mantel. A suggested shrine, until you remembered other people's houses and their displays of photographs. The only difference was that my son stopped aging in our photos.

You know the story of what happened. Though it was preventable, it could not be undone. Not ever. But often in the darkened stillness of grief-thought, I did think that it could be undone if I tried just a bit harder, that none of this was real, that yes of course I could have saved him I should have saved him could still save him. Grief-thought convinced me of possibilities. Of hope. Even now.

Hope is a dangerous thing.

Slow motion these grief-thoughts were. Like a slow melting of ice that changed without fanfare and all at once it was a whole other shape you never noticed was there but was the entire time.

Underneath. How did you carve an elephant from a huge block of granite? Just removed everything that wasn't elephant.

if only if only if only

And he'd still be here.

Yet sometimes too grief-thought could be easy to push down, almost even forgotten about, any hope becoming frosted over and hard, covered with a layer too thick to scratch off with a fingernail; you needed something more substantial like a chisel, wielded without concern for flying fragments, shrapnel that pierced, shredded, destroyed what it hit.

This could not be undone.

But then a trigger came seemingly out of nowhere, like "1979" playing in the grocery store or hearing 40 mentioned on television and just like that I was catapulted back to that week in the hospital like it was yesterday, and I felt just the same as I did then.

Which was better? Which was worse? To cry and hope for what I knew could never be? Or to cry and numbly accept our unacceptable loss?

How could I even hold this dilemma in my hands in the first place? I knew then that there was no hope for a miracle anymore, and at the same time I planned to take Derek home and help him recover so he could keep on living his life. Impossible to wrap my mind around that, on that day, in that place, and impossible to live with ever since.

Intense doubt plagued me as well. Did we do the right thing by letting Derek go? Were we absolutely sure? *Were the doctors?* How could we ever know that what we were told was indeed the truth? Especially looking back now after we got the email that revealed that everyone who said they didn't know what happened knew exactly what had happened?

Oh I don't know... I don't know. Could everyone at Shock Trauma have been keeping the truth from us, too?

He should still be here.

I can't know what I don't know.

Yet I knew grief. Quite well. And at the same time I lacked the words for what I knew about grief.

Grief is my constant companion: My best half. My loathed half. Grief keeps Derek close. Grief stays long after most have left. This I know. This knowing

222

is a struggle, a struggle with living with the constant pause and continue of life and feeling guilt and anger at everything that happened.

No one watched me wide awake in the early morning darkness. No one knew about the bargains I made with myself and then ignored. No one knew what I started and failed to finish as I waited tirelessly for my son to come home. I spent a lot of time in very dark places, so much so that grief-thoughts folded over and over, under and around each other. A tangle of hope and despair: pull it and it unraveled.

I unraveled.

Nothing I did seemed real anymore anyway. What would it be like to slice myself open? What did I think was inside me now? Would the hopes and dreams I saved for Derek finally spill out?

I don't want this to get easier.

I don't want this to get easier. I don't want this to get easier. I don't want this to get easier. I don't want this to get easier. I don't want this to get easier. I don't want this to get easier.

I don't want this to get easier.

♥ ♥ ♥

Denial, anger, bargaining, depression, acceptance. In the late 1960s psychiatrist Elizabeth Kubler-Ross worked with dying people and identified the five stages they went through as they navigated their new realities of being diagnosed with a terminal illness. Unfortunately, the five stages of dying were then hijacked and renamed the Five Stages of Grief, and ever since, grievers have been labeled and pushed to go from the first to the next and the next as quickly as possible, with the brass ring at about the six-month mark after your loss being acceptance.

Not much changed since the 1960s.

Sure, I discovered modern takes, like Megan Devine's book *It's Okay that You're Not Okay*, and I've read Dr. Joanne Cacciatore's book *Bearing the Unbearable*. I found Rebecca Hensler's *Beyond Belief* grief group and *Modern Loss* with Rebecca Soffer and Gabrielle Birkner, and *Grief is a Sneaky Bitch* podcast with Lisa Keefauver. I've read Dr. Mary-Frances O'Connor's *The Grieving Brain*. I have notes and quotes, passages highlighted, their precious iambs stepping softly on fragile feet.

I was well beyond the six-month mark, and I was still sad. And according to my family and friends out there who believed that the Five Stages of Grief were the be-all end-all model of how to do grief, I shouldn't be sad anymore. Besides, they insisted, Derek would not want me to be sad. By now I should be entrenched in acceptance. But I wasn't. And if Derek wouldn't want me to be sad, was I even betraying Derek by being sad? Was there something really wrong with me? According to the latest *Diagnostic Statistical Manual of Mental Disorders*, the *DSM-5*, there might be – I could have a disorder, even, prolonged grief disorder, a label in small, neat font. What cohort of researchers decided that grieving for my child past an assumed expiration date was apparently pathological?

Path-o-log-i-cal, I thought to myself as I walked. It was December, cold but sunny, and I kept my head down, as if bracing myself against a heavy wind, which I was. The passing of time was obvious and loud as it pressed on me, stealing my breath, and with every second that passed I got pushed against my will further and further away from Derek unless I did what I could to stop it. Then I realized, I was more than 60 months up an impossible mountain to climb, and it kept going higher and higher. I was too small and insignificant to keep carrying what I carried up this mountain, so let's just not. *Remove everything that wasn't elephant.* A loss like this was the eternal presence of an absence. And grief for this absence was the elephant I carried. My arms ached; let me rest. The-little-engine-that-could slightly edited into *I hope I can, I hope I can.*

Was I back to hope already?

Shouldn't I keep hoping for my child?

But there was no magic to be found here, in this hope. None. How could there be? I couldn't believe this was what I had to think about, these grief-thoughts: The death of my son.

No – no – no – no!!!

And then, before I realized it, 60 months became 72, 84, 96 months and yet there was no peak in sight. Still, I kept climbing the mountain, alone, and my grief-thoughts were as sad and scattered as ever, disbelieving the blurred reality.

VERY DARK PLACES

♥ ♥ ♥

Do you want to go for a walk? I asked Ken. He was in the bedroom, unpacking. We hadn't seen each other for almost six weeks, and he was at Penn State for a long weekend.

Sure. Did you finish those photo things?

Almost. They're on the dining room table, I told him. I'd been sorting through shoeboxes filled with photographs, looking at but without seeing the static images of the four of us, our extended family, places we'd been, to fill five 16x20-inch frames with collages of our life. I glanced past my own face in photo after photo – me: Before – *who was that?* She was gone. My son was gone. The sharp realization was brutal and foreign, any attached memory lifted up and away like burnt paper. Nothing looked the same as it used to. Was I my own hallucination, trying to remember what life was like Before and who I was Before, and all the while forced to navigate and cope with this new reality of After that I did not accept. And all I could do was float from one unreal moment to the next – floating while dragging my feet.

Where did you find some of these? Ken asked as he studied the collages. He pointed, I don't remember this one at all.

I shrugged and shook my head. I think it was in one of the old photo albums, I said.

In the photo, Ken's dad was on the front porch, his pipe clenched between his teeth and three-year-old Derek perched on his knee. They both wore red t-shirts and matching baseball caps. The photo was from an instant camera and looked a bit out of focus, Derek's smile almost like it was moving.

I have no father, and I have no son, Ken gasped and looked at me.

♥ ♥ ♥

Ken's dad was the youngest of three children (according to family lore – and depending on who shared the story – he was 10 or 13 or 16 pounds when he was born; the risk for gestational diabetes maybe not recognized nor diagnosed in 1943). He was a soft-

225

spoken, hard-working, introvert from a blue-collar Lutheran family who grew up on a farm in southcentral Pennsylvania. Unlike his older brother who took over the family farm, Ken's dad was a professional truck driver by day and a volunteer fire fighter 24/7. As a fire fighter, he rose up through the ranks to become the Deputy Fire Chief, leading by example, ensuring his team was doing things the right way, the safe way. He was a strong yet slender man until back surgery in the 1980s laid him up for months and caused him to gain weight while immobile in bed. I knew him not by what he said but by what he did: always with a pipe in his mouth and a baseball cap on his head when not at work or the firehouse, he could be found splitting wood, cutting the grass on his riding mower, raking and burning leaves, riding snowmobiles, or stoking the wood burning stove in the family room to literally 90 degrees on cold winter days. Not one to wear shorts even on the hottest summer days, he would roll up his pant legs while lounging on his blue recliner doing a puzzle. Ken would tell me stories about his dad in his younger days when he competed in fire-fighting competitions, where teams would try to knock a bowling pin off a 55-gallon drum as fast as possible using water from a hose 40 yards away (I had no idea these types of competitions even existed, and Ken said his dad was really good and won a lot of them).

Opposites attract.

Ken's mom was a gregarious gesticulating extrovert, one of four children (the eldest girl) in a white-collar Catholic family, and raised in the biggest house in the development. She met Ken's dad and immediately after graduating high school, got married, and had Ken (or, was the order marriage and then graduation?). She was 17 (soon to be 18) when Ken was born (disconcerting) and his dad was 23 (more disconcerting). At first, a trailer park that was mere steps to the firehouse was their home, but after Ken's sister and brother were born, the family moved to a house built atop a steep hill, surrounded by trees. The three-acre property was a gift from Ken's grandmother, land portioned from the family farm, land that couldn't be tilled but perfect for a homesite.

When the three kids got a little older, Ken's mom worked part-time as a server in a restaurant, but her passion remained being a full-time wife and mother who always volunteered to be homeroom mom, fieldtrip mom, boy scout den leader, and every similar opportunity that appeared. She also was the disciplinarian, armed with a wooden spoon and a sharp tongue. Unequipped with a filter nor the ability to self-regulate, she never hesitated to share exactly what she was thinking as soon as the thought popped into her head.

Ken told me when we were dating that he grew up in some isolation, as his house on the hill wasn't near the homes of any other kids. His closest neighbor was his grandmother's farmhouse several football fields away. Playing after school with the neighborhood kids was not a thing, not ever. For Halloween, he was even driven to his cousins' neighborhood so he could experience trick-or-treat like all his friends did. Incidentally, his cousins lived right across the street from where I lived, so maybe our paths crossed one All Hallow's Eve, hopefully the year I was dressed as Princess Leia.

Ken and I spent more time at my house than his when we dated. His house had no central air or cable television, and when that wood stove was alight, 90 degrees was way too hot for me. And his house had fire monitors and CB radios, foreign-to-me gadgets which beeped and chirped and squawked every hour of every day for some reason or another. We could be studying or even making out, and when Ken's dad recognized the correct orchestra of tones and beeps over the monitor, he'd jump into his waiting boots and overalls by the door, tell us See you later, and trot out to his red and white pickup truck. He'd race off to an accident or a fire, his custom lights swirling and sirens wailing.

♥ ♥ ♥

My dad bought a video recorder soon after Derek was born. A camcorder. It held videotapes, which were paperback-sized, so the camcorder rested on your shoulder while you filmed. Imagine! Cumbersome was the camcorder, but it was pretty cool to have in 1989. I remembered filming particular moments myself: of my dad feeding Derek pinches of homemade apple cake at the dining room table; of my grandparents holding Derek's hands as he walked between them on a sun-dappled trail atop Sandia Peak the summer we lived in Albuquerque; of a can't-walk-yet Derek dancing to the "You Can't Touch This" video while steadied by the coffee table.

We kept every single one of the many, many tapes, so perhaps one of these days I could look at them for Derek's baby laugh or his crawling or his attempts to stand.

I could. One of these days.

Did I just *maybe someday* myself?

Fuck.

Would a 30-year-old videotape even work in the old player we still had, hidden in the eaves behind the blue plastic bins in the room at the top of the stairs? What if I ruined the tapes with too much fast forwarding or rewinding before I found what I was looking for? Could I bear to watch these tapes in the first place when mere photos of my dead child were impossible to look at without crying? I didn't know. But I knew for sure that I wanted the real thing, not Derek's image on brittle cellophane.

I wanted him here for all of the reasons. I wanted to talk to him, to sit across from the little boy who was called *too sarcastic* in third grade, so sarcastic most of his peers didn't know Derek was joking around. This one made me cringe as I remembered when his class was asked to imagine what life was like before the Civil War, and he commented to his Black friend, I guess we all know what you'd be doing. I got a call from his teacher for that one.

And I remembered when the mom of one of his friends called me out of the blue very upset that Derek had supposedly pushed her son to the ground at recess, and when she said her name I recognized who her son was, by far the tallest and heaviest boy in the class. Oh sure, I thought, Derek went after her son, the one who outweighed and towered over everyone. I accepted her story, asked Derek what had happened at recess, and he shrugged and said the two of them were playing catch with the football, diving and sliding to make great catches. I didn't push him, Derek said, shaking his head. I found out later that since the other boy's mother had told her son not to come home with grass-stained pants anymore, he had decided to lie to her to avoid trouble. Good thing I made it a habit to believe my kids.

And I remembered when Derek had been accused of cheating in college because he didn't cite his sources in his English class for the paper about Dostoevsky. He could've gotten kicked out of school for plagiarism, but Derek stood his ground and at length discussed with his professor *Crime and Punishment* and *Notes from the Underground* alongside detailed Russian history facts, declaring there was no need to cite anything since he already knew it. Convinced, his grade was changed to an A.

I wanted to sink into these memories. All of them: Vacations to Stone Harbor in New Jersey, the Outer Banks in North Carolina. Hersheypark. Disneyworld. But at the end of every single one was the flashing warning light that meant, Guess what happens next: Your son was dead. No matter how lovely or real or oft-repeated, the ending was always the same. Derek was dead. I didn't think I could watch that truth in living color, on a whirring tape playing on a screen in front of me. With sound. And I likely would catch sight of a person who resembled me, but any recognition proved uncertain. It wasn't about aging or my hair or clothes being outdated, or whatever. It was worse and far sadder because that person in those memories, on those tapes, was gone, and I didn't know where she went.

♥ ♥ ♥

The two of us used to float together as we slept, dreaming of the future, or even of just the next day, in the Before. But now all Ken and I could do was sink together, sink I think, until we'd sunk below, far below, the place we used to be. Laden with guilt and sorrow, the heaviness of the loss of Derek weighed us down while at the same time tethered us together. We'd known each other since I was 16, and Ken knew me far better than I knew myself. If nothing else while living in grief, we were reminded again that we're each other's best friend; breathing the same air day after day we felt safer with each other than with anyone else. Ken even remarked that he felt closer to me than ever, and I knew this was a good thing, an enviable thing to be found in long relationships, perhaps, but I couldn't help but sense sadness about it because I knew the main reason why. We'd spent nearly the first decade after Derek died watching each other leave as we traveled alone from one house to the other, and now, we shouldn't be happy, but we were, we were with each other anyway, peaceful while we're in such hollow pain. It made no sense to hold both of these beliefs at the same time.

Stock was taken, assessed, recalculated. With the loss of a child, wondering what could have – should have – would have been never ended. Years and years in this, this state of otherness, had us not seeing and knowing what Derek *was* doing as he made his way in the world, we were forced instead to be satisfied with wondering what he *might be* doing. So in the evenings on ordinary days, there I sat with my broken-hearted love on the couch, both of us on our phones, each a reminder to the other that we had a broken future, with only the past, reliving the past, the passed, days of the Before times when we used to fly.

♥ ♥ ♥

Ken's dad died of a sudden heart attack the year Keyton was born. He was 50, and Ken was 27. To Derek and Keyton, Ken's dad was Pap and Ken's maternal grandfather (Derek and Keyton's great-grandfather) was Great Pap. When we told four-year-old Derek that Pap died, he couldn't understand how Pap died before Great Pap. It didn't make sense to him. He asked question after question that we tried to answer.

When we gathered with Ken's family to plan the funeral, practical matters were discussed, like the design and cost of the casket, vault, and grave marker and which hymns to have playing before and after the service. But the actual loss, to lose your father like that, with no warning, and then, to have no conversations afterward about any of it, was bizarre and strangely expected, and accepted, because Ken's family was so similar to mine. *We didn't talk about hard things.*

Nevertheless, Ken felt compelled to act, and almost immediately, he planned an award to honor his father, a lifelong volunteer firefighter in his community who rose to the rank of deputy chief, an award to recognize a leader who sacrificed for the greater good and who saved others in times of peril. Losing Derek not even 20 years later sparked in Ken the same energy to establish lasting elements that would highlight and preserve Derek's legacy.

Establishing the foundation and a scholarship were first, followed by a ceremonial white oak tree planting at Derek's high school. And the ironwood tree at our house. Then we commis-

230

sioned an engraved granite pillar to be positioned near the tree outside the football field at the high school, along the path the team walked from the locker room to the field, their cleats clacking to the tune of Darth Vader's "The Imperial March." *Derek Thomson Sheely* was inscribed on the top of the granite almost-obelisk, and the sides read, *tradition, dedication*, a description of the significance of the white oak, and the poem recited to the team before every game, *This is the beginning of a new day.* But with each new football season, a feeling of panic crouched next to me that no one after me would remember him. Coaches came and went, and I wondered whether the team still touched this marker on their way to the field. Did they read Derek's name, and did they recognize his commitment, his integrity, his legacy? Did they remember the name?

Yet as much as these permanent reminders did to memorialize both Ken's dad and Derek to the outside world, they did very little to help us share our grief with others, especially our family.

Aww, Ken's mother said when we told her about the pillar at the school, describing for her the inscriptions on all four sides and the top. That sounds nice, she said, Though you know Derek's getting his reward in heaven.

He's getting his what? I asked Ken when he hung up. What does that even mean?

Just ignore it, he sighed.

I sipped my drink. I was sick of ignoring things. I thought of the angel card and the angel pin and the angel wings adorning Derek's senior portrait on my mother-in-law's mantel. And tell her he's not a fucking angel, I added, my voice rising in anger.

Oh, like you tell your parents when they say shit? Like that?

I sighed.

I'm going to look at some emails, Ken said as he went upstairs.

Of course! Go do some work! I yelled at his back. Talk to me, I said to myself. I sighed and my legs shook up and down.

I wanted to text Keyton, talk to her, fill the silence. She's working; don't bother her, I thought. What about Derek? I gasped at the disconcerting counterfactual thought, wanting to text him, call him, write him a note every night asking him to come home (*but he's gone*), thinking I should have saved him (*but I wasn't even there*), my brain trying to comprehend the incomprehensible. And it failed and failed and failed. *Did Ken feel these things?* My thoughts looped over and over onto themselves in my mind, every last corner filled with these rambling wonderings. Times like these painted a clear picture of madness, and I felt like I did in early grief, like I was going crazy, and this was why conventional wisdom said I was better off keeping everything I was thinking to myself.

♥ ♥ ♥

Then in a blink, I saw the first crocus yesterday morning. Lavender, tiny, fragile yet strong enough to push its way from the dark into the sun. Six squirrels circled by the tulips. Trees with bits of young green swayed above my head. A cardinal landed. On an early morning walk, I glimpsed three elegant deer leaping across the field in the fog like ghosts. I dreaded the thaw. The first snowdrops, that delicate crocus. But the world would never be beautiful again. Not completely. There would always be ...*and yet, Derek*. Always. In everything.

Sometimes in this used-to-be-beautiful world I felt like I never stopped falling. I could be sitting quietly, maybe writing just like this, and then, all at once pushed, as if down the stairs, so abrupt I could barely recover. Or I could be out running, lost in thought, and then it happened again: a sudden push, and I stumbled, tripping over my own feet. This predictable unpredictableness perhaps had a way of grounding me, albeit for just a moment, as I got used to it. It's familiar. It's Derek, maybe, wielding a wand of *beannacht*. In that case, why should I ever find a place to land when, really, all I wanted was to feel like I never stopped falling?

♥ ♥ ♥

Over the years, Ken and I made countless connections in the so-called concussion realm, and I tried to find my footing there. Kind and gentle hands were offered, and I accepted every single one. But it wasn't long before I felt on the outside again: Derek hadn't survived, and I had next-to-nil motivation to help others who did. I felt I had nothing left to give – a shadow of a shade was left of me. Terrible, I knew, to realize I didn't belong in this particular arena of preventative care. What would embrace me wasn't here that I could see. I was looking for grieving people, and they weren't here amongst the ones I knew.

Was I again putting myself to the outside? Again becoming the other, that thing I hated being? Why couldn't I just force myself to fit in so that maybe I'd find what I'd been searching for?

Losing Derek wasn't the only thing I lost. Like everyone who has ever grieved a death, the associated, ambiguous losses that stacked up and toppled over were confounding. You lost your temper, your memory, your friends, your family, your planned future. You lost trust, you lost faith. You lost sleep. You might lose weight, your sense of humor, your mind. You might lose your partner. You felt like you're in a constant state of stress, enveloped in that feeling of knowing you lost something, and you wanted to know exactly how you lost it and what you could have done to prevent it.

I lost my voice.

I had no say in this, pun intended. And I didn't know if I'd ever fully find my voice again. Find it enough to keep it, anyway, because I did get glimpses, reminders, of my voice every now and then. I might write a poem that just – whew – tumbled onto the page as fast as I could write it, and it's perfect, at least to me. And I might write a paragraph here and there that when I reread it, I had no memory whatsoever of writing. Maybe too woowoo here, to laud and praise the muse, but it was pretty cool when that happened, and it's precisely that glimpse of my former self that turned out to be what I kept looking for. And piecing together these fractal glimpses could create a picture. Not a whole one, but maybe an upside down Picasso one, with enough lines and gradations that resembled me.

When part of the settlement included a fully funded conference at George Washington University where I would speak and tell Derek's story, I first thought, *Oh no, I do not think so. All eyes on me? No, thank you.* But then I reminded myself that people wouldn't care unless we compelled them to look at Derek and listen to his story. Pressuring people to care was the only way change would ever occur so that all the failures that contributed to what happened to Derek

233

hopefully would be corrected, and what happened to Derek would never happen again to another child.

Besides, what would Derek say?

Don't be complacent.

Before it was my turn to speak, a handsome young man hugged me (he was Derek's age), a beautiful young woman hugged me (she was Derek's age, too), and I looked past them into the audience: All of the GW students I saw there were Derek's age. College students always would be.

And then all at once Ken was done talking, and as I rose from my seat and moved to the podium, blood rushed to my face, a tilt of red wine in a glass. I kept my eyes straight ahead as I walked: The slide deck of photos of Derek I'd created for this event was still playing on the huge screen behind me, and I knew if I looked at Derek's face for more than a few seconds, I'd get lost there. I paused and found my breath, tried to find my voice, and then I told everyone what happened. Ten or 40 or 200 in the audience, I had no idea, and it really didn't matter. I was standing up. I was speaking. Finally. Unlike the interviews we gave, in which I barely uttered a word, words flowed out of me nonstop like blood from a vein. I had prepared pages, but I hadn't practiced a word of what I was going to say because how could I have rehearsed this? I had to tell everyone what happened and I didn't want to believe what happened, let alone speak about it. My voice prevailed, and I somehow told the story – Derek's story – and my tears came, as I knew they would, as I wanted them to. I told everyone what happened, even sharing the anonymous email, enunciating its horrific slurs, and everyone cried with me. Now they knew, now they really knew. Because of my voice.

Afterward, people I had never seen before or since told me how moved they were by Derek, how they wish they'd have known him. Me too, I said, over and over. I was embraced, I was prayed over, and I was frozen when someone from the organization that failed to investigate what happened to Derek hugged me as if in alliance. Derek's high school coach had lunch with us, leaning toward us as he spoke, earnestly promising his support of Derek's foundation. We heard quite a few promises of support that day. Promises to stay in touch and never forget Derek. Promises were appreciated, but so was just sitting with me. It's okay to just enjoy the silence.

♥ ♥ ♥

In spite of the fact that Derek was dead and I believed that no one understood a damn thing about it, and that, except for giving an interview or a speech at a conference, people pretended like he never existed instead of asking me about him – yes – I knew no one wanted to talk about stuff like this – difficult things were difficult for a reason, and it wasn't fair. It's difficult sometimes not to be anxious about saying the right thing or the wrong thing when you didn't know how you're supposed to know what the right thing to say and the wrong thing to say even were in the first place. It wasn't fair to not know these things. I could admit that. In spite of the fact that Derek was dead, these were the details I thought about as I compiled my notes and sorted through the fodder yet again to try and structure a more readable report, much like this one that's in black and white type – yet, I had to ask, why was my report so hard to understand even after so many revisions?

I didn't used to be angry all of the time. Maybe. It's difficult to know for sure. Like all the faces of grief, seething anger was just below the surface now, lying in wait alongside the sudden sting of tears. They both threatened to reveal themselves, usually at the same time, usually when I thought I was fine – whatever that meant that day – and they were very likely to gang up on me. I tried to listen to my dad's advice: Don't let anger take hold of you (again, his well-intentioned advice was more about him controlling my feelings). But the more I focused on controlling my anger, the more out of control I felt. There's just so much of it. And I could try all I wanted to ignore it and push the anger down, but like grief, it would rise up when I least expected it. Heavy emotions like these were somehow buoyant enough to invariably resurface. Always with the weird physics. And so I tried to shut myself off completely, or totally surrender so that I was either numb, or I felt everything all at once.

And with Ken, my beloved, I felt every single thing and pelted it at him.

I needed someone to listen, and I knew he would.

I needed someone to understand, and I knew he would.

I needed someone to support me, and I knew he would.

But what about him? Was it fair to lean on my husband like this when we'd both been through the same nightmare? What if I launched all my angst and madness and grief all at once in his direction and he fell under the weight of my burden and we crumpled to the ground together and we never got up? He stoically absorbed whatever I threw at him and then became consumed with work, only to go quiet at night. We bickered, we drank, we what-iff-ed, we desperately clawed at impossible solutions to fix what was wrong. I coaxed him to talk. I asked him to read the grief books I had, but he wouldn't. I'm fine, he insisted. But *we* weren't. He couldn't protect me from this horror, and I couldn't protect him.

Our disconnect grew and swirled.

When I confided in my mom, she scolded me a little for not noticing the obvious. You shouldn't be living at Penn State and Ken in Maryland. You should be living together, she said.

But he's at work all day anyway. And it's very hard to be in that house.

Maybe someday it'll be different, she said. It's just not right you're not living with your husband, Kristen.

Though her tone was gentle, even through the phone, I could tell she was shaking her head in disapproval.

Just because we'd be living together doesn't mean we'd be talking about our grief, I said.

Maybe you should go back to church, she suggested.

Thanks, Mom, I thought.

♥ ♥ ♥

Months later, Ken called at seven-thirty one night, and I knew right away something was up. Whenever he was in Maryland and I was at Penn State, he'd wait to call me until he'd gotten home from work and eaten dinner, usually around nine, and Ken didn't veer from the schedule, like ever.

The basement door was half open when I came in, he said, sounding out of breath. It's never – I don't know; I feel like someone's in the house.

What? Get out! Call 911! Oh my god, Ken, I shrieked. I broke out in a sweat and paced, waiting for him to call me back, text me, something.

Forty long minutes later, he finally called me after he filed a report with an officer, who told him we'd probably never recover our stolen items again. Kids, likely, had ripped open a window screen, forced a window open, and crawled inside our Maryland home.

Ken's laptop for work was still on the kitchen table, likely because its sticker read *Property of the US Department of Energy*, but a half-empty box of wine was gone. They found Derek's Xbox and took it. They also took a PSP and a Game Boy. Our strongbox under our bed was taken down to the basement, where it apparently was dropped repeatedly onto the concrete floor until it cracked open. Nothing but our outdated wills inside. All the shoe boxes in our closet were turned out, revealing only shoes. And my jewelry box contained only cheap earrings and necklaces and Derek and Keyton's baby teeth sealed in two labeled baggies. They missed an old empty coffee container that held coins; and Ken's coin collection from when he was a kid was safely hidden beneath five years of *Oprah* magazines in the corner of the closet. The burglars had picked the wrong house – old worn furniture and outdated televisions, one literally a wedding gift – no hidden hundred-dollar bills amid lights on timers and silence within the walls – didn't they know this was a house of grief the moment they broke in?

♥ ♥ ♥

Time passed as a strange alchemy, stopping as much as marching by at a fast clip. Days were white space waiting to be filled, and I spent too much time alone scrolling on my phone. I read day after day that sporting events were suddenly cancelled, schools closed, and then bars, restaurants, gyms. The news wasn't clear in that there was no official announcement about a pandemic (yet), but I was afraid people would start to panic buy, so I told both Ken and

Keyton to buy a few extra cans of beans and a pack of toilet paper every time they went to the grocery store. Just in case, I told them.

And then the whole country shut down, and we all became nothing but white space. I did what I could to fill that space as Ken and I waited in isolation. He came up to Penn State as soon as it became clear that working from home for the near future was his future. And just as suddenly, we were together all day every day. Filling space, filling time; time was all there was, really. One long hour, day after day after day after day. Yesterday, today, someday, the-other-day. Staying inside together seemed to cause a cosmic rewiring to our individual worlds: I stopped counting the hours until we would see each other, and Ken stopped spending stressful weeks at work and then weekends alone or hours in the car driving up to Penn State. Together, we didn't count the hours or care which day of the week it was. I learned how to bake sourdough, we planned a garden, we binge-watched *Arrested Development*. We ordered masks after I decided my homemade ones made out of two elastic hair ties and a scarf from the 90s wouldn't cut it, and we waited patiently until it was our turn to get vaccinated. Maybe it wasn't a cosmic rewiring, but isolation didn't mean annihilation nor extinction. For us, isolation meant reunion.

Ken and I were together again. Inseparable.

We stayed up late, and in the dark, the ice in our glasses melting, we held hands and cried. I shared stories about the unhelpful advice I'd read online or heard from friends or my parents, and he nodded along, telling me similar suggestions he'd gotten from friends and coworkers. We diverged when I tried to talk about the week in the hospital, begging him to tell me something he remembered that I didn't, but he didn't want to revisit that time. We came back together when we talked about our concerns for Keyton and how massively we screwed up. How instead of focusing on listening to her, we focused on not being able to bear seeing her sad, so we tried to fix her the same way we didn't want to be fixed. And then we talked about Derek.

We should get out those photos from the Outer Banks, when we rode those ATVs on the sand dunes, Ken said.

Keyton had ridden with Ken, and Derek with me. He had been annoyed that he wasn't allowed to drive his own vehicle; since he was too young to have a driver's license he'd had to ride behind me. The whole time he'd coaxed me to go faster and faster. They're ahead of us, he'd yelled over the roar of the motor, and my helmet shrouded my head in near silence so I barely heard anything. Go faster! So I went. His joy was deafening as I accelerated, and he even grabbed my waist to hang on.

And then those Bermuda ones, I added, wiping my eyes.

On the beach, Ken nodded.

Derek had dug a hole in the sand deep enough for him to sit in, and the waves filled it until he had his own personal pool.

I can't remember what else – I'm forgetting him, I'm forgetting everything, I cried.

Ken moved closer on the couch until he put his arms around my shaking shoulders. And then he went out into the ocean with you and Keyton and you jumped waves together and you wanted me to come in and I said no way and you kept laughing together and dunking under the water and splashing each other and you're not going to forget anything, he said into my ear.

♥ ♥ ♥

We should go down to Maryland this weekend and check on the house, Ken said. Our neighbor had been taking care of our lawn as the lockdown weeks passed, but for all we knew a raccoon family had moved in.

Should we think about selling? I asked. Uncertainty hung in the air, as schools reopened then closed again, mask mandates became voluntary then mandatory, vaccines were required yet demand was exponentially higher than supply, testing kits were scarce, and on and on. Ken had zero confidence of when he'd have to report back to his office, so there we were, luxuriating in living together for the first time in years while at the same time panicking about how to maintain our other house.

I don't know. Maybe, he shrugged.

After we got home, we started a list, a to-do list to (maybe) ready our Maryland home for sale. Before I knew it, the to-do list became extensive enough to need sub-lists and sub-bullets, annotations and asterisks.

In the morning while Ken cut the grass, I went down to the basement.

I looked around, dreading my decision to start here. Every corner held a memory, held Derek. Even all of my old toys, the good ones, mine from the 70s, the ones I'd salvaged from my parents' house before they moved to a small condo, had Derek's fingerprints all over them. There were legos and matchbox cars and dinosaurs star wars polly pocket thomas the tank engine books and more books (sorted) and school papers (not sorted – I couldn't – I'd just – here: my hands pressed together around as many papers as possible and then dropped into a plastic bin) and (same with photos). *I can't do this.* I sank to the floor and cried.

Minutes passed, maybe hours, who knew, and then I heard Ken come in from the garage. Kris? Where are you? He called.

Nowhere, I thought. I went upstairs.

We ordered pizza and salad that night, and I ran into the liquor store next to the pizzeria and grabbed a box of wine.

I'll go downstairs with you next time, Ken said as we ate. He would try to protect me like he always did as we moved through the to-do list. Don't look, he'd say when he saw an artifact that he knew would trigger me. But who warned him not to look? Who protected him the way he protected me?

♥ ♥ ♥

We met with a realtor who assured us our house would sell, and quickly. Her advice added a number of items to the to-do list, like fixing long-ignored things like our nonworking doorbell and polishing the house's curb appeal, like painting the faded front door.

Trip after trip, hours in the car back and forth from State College to Germantown, Ken teleworked some days while I painted and packed. He replaced torn window screens and helped me refinish the deck. We gave away furniture to friends and family. As the house slowly emptied, the packing still seemed never ending.

And everything we trashed or donated gave me pause. Derek had wanted our coffee table and one of the couches for his first off-campus apartment, and that same worn couch should have been replaced by now, but we'd kept it, because he sat there.

How much of our old life I tried to keep versus how much of our old life I threw into the pile to be carried out of our family home by the one-two-three-junk men I did not know to a place I would never go. Sure, they were just things, easily dismissed, but I needed to carry these things always, just like I carried my grief. These things held my son in them.

Indefatigable grief, this.

When we leave this house for the last time, I must leave claw marks on the door frames, scratching till I draw blood.

Inside the pantry were penciled lines drawn and dated by me on the molding to say *Derek* or *Keyton* and how they'd grown. I wanted to wrench this molding from the wall and save the carefully penciled marks that climbed higher every year until they stopped. Did we stop measuring because they stopped growing or because years ago we stopped just about everything?

There's the fridge to clean out, a task that took much more time than I ever thought it would. And there's that package of savory pastries in the freezer, left behind, forgotten when Derek went back to school nine days before we got the phone call. The small package we kept, chicken and broccoli frozen solid, saved for when he came home. Throwing away this expired food now shouldn't matter. But it did: It's yet another reminder and I was throwing it away. Seeing it every time I opened the freezer made me think of him, and while I didn't need reminders, I looked for reminders everywhere. They were like touchstones. I wanted to think of him, because every bit was him.

Pack up Derek's room was number 14 on the to-do list. How to pack up his belongings without looking at them was a necessary and difficult endeavor, and why should any of this be easy? Derek deserved my sadness, and that's what he'd get. I packed his books and emptied his top drawer of notebooks and essays and himhimhimhim. *All his things I would fit like tetris into the spare room at the other house.* I checked his closet and patted his clothes hanging there all in an ordered row. His dress shirts smelled clean still, clean like him, and I folded them into neat squares without looking at them and without remembering exactly when I last saw him in this shirt and that shirt, and I packed his trophies and awards and diplomas without looking at them and without remembering exactly how old he was when he won this trophy for this and that trophy for that, and I emptied his dresser drawers into plastic bins without looking at a single fucking thing.

♥ ♥ ♥

Keyton was less than thrilled when we told her we were thinking about selling the house. Do you think I'll be able to see it one last time? She asked, her voice catching.

Maybe we'll have trouble selling it, Ken tried and looked at me shaking his head. Interest rates were at historic lows; it was an ideal time to sell our dream home.

We can facetime you when we go through your room, I suggested.

I don't care. Whatever, I don't know, maybe, she sighed. But you know what? I've been thinking about another tattoo, and I need your help.

When I went back down into the basement, I was on a mission. I sat in front of the plastic bins that held Derek and Keyton's school papers, took a deep breath, and plunged my hands into the first bin. I looked at paper after paper, scrambled subjects and grades, math and spelling and handwriting and art, science and social studies, Keyton's pen and ink drawings and Derek's crayoned doodles, every glance scalding my eyes, searching for what Keyton had asked for: her name in Derek's handwriting. I must've looked through thousands of pieces of paper before I finally found a page that read **Kiwi**, Derek's childhood nickname for his sister.

kiwi

I taped balloons to our fence the morning of Keyton's graduation from Penn State, and then stood back a few steps from the cardboard numbers I'd made. The five was crooked. I tried to straighten it, to align it with the two, the zero, the one. I had printed a bunch of black-and-white photos and arranged them collage-like on the large cardboard cutouts of her graduation year. Derek's face was close to hers in photo after photo. It was the only way I knew to have him here with us.

That afternoon, after a few cups of fruity vodka punch to steel our nerves, Keyton's degree in Anthropology was awarded early in the ceremony for Liberal Arts students, and I watched her climb the steps to the stage, her ironed navy blue gown swishing as she walked in new heels. Tears filled my eyes, and I told myself, *don't blink...don't blink.* On Keyton's first day of college, we got the phone call about Derek. And for four years she fought with her own grief and graduated from Penn State on Dean's List and on time. That she was able to function, let alone achieve academic success like that, was astounding. Pride took my breath as I watched her shake hands with the dean and accept her degree, and I thought, Derek should be here for this milestone, like when he trotted across town on the second day of his internship to attend her high school graduation. I blinked and tears spilled onto my cheeks. I squeezed my eyes shut and clenched my fists. I was so proud of my daughter, yet grief sat right next to me, pushing its way in. Grief with a beckoning finger and a soft hand to brush away tears. Joy and grief, happiness and sorrow, sat side-by-side.

I wanted to feel both, but how?

Grief told me what no one else did: *I'm the only one you can count on. No one else pays any attention to you, so aren't you lucky to have me? I'm your only true friend, and we go everywhere together, don't we? I'm the only one you can trust to tell you the truth. Thanks to me, you're never really alone. How does that make you feel? I'm not going anywhere. You can try to ignore me, but*

I'm right here, always close by, whether you like it or not. Everyone else has left you, remember? They can't handle this, not like I can. They don't like who you've turned into – it's too much for them. And your new friends? You're too afraid to tell them about me. But I know everything, and I can handle whatever you can dish out, because it's nothing compared to what I can do for you. Deep down you know that I'm your protector, your armor against the world. I make you cry, retreat, shout, scream, whatever you need, all on cue. There's no one else out there like me. With me you're never alone. Never. Look in the mirror: there I am. I am you. I have become you. We will always be together. No one else loves you like I do. No one else can save you. I'm in everything you see, everything you do. Close your eyes – I am there. I will always be there.

I am your love for Derek. That's why I will never leave.

Grief said the same thing a thousand-thousand times, and I finally understood.

Grief said: *I catch you looking at me, and sometimes you stay and stare. Most of the time you look away. Why? Why do you look away? I've told you before that I'm not leaving you. You can ignore me all you want, but I'm not going anywhere. I know it's bitter to need me. Bitter to look at me and let me wash over you. You'll never be clean again. Go ahead and try. Scrub away. You love your son too much to be rid of me. There's no distraction, not even Keyton's graduation, powerful enough to ignore me. I just come on stronger. And I push your hair out of your eyes – I touch your cheek – I tuck you in – I wake you up, so softly you don't know it's me at first – and then you rage – like a storm – keening for Derek. I've told you a thousand-thousand times. Don't make me tell you again: I will never leave you. So that your love will never leave you. So that Derek will never leave you.*

♥ ♥ ♥

I believed we'd have another boy when I was pregnant again a few years after Derek was born. Old ladies divined the shape of my belly and my mom did the thread and needle test, where the needle either spun in a circle or swung back and forth; both amateur forms of magick predicted the same thing: a boy. An ultrasound had been done, but Ken and I didn't want to know. Gender reveal parties weren't a thing in 1993, and I definitely wasn't one to adhere to gender stereotypes: Derek's baby clothes would be perfect for the next baby, boy or girl. Names, on the other hand, were a challenge.

I wanted the name Wren for a girl, but Ken did not. And since he had a list of at least ten names for a boy, with Drew Robert as the front-runner, I was further convinced we'd have a baby brother for Derek. But as my due date grew closer, we wanted to cover all the bases, so while watching the women's college basketball tournament, Ken spotted the name Keyton.

What about the name Keyton?

I like it, I said. But it's gonna be a boy, I thought.

Keyton was born precisely on her due date of April 26, a feat accomplished by merely 4% of babies. No waiting around for her. I had called my mom the moment I knew I was in labor and asked if they would come down to watch Derek when Ken and I went to the hospital in Frederick, Maryland. For some reason, my parents were a bit surprised when I asked for their help, but they came.

I can't do this I don't want to do this, I wailed to Ken as a contraction twisted me nearly inside out. He patted my foot, Yes, you can...you're doing this...I'm here, I'm here.

I stared at his blue and yellow striped polo shirt. I hated that shirt.

It hurts too much get it out!

Breathe, honey.

You breathe! I can't breathe anymore I can't I want it out of me!

And there she was, a girl.

I started crying. A girl? A girl, Ken said.

I cradled my baby girl and moved the blanket a bit from her face. She blinked her blue eyes. A little girl for me to mold, I whispered to her.

Later that day, my parents brought Derek to the hospital to meet his baby sister. He held her carefully, and he giggled when she grasped his finger in her tiny fist.

She's so little, he said, his voice rising. Little Keyton. Little Kiwi, he sang.

His nickname for her stuck.

Keyton was a good baby, eating well and sleeping on a fairly regular schedule. At three months of age, she managed a cross-country flight to Phoenix without crying once. Born two days after my birthday, Keyton's a Taurus like me, so when she grew older, her stubbornness should not have come as a surprise. She spent several hours each day in day care when I went back to college after our move to York. When I picked her up after my classes, I was told how wonderful and sweet Keyton was. But within moments upon arriving at home, she turned into a little demon in my arms, frowning and shrieking *No!* and swatting Derek across the top of his head. Her determination to articulate her thoughts and ideas often ended in frustration directed toward her big brother as she stuttered to express herself. Derek had never acted this way, so I had no idea what to do, and my three semesters of studying speech pathology were of no use. I definitely didn't want to silence her nor force her to become small, so at her next well-child appointment, I asked the pediatrician for advice.

Sounds like just a phase, she assured me.

Keyton found her groove when she entered kindergarten. She loved school, and her language skills finally caught up to the thoughts she'd been trying to express. Wanting to keep up with her big brother, she asked to sign up for soccer, and she learned the basics, but soccer for five-year-olds was mainly 11 kids chasing a ball from one end of the field to the other.

With Ken's commute from York to DC, he unfortunately missed every single one of the games of her first soccer season.

Soon after we moved from York back to Maryland, Ken's job had shifted from DC to the Department of Energy building in Germantown. His commute went from five hours round trip to just one song on the radio. He helped with chauffeur duties, taking Keyton to girl scouts and Derek to soccer practice. Then Derek to flag football and Keyton to soccer. He volunteered with me at church. He was home *all the time.*

When Keyton expressed an interest in horseback riding, I eagerly filled out the form and took her to the barn in Potomac. I'd always loved horses, to the point I'd scoured the classifieds under *Horses for Sale* when I was in middle school, vowing to purchase a horse for my very own. I'd shown my parents my circled choices in the newspaper and begged them for a horse, which was, of course, not practical; but, they never even offered to sign me up for riding lessons.

The bay horse chosen for eight-year-old Keyton was a gentle giant. She adjusted her helmet and climbed aboard from the small set of stairs for that purpose. I leaned against the fence and tried not to cry. She was so cute, so small in her riding pants and black boots, doing such a brave thing, and I was so proud of her. I hoped she loved it as much as I wanted her to.

Round and round the ring they went, Keyton and her horse following two other young children on their horses, and when the lesson was over and Keyton dismounted, she led her bay horse out of the arena and waved her hand for me to join her.

We have to bathe him, she said.

Bathe him? How? I asked.

I don't know, she shrugged. But we go this way, she said. That's where the hose is.

In my sandals I tiptoed from the arena up a sloped path to where the hose was. I wasn't prepared whatsoever to bathe a horse. Keyton wasn't afraid, and that's what mattered.

After riding lessons, or soccer practice, or whatever the kids were into, was homework time. Since Ken was home, he helped both kids with their homework. Once Derek started high school and Keyton still in middle school, he wanted to motivate them to do well and get good grades, so he drafted a two-page contract: Instead of Derek and Keyton working after school to earn money, we'd pay them for their grades. In theory, this was supposed to be a good thing, but lots of things looked good on paper. (We found out years later how traumatizing these two pages were for Keyton.) (A version of this same contract was what Derek initialed and signed when he wanted to transfer from Penn State.)

Keyton always looked up to her big brother, wanting to do everything he did. When Derek signed up for lacrosse as a senior in high school, she signed up the following year as a freshman. To our surprise, Keyton was a natural lacrosse player, better skilled than Derek, who used his size and strength to stand firm as a defender, allowing the offense to literally run into him only to bounce off and onto the turf. Keyton's cradling, passing skills, and athletic endurance got her called up to the varsity at the end of her first season, pretty much like Derek had in football. She was one of the captains her senior year.

She also looked to Derek in their free time. Playing computer games together was one of their favorite activities, and she was content just watching him play games like *The Sims* and *Civilization* and *Railroad Tycoon*. When Keyton was old enough to play games by herself, she still wanted Derek close by, especially to help her solve *Nancy Drew* mysteries. They'd sit together for hours, unraveling intricate puzzles and piecing clues together until they finally solved the crime.

So alike yet so different, my son and daughter.

Derek was pragmatic and deliberative, a sarcastic comment just below the surface. I pictured him, about to graduate college. Keyton was fiery and confident, her sarcastic comments also ready and waiting. She was just starting college.

The future was bright, then.

♥ ♥ ♥

I used to be a lot of things. I looked forward to the future. I was even a half-full kind of person. I had hope. I had purpose. I had a life. And now I could spend hours spinning, walking in circles, looking for the right word to describe the pain I felt, trying to find it, desperately looking over and under everything, pausing every-thing around me while I parsed pages of the dictionary, flipping back and forth searching so I could write it down, this right word, because that's what would explain everything. I clung to this craziness, rifling through pages for that right word that was missing, lost, perhaps not invented yet.

Sure, I could pull up the Sanskrit word *vilomah* from the interwebs. Its meaning, against the natural order, that the grey-haired shouldn't outlive the black-haired, sounded just about perfect, and it was gaining acceptance in grief world, but there's no specific mention of child loss. Vilomah: close, but not quite.

What words were there? A dead spouse meant you were a widow or widower. Dead parents meant you were an orphan. Wasn't it inappropriate, even offensive, to describe the indescribable, the unacceptable? Revolting, actually, to try to use language and words in this case. Child loss was beyond language, beyond known words. No word for what to call a person with a dead child.

It was the same as it ever was: There's no name for this grief.
Maybe I was working with the wrong alphabet.

And all the time I spent ruminating over syllables, lost in thought, was time not given to Keyton, who was also lost. Missing words as well: There's no word for a person with a dead sibling.

I remembered what she had said back at the rock dedication, when Ken's sister had asked her how she'd been coping. I'm not, she'd said. I was chilled by her admission then, and I still was.

Just 18 when Derek died, Keyton was labeled too old to get the care and support available to grieving children, and too young to *handle it* like an adult (which wasn't saying much). Just 18 when her world collapsed. Her parents collapsed. She collapsed.

Again with the poor word choice. Derek was the one who collapsed.

Keyton needed us more than anything as the rest of her world fell apart, and we failed her as we sent her back to school, first during the week in the hospital when we believed Derek was on his way back to us, and then back for good after having barely two weeks off to grieve. We thought it was the right thing to do: Go and try to find a new normal as soon as possible. But we couldn't have been more wrong. We were in shock, and we didn't know what the right thing to do was when we were in shock. We thought we were helping her as we encouraged her to live her life. We thought we were helping Keyton when we tried to lift the burden from her of being two children, of literally being Derek's stand-in, instead of being herself. But what we were doing was the opposite of helpful; we were trying to do exactly what we didn't want others to do for us: we were trying to fix her. Doing the best we could wound up being incredibly, incredibly unhelpful. Why didn't we know any better? Why didn't we know what she needed? How much did our insistence that she stay on schedule in college hurt her even more? What should we have done instead?

Ken and I took Keyton to Student Affairs, got her an appointment for the following day with a counselor. She never showed. When she found a camp for grieving kids, but the dates and location seemed impossible to coordinate, we should have done whatever we had to do to make it work. She was on her own, skipping class, blurring one day into the next, and I didn't know how to talk to her. I fell into the same trap I blamed others for: I didn't know what to say, so I said nothing. Or next to nothing, anyway, because I was afraid to upset her more.

Keyton told me later that for weeks and months After she stayed in her dorm and didn't go to class for days at a time. That late at night she cried in the shower so no one would hear her. That she spent most of her time talking and going out with friends she had made over the summer at Penn State, people she met Before and as everything happened that last week of August. Friends who then stuck around. New people didn't interest her very much; the only people she wanted around her were those who remembered her from the summer and now knew her as the girl whose brother died. She had a harder time than anyone knew, including me.

What did losing her brother do to my daughter? How did she survive, living in trauma's shadow, with my mother-ness forever changed in relationship to her? I made so many mistakes. Big mistakes. I still hold such bitterness inside for my role in her struggle: I'm so angry at myself for failing to protect both my children.

I tried to organize my thinking, but thoughts about Keyton came too fast for the pen, and a headache started in my temples. She was beginning her next chapter, starting college, and supposed to be loving life and excited about the future, but instead was completely devastated when everything in her world changed. And yet: Keyton told me that the only way she knew how to manage her pain was to believe Derek was away at school. Like Proust had explained, as if her brother were traveling abroad. This belief lasted until her graduation from Penn State. Her graduating, with Derek not graduating nor coming home, hit us both hard. And I fell into the same patterns I'd learned, the same patterns I hated in my parents: I didn't talk to her about the difficult, worst, and most important thing.

♥ ♥ ♥

For sure, I didn't want to share the very dark places of my own grief with Keyton. Putting that burden on her was not an option. But she knew. And she tried to help me. When Cinnamon began having accidents in the house, trouble seeing, and eating less and less, about the time when we were building our case for the lawsuit, we knew she was ready to go. At nearly 15, she'd been our devoted furry companion as long as she could. Keyton sensed that we needed to have a dog be a part of our lives. Not replacing Cinnamon, but to continue that bond.

What do you know about greyhounds? she asked.

Not very much, I said.

Did you know there's a greyhound rescue near here?

I did not.

They have a meet-and-greet at the pet place up the street. You should go, she encouraged.

I went. I petted a pale doe-eyed boy for an hour. When I stopped he nudged me with his slim nose. His fur felt like silk and his long dark eyelashes didn't look real.

Fill out an adoption application and come by the kennel sometime, the rescue volunteer offered.

Keyton and I drove out to the kennel the following week to meet a red fawn girl so shy her back was to us the entire visit. She needs a quiet home, we were told. She's a bit spooky and needs a lot of patience.

Sounds like me, I thought.

Some coaxing got her into my back seat, and we took her home.

We named her Cairo, as she reminded us of the hieroglyphic figures of pharaohs.

We'll never know everything about her, about what came before; I only could imagine how she got her scars, why she's so fearful of sudden movement from the side, what she saw within her yipping dreams. Her red fawn color made her look like a small deer, fleet on her feet as she raced in circles in the backyard, or curled tight as a ball on the couch. She quickly became incredibly affectionate, playful, and eager to please. She was also very shy, needy, and nervous: Perfect for me. Perhaps we're peas in a pod.

After a short time, she acted even more at home, rolling onto her back, one paw stretched into the air, *roaching*, as they said. It was wonderful to see, considering what happened on what was supposed to be a tranquil walk a few weeks after we brought her home.

We were out for a walk on one of the sunny days, a feeling like the water was lovely and warm, my raft that carried me through life gently floating until something happened that made it almost sink to the bottom. Cairo and I passed by slender purple thistles and milkweed pods that were still green and hard. We looked for bunnies, as black and blue butterflies flitted just ahead. Fluff and seeds floated in the air like so many words I longed to say to Derek. But silence was all there was.

As we turned for home in sight of the Penn State Arboretum, that lovely open space of countless trees and gardens of manicured shrubs and flowers, Cairo was spooked by an unleashed dog, and she bolted. Her leash flew out of my hand, and the abrupt force made me fall forward. I tried to follow where she went, and I gave aimless chase, all the while out of my mind screaming at the owner of the loose dog. You bitch, I screamed, You fucking bitch! She probably recovered her dog in moments and went home, not giving us a second thought. Meanwhile, I raced around the grounds, my course a fingerprint whorl, calling Cairo's name, panicked, desperate, terrified, cast suddenly upside down in the ocean, my raft far out of reach. Was Cairo in the woods back behind the gardens of the arboretum? Was she acres away on the other side of the law school? Or did she cross busy Park Avenue and head onto campus? My greyhound could be anywhere – she could hit 40 miles per hour in less than four strides. Would I ever see her again? Hot tears hit and I could barely breathe. Again, I failed someone who depended on me.

I didn't know what to do.

Then I saw her before I realized it was her. Like that flash of recognition you get when you're trying to think of someone's name or why you went upstairs and then it comes to you suddenly. I ran to her. Her leash had gotten caught in a fence that defined the butterfly garden, and there she was, panting, bleeding, waiting. Three thick parallel wires made up a fence meant to train grapevines, and Cairo must have crashed into it, catching her leash but lacerating her front leg. She appeared unconcerned as blood dripped onto the dirt. A lot of blood. These hounds were known to be stoic beasts, but I was not.

I picked her up from the vet that afternoon. All that blood required only one stitch, but it was right where her front leg joined her body, like her armpit. The bandage was cumbersome, and she had to negotiate stairs to go outside, so I rigged an old door we had in the basement like a ramp down the deck stairs to the yard. I covered the door with a carpet remnant for traction, and thanks to a lot of encouragement, Cairo figured it out after a few minutes. Her leg healed well, but when she was physically ready to start taking walks again, new fears appeared: leaves rustling, a random bicyclist, other dogs on the opposite side of the street. Cairo literally would freeze just steps past our driveway. It's called *statuing*, in greyhound-speak. Patience won out. Patience, and a ton of treats. Bribery got my grey moving, and eventually our walks got longer and longer, our ride on the raft in the ocean lovely and smooth once again. Cairo stalked chipmunks and squirrels, and one time startled four deer. I was thrilled to see them, but she didn't seem impressed. To be fair, I still had many days when my raft dipped and capsized quickly; other days I was drenched but stayed afloat somehow. On those days Cairo stopped and leaned against me, patient. Like her, I had many new fears too.

Peas in a pod. Thanks to Keyton.

♥ ♥ ♥

I don't want to talk about it, Keyton said. She didn't look away from the television.

We have to talk about it sooner or later, I said. *Look at me*, I thought.

You keep saying that, she sighed.

I had discovered a small wooden object I'd forgotten about – a napkin holder (now partially broken) I had made in shop class in middle school and given to my mom. She'd actually used it for years and then at some point given it to Derek, probably because he commented that he liked it for the Nittany Lion depicted on the side, cut to shape and then painstakingly wood-burned by seventh grade me into the light-colored wood. My nine-fingered shop teacher who wore safety glasses 24/7 gave me a B-minus because the burns looked hesitant, weirdly starting and stopping as I fought against the wood's grain, lighter into darker lines overlapped in a haphazard way, but Derek liked it enough to use it as a pen organizer for years. I wondered whether Keyton wanted it now. Whether she wanted anything of Derek's.

What's the hurry, anyway? It's not like he's coming back for anything, she said and stomped upstairs.

I sniffed, leaned back against the living room wall, and slid to the floor. Cairo padded over to me and touched her nose to mine. Oh, Cairo, I said, and cried into her fur.

♥ ♥ ♥

Do you want more coffee?

Yes, please, Keyton said and stretched her arms over her head.

How long have you been up?

A couple hours. Once I start looking, I don't want to stop. I found four I want to apply to.

Keyton's job hunt was now in month five post-graduation. Her phone interviews went well, but then an email would arrive, dashing her confidence.

How can I get more experience if no one ever hires me?

You're an apple high up in a tree, I reminded her with a nudge.

Ha ha, very funny. Wait – look at this, she said, pointing to her laptop screen. You should do this.

Writing Your Grief 30-day online course, the homepage stated. I squinted at the screen; my glasses were upstairs. Who is Megan Devine? I asked.

A psychotherapist. You're a writer, and you should be writing, Keyton said, once again trying to help me cope. You can write about the things no one wants to talk about, and no one can make dumb comments like what happens when you post on effbook. You should do this, she repeated. I'll send you the link.

I thought about what she'd said. I'd always loved to write (one of my early what-do-you-want-to-be-when-you-grow-up memories was declaring I wanted to be *an arthur* – how young was I that I misspelled *author*, and how young was I that I dreamed I'd always be surrounded by the endlessness of stories and books and imagined becoming someone who filled pages with my words…my own thoughts…about pretend people and worlds).

I signed up for the 30-day course, and the writing I learned to do there literally opened the floodgates. Please look up Megan Devine's outstanding course for yourself or someone you care about. Her website is full of vital resources, and her book, *It's Okay that You're Not Okay,* meets you exactly where you are in your grief.

The grief writing prompts appeared simple and straightforward, but they were deceptively complex. I wrote as little or as much as I wanted, and sometimes I was compelled to write about something completely different. No one was looking. The feeling of safety that gave was priceless. So on the days when I droned on and on across the page, writing seemingly everything that'd ever been written and feeling seemingly everything that'd ever been felt, I still wrote everything and I still felt everything and I somehow kept going, wilted along with my words. I found that it was my words that were the only things strong enough to continue to prop me up (my words, along with Keyton and Ken). These were words I could not speak, but only write about, and they were like scrabble tiles, square and unyielding in my clenched fist, sharp pokes against my skin, yet different vowels and consonants that, if I arranged them neatly, might spell out what it was I meant to say.

How many times in a day I thought about Derek, but most every day I said nothing and nothing and nothing and nothing was said to me. But with writing, I could say everything. I carried words with me: I ruminated on his 10-year-old honesty and innocence back when he pointed out to our realtor that our refrigerator wouldn't shut completely unless you pushed it closed with your foot. I lamented how Keyton and I tried every password combination we could think of (but to no avail) to unlock his laptop so that she could use it when she got the dreaded blue screen sophomore year at Penn State. I described in every imaginable iteration our last hug that morning when I told Derek to have fun and be careful or how I wrote more thank-you notes after he died than when I got married and wondered why in the world I was thanking anyone. And sometimes I ranted and raved, my anger spilling across the page, words like *unfair* and *injustice* and *preventable* in all caps. How amazing all of this was to someone like me who loved to express myself yet never learned how to protect myself with boundaries when well-intentioned people tried to control how I felt and how to handle grief.

And it was more than freeing to say the least to find no punctuation in grief writing but a run-on sentence looping paragraph after paragraph yes it's a fragment chopped into pieces also it's interrogative yes questions that had no answers it's declarative. It just was. It's exclamatory because I am fucking grieving! And it's of course certainly imperative it's imperative that I remained here right here in this grief unmoving.

More than anything, writing made me look directly at very dark places. And it was here, on these pages and on all the others, where I wrote the truth and could be as raw as I wanted to be. I could finally use my voice to be as honest as possible about the unacceptable. The writing didn't always make sense, with the words failing me – or was I failing the words? Either way, I kept going, hoping to capture a phrase here and there that was worth saving and holding precious, the words themselves keeping me safe from all those good-intentioned-yet-invariably-say-the-wrong-thing people. The page as my shield, and ink as my arrows. Here on the unflinching page I didn't have to watch another person's face change as I explained myself in 40 million different ways why after all this time I was still angry and sad and full of guilt, because I just did that. Once. And in clear, literal black and white. The one time was enough. Here was where I could lay my burden down, finally.

But I had to be careful. It wasn't unusual for me to dedicate pages and pages to darkness and anger and hopelessness, such weighty themes, which was no wonder, as the word *grieve* came from the root for *heavy*, and I often wrote so quickly in whatever notebook that was nearby I had trouble re-reading the words, for they looked like another language, which, technically, they were, because only those fluent in grief-thought could understand. Or, I typed without spellcheck so that word after word became a messed-up jumble of wrong words, and if I didn't proofread immediately what I actually meant to say would be lost forever. Even more convoluted was my prose when I dictated my pithy thoughts into an excellent app called Cocoon as I walked, since for me walking inevitably generated the absolute best ideas and phrases, but if the voice memo heard me wrong, who knew what would be transcribed on the other side.

And yet. How could I put Derek on the page and tell a story I did not want to tell? Stringing together words into patterns into the shape of my son's life so that its creation on these pages would live on for him and somehow sustain me? Scribbling down some anecdotes from an idyllic childhood? Doting grandparents, adoring cousins, bestest friends in elementary school? Baptisms, birthdays, vacations. Loving parents. A devoted sister. Was Derek's life a lovely two-decade-plus stretch of perfection? I'd love to say yes, and sigh, and switch here to writing about rainbows and unicorns and the inevitable fairy tale happy ending. But that wasn't real nor true. Not only were we a very normal, very boring, family, making mistakes and being jerks to each other sometimes, our story also included too many shifting storm clouds swirling around hellish demon horses and rabid dogs. To read through everything then, beginning with the very first draft, and to make myself reasonably and calmly analyze the story's structure and then look for misplaced commas, critique word choices, spot spelling mistakes. How could I even write about this? What was I doing? Nothing made sense.

Writing about my grief changed nothing, as it changed everything. Thanks to Keyton. Again.

♥ ♥ ♥

It took almost a year for Keyton to secure her first job after college. She found an apartment in Beacon Hill practically right across the street from Massachusetts General Hospital, where she'd be a nonprofit coordinator, with an @harvard.edu email. Close to Boston Common, an organic grocery store, and countless other amenities, the studio apartment was wicked small in a recently refurbished brownstone, complete with a heated floor in the bathroom. Helping her move to a city she'd never even visited was exhilarating while at the same time marked yet another loss in our ever-growing list of losses. Not only were we losing her as she was moving away, far away, almost 400 miles to ship up to Boston from our house, but also we were losing part of our Before.

When your grown child leaves home, it should be an occasion to be celebrated. First real job! Or getting married! Or both! Should be. But just like I felt when Keyton graduated college, my happiness and pride was clutched close to my grief, three flowers in a bouquet, as I helped her arrange her new apartment. I hid my eyes and tried to keep from crying as we explored the new city together, a city that would become her home, a city Derek would never see. And I absolutely couldn't keep it together when I hugged her goodbye and watched her alone on the sidewalk in my side mirror as we slowly drove away. Would Derek have stayed in the DMV like so many of his friends, or would he have gone to another area like Los Angeles, New York, or Boston first, with Keyton not far behind, just like so many times of their childhood: Derek blazing the trail and Keyton close by his side. Now she's the one with the machete, but I wondered whether she'd enjoy her adventures as much without Derek by her side.

Almost seven hours by car or a non-direct flight away, my being separated from Keyton was palpable. We texted, we talked on the phone, we shared videos. But it wasn't the same. She visited us, and we visited her. But it wasn't enough. I tried yet failed not to envy people I knew who saw their grown children all of the time. I clenched my jaw when I heard people complain about their grown children. I forced myself to ignore what looked like the flaunting of safe and healthy offspring everywhere I looked. I would love to talk to Keyton and Derek every day. See them every day. But one of my children lived hundreds of miles away, and the other was dead.

♥ ♥ ♥

We visited Keyton for five days one July, and instead of walking down the hill on Wednesday night toward the Charles, trying to cram our sweaty selves between sweaty strangers on Storrow Drive for fireworks over the river, we stayed in her warm apartment and drank boxed red wine in front of her small fan.

On this particular fourth of July night, all we did was talk. And the three of us sat together, alone in our grief.

I watched Keyton closely as we shared stories, hopelessly sad, darkly funny stories, re-creating the past in the present tense. She smiled and laughed when we did, and she got choked up once when she recalled hiking in the Poconos and Derek had spotted a small snake on the path. Red and yellow will kill a fellow, he had called to Keyton, who almost leapt into the nearby creek when he pointed the snake out to her. This one's green, he teased. Don't worry. But except for a handful of moments, she looked numb and flat. Maybe it was the wine, or the July heat that subdued her. Maybe she was out of spoons. My mind raced as I studied her, so quiet and controlled, her affect the same as she seemed on our phone calls. Ever since the last night in the hospital, when she'd screamed and I wrapped my arms around her, she'd been almost frozen. Where was my emotional daughter? The one who shrieked with happiness when she opened a *Nancy Drew* computer game Christmas morning, the one who had cried on my shoulder at her great-grandfather's funeral, the one who was so angry when she wasn't allowed to play with a friend one night after dark she kicked her bedroom window with a fury that cracked the glass, the one who screamed in anguish when her brother died.

Her big brother. Derek was always older than she was. But she's older than he was now. What sick riddle was this? A puzzle I could never solve, no matter which piece I picked up, no matter how long I stared at the negative space. I had no instructions on how to hold this in my head.

And I thought about Keyton's ideas to adopt Cairo, and then her insistent encouragement for me to write about my grief. She tried to help me. What had I done of significance to help her? Her grief was just as intense as mine, yet it was completely different. The loss of a sibling was a loss of a lifetime because who else could Keyton expect to have a relationship with that stretched her entire life? Her oldest companion was gone, and no one talked to her about this. Keyton should have had Derek in her life for her entire life, the two of them together in the world, but ever since the week in the hospital, our friends and family worried about Ken and me, but hardly anyone mentioned Keyton, and even then only in passing. *Were you close?* A dreaded question asked of her often, so thoughtless in its simplicity. My mother-in-law, when I confided once how much I worried about Keyton, told me that it would always be much worse for Ken and me than it ever could be for Keyton.

There's no *much worse* in grief world.

♥ ♥ ♥

I need some space, Keyton said one day. I didn't understand. We lived three states away. That was enough space.

How can I help? I texted. No response. I called. Voicemail. Finally after what seemed like hours, she texted back, I'm okay. I just need space. That's how you can help. And that means no texts or calls until I'm ready. Followed by a heart emoji.

Okay, fine. I had to give her space. To her, a Millennial, not a big ask. But the last thing a Gen X person like me (and a grieving parent at that) wanted to do was pull back. So against every instinct, I gave her space.

How long do we have to do this? I pestered Ken after a week had gone by.

It'll be okay; she'll let us know, he answered.

Would it be okay? I wondered to myself. Or would this space between us grow and grow until that was all it was: an abyss. Unnavigable and uncrossable. Forever separated.

Like whenever I settled myself in the rabbit hole of grief, I spread my arms in this space Keyton needed. Months ago she'd told us that she wanted to try and build new memories and not talk about the same old stories, the stories Ken and I told and retold, the ones that included Derek, and I got so defensive I shouted, I will not move on! I will not leave Derek behind like he never existed!

Through angry tears she declared that that wasn't at all what she meant. You're living in the past telling those stories over and over, she said, and I want us to move forward, all of us, including Derek. Frustrated silence punctuated that phone call.

The space Keyton needed, like the space between her and me, the gap, was what was real, the distance from point A to point B. The *lacuna*, the blank space or gap in something, like the space between seconds, the words not said, the breath in and the breath out, the life unfinished.

And all of this space suddenly made sense to me. Keyton would fill the space.

Beannacht.

It would be okay.

steps

As I waited for Keyton's call, I opened my journal and wrote, *Is hope the same as optimism? To have a glass and see it as half full?* I added, *Or maybe the only way to see beauty in a spring flower is to sigh and be grateful and avoid pain by putting Derek off to the side because it's impossible to hold beauty and pain at the same time.* I shook my head and thought, I'd rather never see a beautiful flower again if I had to consciously put Derek off to the side even for a second. I wrote, *Hope is about holding Derek close as I hold the flower, cry that he's not here to see it, be sad, and miss him.*

I wiped my eyes; Keyton was about to call, yet I had to keep writing, *Hope is about handing Keyton the flower and seeing the light in her eyes. That's about all I know of hope.*

Pull it together, I told myself. She'll know if something's wrong in two seconds if my voice sounds off.

But I wasn't done. *In hope,* I wrote, *I could look for that elusive feeling of belonging. There's no name for this grief of mine, so was it still possible for me to have hope? Could I have hope even in my grief?*

Jeez, you took forever to answer, Keyton said when I picked up.

Sorry; I was writing.

That's good. Hey, I have a question, Keyton began.

What's up? Should I get your dad? He might be in a meeting –

No, she interrupted. This is just for you.

For me? Uh oh, I joked.

I'm serious, she said. What would you say if I asked you to run the Boston Marathon with me?

♥ ♥ ♥

In less than six months after her move to Boston, Keyton left her first job out of college over principles. What began as connecting with patients and families who were likely facing terrible news like a cancer diagnosis morphed into strict daily quotas of registering a certain number of patients for various studies. Data collection became more important than people, and Keyton did not want to feed that machine. Besides, standing steadfast for principles guided her through life from an early age, just like her brother. She wasn't even in high school yet when she heard a pair of good friends talking about another friend, and Keyton not only went to that friend and told her what the other two had said, she also severed her friendship with the two mean ones.

She found a position in development at a small nonprofit that helped unhoused women, and this cause suited her. Like Derek, Keyton stood up for people who needed help. She found her inner social justice warrior as she organized clothing drives and fundraising events, built relationships with donors, was trained to identify an overdose and administer Naloxone, and in her spare time she volunteered at a rape crisis hotline.

Keyton even committed to be a volunteer counselor at a grief camp for kids, a place we should have sent her to. Meeting children who had lost a sibling or parent and helping them write a poem or create art about their feelings moved her to do the same as her grief rose to the surface.

Then, after less than ten years in the nonprofit sector, Keyton became a Director of Development at a national charity that addressed generational poverty.

She also met someone.

On a dating app.

And then he moved away to begin graduate school at Tulane.

They kept talking. And alternated visits. On one visit to New Orleans, the whole country shut down, and she didn't know what to do. Stay put, we said. Fly back next week.

Little did we know.

Keyton wound up staying in New Orleans for six months, her long-distance relationship transformed by Covid-19 into living together. And when grad school officially ended with a final project, he found a job in Boston, and they made their way north. When they stopped at our house for the night, we met Oren.

♥ ♥ ♥

What? Me? Why? When? How? I sat straight up in my seat, almost dropping the phone, tension gripping every square inch of me.

Jesus Christ, Mom, you sound freaked out.

I guess I am, I said. I'm a wee bit shocked.

Would you run it with me? She told me we'd be charity runners, raising funds for a nonprofit in return for a once-in-a-lifetime chance to run the Boston Marathon.

I just shook my head in disbelief: *How in the hell was I going to do this?* The marathon was right around the corner – how would I be able to train properly in the brief couple of winter months before the race? Was I going to be able to raise the dollar amount a charity runner was required to contribute? *Did these worries really matter?* What really mattered was that I'd be running with my daughter.

I'd worked out just this morning and went running yesterday, but I hadn't always been a runner. I played softball and field hockey when I was younger, and I hadn't been interested in track. Maybe I didn't really have the build for it. Thick thighs and curvy butt and quite short, I seemed more suited to gathering berries that grew low to the ground, than I'd be to sprinting after swift animals to kill with my spear, evolutionarily speaking. As an adult, however, I'd run five marathons, a bunch of half-marathons, shorter 10Ks and 5Ks, and helped direct our 4-mile Lead the Way run/walk for Derek for seven years. Nevertheless, no matter how much I ran, running never got easier. After all, who needed to run when you could drive? And training for a marathon, especially one like Boston, was physically taxing, time-consuming, and actually pretty crazy. For starters, Keyton and I would have to train to be on our feet for likely five hours in unpredictable and often wild New England weather, negotiate fast downhills, and finally climb affectionately known *Heartbreak Hill*, a half-mile incline late in the race at mile 20. But we'd get a medal, a shirt, and bragging rights, so in the twisted world of distance running, the blisters, bruised toenails, and battered legs would be worth it.

I'll do it. I'll run it with you, I said. And then I told Ken.

♥ ♥ ♥

I had to start somewhere, so the next day I sketched out a rough running schedule, and I texted Keyton to set up a time to talk later. In the meantime, I went to the gym. I felt a little tired and achy, and I thought a workout would cure the rest of me.

Time at the gym was when my mind turned off for an hour. I didn't have to look for Derek there, because instead he always found me and pushed me along. Especially near the end of a tough workout, I desperately needed Derek's hand at my back.

Disclaimer: I know he's not really there; I just prefer to think that he is.

As I got out of breath and sweat dripped off me, I could see the proof that I was still here. The stair-climber was no joke, and nothing-everything had changed when the time's up. The machine did not care at all how sad or grieving or tired I felt. It climbed, I climbed, we went together up the summitless mountain of grief, my burden just as heavy, and since I started lifting weights, the burden settled against my smallish muscles more comfortably. More suited. The same, yet better.

After my workout, I went home and showered, and I watched a few episodes of Ricky Gervais' series, *After Life*, in which he's a widower who's sad, depressed, miserable, and the only reason he's still here was because he must care for their dog. It's perfect.

Besides the numerous funny and absurd moments in this show, there were some hard-to-watch ones, brutal moments, that literally made me cry, nod, and applaud. *I'd rather be nowhere with my wife than somewhere without her*, the lead character stated. Exactly. The truth of grief in this show was recognizable, honest, and so very necessary.

While the show centered around a widower, and there-was-no-name-for-what-I-was, grief was grief, loss was loss, and sadness was thick and real no matter how it originated. There was no grief olympics in grief world because competition in grief helped no one. All competition did was separate sad people from each other. Understanding and compassion brought sad people together. Not only was compassion not a zero-sum concept – as in, if I got some, then you got none, and to quote Megan Devine, *It's not pie* – there's plenty of compassion to go around – it's a renewable resource – we will never run out. Not ever.

♥ ♥ ♥

I opened my journal. But I didn't write anything yet.

Thinking about tears, the sharp sting behind my eyes, eyes that used to be bright, lifted, but now ritually, habitually downcast, ringed with smudged, dark circles. Thinking about my search for *best eye cream* on the internets, and then trying serum after serum, but there's no remedy for what looked back at me in the mirror. Thinking about the sharp dagger of pain in my lower back that came and went – cause unknown/cause, of course, known. My body ached not for more ibuprofen, nor an expired opiate, but because it's missing Derek. A phantom twinge appeared in my right leg, a twinge I got used to until one day it disappeared. Maybe it would return, and maybe it wouldn't, but in the meantime I couldn't lean on Ken all the time; besides, as close as Ken and I were in our grief, sometimes how we carried grief drifted apart, separate, like two falling leaves spinning in two different directions.

I took a deep breath and wondered, again, why did I even get out of bed today?

Because if I didn't I never would leave it.

I picked up my pen and wrote, *I don't know what to write.*

Maybe it would be easier to smooth the sharp edges of everything and embrace whatever form of denial would be most appealing. Drugs, religion, work. Try books, exercise, television, alcohol – surely one of those would be the beckoning hand that lifted me up. But what if grief inhibited concentration and all I could read was the endless scroll on my phone? (Try a coloring book.) And what if running and yoga turned off my mind for a time, but then guilt returned and reversed any endorphins created, leaving me in a worse place than when I started? (Try prayer.) And what if I enjoyed a niche Scottish crime drama subtitled in English, and again, harbored incredible guilt for embracing that distraction? (Try a computer game.) That left alcohol, but instead of calming and numbing me out, drinking seemed to sharpen things more, making me even more emotional.

To be fair, I didn't want things to become smooth, soft, and safe. I felt like I'd lose Derek all over again if that happened. Well-intentioned people told me that I'd learn how to cope because the pain of loss lessened over time. But for me, the pain did not become less. For me, the pain grew until it became a part of me, transforming into a headache or a limp or something else physical. Real. Before I realized it, I looked in the mirror and it was the first thing I saw, like my shadowed eyes, my reflection an image I almost didn't recognize. Grief *had* become me – it had knifed its way in, and it shared space with me, within my body, because I let it. I wanted it. I welcomed it.

♥ ♥ ♥

Keyton and I compared notes as the days passed, each keeping the other on track. As the miles grew, instead of circling the same nearby park a few times, she started running the actual course we'd face on race day. I was envious she had this option, as I circled campus over and over to tally up my miles, hours by myself in the cold air, alone on the road, alone in my thoughts. Every step I took brought a hushed and profound awareness that nothing was as it should be in our family. All I could do was run with grief, not away from it. Run with my daughter, not away from her.

At the same time, every run brought Derek with me. Maybe my morning runs were mourning runs, maybe I lost myself in every mile, maybe that mysterious runner's high enveloped me. Maybe. The truth was that I carried my grief wherever I went. Marathon or no marathon, my grief was with me. My loss was heavy, so very heavy, every mile felt uphill, and I carried Derek every step of the way. It was a compulsion, like how I carried him before he was born, like how I carried him when he was little, so now I carried the heavy weight of his absence.

If running worked to heal me, I'd be out there all day every day. I would think of him: how freshman year at Penn State I mailed him fastnachts in February when a snowstorm prevented us from delivering the sweet fried treats in person; how I volunteered every year he was in elementary school to go on field trips, to help with the Halloween party, the Valentine party; how he watched me play *Civilization* and *Railroad Tycoon* on the computer until he mastered them. Running might lend a quiet even hopeful confidence on even the worst days, but it did not bring healing. Nothing did that for me, not even hoping for Derek's hand to be at my back, pushing me along. Running was simply something I could control when everything else around me seemed out of control.

Running gave me a purpose, to do this marathon with Keyton. Running helped me process emotions that I kept hidden for the most part – maybe the endorphins that fired on a long training run brought everything to the surface. Maybe on a run I could be my true self after all: when alone, whatever came up I could let out, unlike when I was around other people and had to pretend to be fine, strong, and normal. Being my true self meant I could be so overcome with emotion I had to stop and walk. A wink of light peeped through the clouds, and there's a small flower by the side of the path, its thin pink petals beautiful without asking to be. Something like this flower in winter made me pause and continue in my grief. And these intense emotions were fine on a long run, they really were, because it's much better to think about all the things I should've said, all the things I should've done, and my mind just kept going, going, going, playing that Derek reel on constant repeat that slowed and then sped up, because these thoughts distracted me from the one-step-at-a-time of my rhythmic feet on the ground, my methodical arm swing, my 1-2-in and 3-4-out breathing, my pace, how many miles, how much longer, why were there so many hills, my feet hurt, I was so thirsty, and then all of a sudden I'd be done, and I could smile and raise my fist John Bender-style: Look what I just did – I just ran 18 miles!

♥ ♥ ♥

I didn't want to risk saying nothing, as if Derek disappeared or never even existed, but sometimes I veered off course and said too much. One point of contention happened over and over, and it started to seem like a no-win situation, at least for me.

One day in the middle of a conversation that began with a benign remark about recalling when we went to Hawaii back when Keyton was in middle school, I added, And I always felt so terrible that Derek wasn't able to come with us because he had finals.

I know. But I was there, Keyton said. Her voice was quiet.

267

I froze. I did it again. During our last phone call, I added onto Keyton's memory of when she was little she'd been totally content playing by herself in her room, by saying that Derek had been the same way. At first she'd been quiet, but then asked whether I could remember moments when it was just her in my memory. I'd bristled, defensive and annoyed to be corrected. Well, I can't help it. Derek *was* there with you all the time, I'd said.

You're right. I'm sorry, I said now. Apologetic and not defensive.

It's okay, she said after a pause. Remember the pineapple on burgers, and that shrimp truck, and the luau we went to? We watched the sun rise the first day because we woke up so early because of the time difference, and then we drove the whole way around the island. It was so beautiful there; I want to go back someday, she sighed.

I think we got burgers with pineapple for almost every meal. And now we're vegetarian!

I know. She paused. But yeah, Mom, I feel terrible too that Derek wasn't there. Her voice broke. And he should be here now.

♥ ♥ ♥

Though the weather wasn't horrific, that day's mourning run seemed worse than the one before. Maybe I was a little dehydrated or my legs overtired, so to distract myself, I thought about the book I'd been meaning to start so I could pass it on to Keyton when we saw her in April for the marathon, but *meaning to start* meant nothing if the book never even was opened. I'd found this particular novel last year at the annual book sale held in the agricultural arena on campus, where the vague scent of manure wafted upward between the pages of the tens of thousands of donated books that lay in wait for the crowd of people like me: those who arrived on half-price day. I usually had to park quite a ways away. No big deal, until I left with a heavy haul of mostly hardcovers.

I'd always loved being surrounded by books, loved being in an endless library, loved reading, writing, and learning new words. All I wanted to be was *an arthur* when I grew up. But grief changed how I read: I no longer devoured books, rather, I savored them now, as if each word I came across in a line of text had to be picked up and turned over, examined from all sides, before I could move past it to the next one. And there were days and days when I didn't read a single word because everything inside me kept combining and shifting and multiplying, growing, and growing until I felt heavy, numb, and completely out of spoons.

Along with the close earthy smell of the arena, it's hard not to notice the number of old ladies. They were everywhere. Most had lists. Careful, methodical, alphabetical lists. Most lists existed in three-ring binders. And as they caned/walkered/sashayed their way through the stacks, the old ladies consulted these lists, determined not to buy a book already... *listed.* They seemed to amble counter-clockwise around the book tables, ending up smack in my clockwise path like an adorable sloth in the middle of a road. They always smiled as I would excuse my tattooed-self and move past them. I was searching for titles for myself but also for Keyton, as she's rediscovered her love of reading, especially female lead character-driven thrillers.

The 50s music that used to come through the speakers had been replaced with 70s music last year, a nod to the fact that I, too, was now part of the old lady cadre, I supposed. Who knew what the 30-year-olds thought when they spied me with my black painted nails and *Purple Rain* t-shirt. Little did they know that we Gen Xers have remained feeling aged 30 ever since we were 12. And sure, I take inventory of my surroundings as well, the Doobie Brothers and Eagles and Donna Summer and Linda Ronstadt as the soundtrack of the vast arena, noticing the old ladies' tightly curled hair, their bright lipstick, their too-much-because-a-little-is-never-enough perfume, their bright freshly coated nails as they pointed to #40 on page eight of their binders. Already read, so moving on.

Me, I've bought the same title three times the past three years. Joke's on me.

I wandered through fiction and mysteries, self-help and biographies, and I never knew what I was looking for. When I saw something interesting, recognizing the title, or the author, or just liking the font on the cover, I put it in my bag. By the time I circled the vast arena at least twice, my two bags overflowing and heavy, my arms were beat. And I nevertheless made one more pass in case I'd missed a gem, like that perfect book for Keyton, weaving through the ladies and the thrillers and the lit fiction until I finally found the check-out line.

The walk to my car was cumbersome. Usually my books totaled some $40, so at $1 or $2 per book, the tonnage was significant. I heaved a hoard of tomes into my trunk and wondered where I would put them. My shelves were full. And I bought faster than I read, my purchasing resulting in *tsundoku*, a lyrically apt Japanese word for leaving books unread. Anyway, buying took far less concentration, since my concentration tended to be on Derek. I spent hours with him, not fictional characters in books he'd never get to read.

♥ ♥ ♥

I sipped my coffee. From the window, I could see Derek's tree, the beautiful ironwood about to burst into green in a few weeks. Its branches stretched upward as if on tiptoes. I couldn't believe how much this tree had grown, yet that wonder was quickly replaced with hollowness. As Derek's tree kept growing I kept shrinking. It's leaving me behind, and I was letting it. There's nothing for me where it's going. Every time this tree met Spring was yet another thing that would happen from now on and Derek would miss it. How could I... why should I... continue along now? Why must I follow along as expected: shopping, making small talk, mowing the lawn, going to football games, cleaning, waking up? Didn't anyone know how difficult these big little things really were? How forced? How laced with guilt the smallest action was? Our porch needed painted, a task put off for years, because something kept getting in the way. Maybe it was as simple as not wanting to do yet another fucking thing without Derek here to see it. That every accomplishment, no matter how minor, pushed me further away from him. This mere act of pouring a cup of coffee could remind me of the time when he was, and then he, and so I, and he was very, and my tears did not stop they did not stop.

My gaze dropped to the windowsill, to the mug upon it Derek painted, the same one I'd pictured his drinking from in a recent dream. It was for display only because I was too afraid to use and wash it too much in case the colors he painted faded away.

Green pears in the blue bowl ripened slowly in the cool indoor air. I could hear the dog breathing. I felt a familiar twinge in my left foot that called for ibuprofen before my next run.

Did I need Derek to die in order to pay closer attention to things? That was the common lore of society, to point out the lesson learned from all this, or to never know what gratitude was until, or to never appreciate the little things until. I always knew Derek was my heart – I didn't need this tragedy to make me appreciate him. Here's a better question: How was it possible that grief made me leave this world while staying in it? Nothing made sense when we got the phone call, and nothing made sense now.

Think of him, just for a few seconds. Think: He should be here.

I needed a sort of quiet touch, a hand on the shoulder, when I started to think like this, especially now. Now it was day after day after day of days coming around again. Counting and counting and counting the days weeks months years the counting never stopped. Until it does.

We made it through the holidays and countless new years, and now Spring came round again for the umpteenth time. It would be crocus and narcissus and hyacinth, with lavender paper white purple soon. The birds would wake me early, and the brown bunny would be back, yet a quiet weariness whispered from the usual corner of the usual room, and my usual hands fell, lost in the box of slick photographs I thought I'd put away. My coffee forgotten for now, I put my head down and suddenly wanted to sort through the photographs and write about them, and then share what I learned so far.

Guess what, I wrote. *What I've learned so far could fill barely an index card – a three-by-five, not even a four-by-six. But that's okay: Look closer and notice that my script is tiny, concise, and the card is soaked with the ink of my learning.* I wrote and wrote, cataloguing flowers and birds I knew, books I'd read, photographs filled with people I loved, and before I realized it, I turned the page. *One thing I've learned so far is that black pansies are my favorite, the deep purple ones with a yellow eye, the ones that love the cool air, and how in the heated months of summer I wonder what they do at night to gather strength for the coming day. To survive. Are they drinking water, lifting their stems, stretching their leaves, braving their petaled faces just to*

endure the scorch of the sun? A workout like no other, this, night after night,
just to live for one more day.

I drew a line across the page.

♥ ♥ ♥

I wasn't a marathon expert, although I'd done this a couple of times
before, yet I shared some tips with Keyton along the way on
preparation and recovery that worked for me: Eat carbs, eat protein,
get and use a massage gun, and run more miles than you think you
should. She's fit, young, and healthy; her go-to were pilates and spin
classes. I was fit, not-quite-as-young, and healthy; my go-to were
long walks in the woods and lifting heavy things and putting them
down. And Keyton was very goal-oriented and purpose-driven. She
ran cross-country in high school and played lacrosse and soccer, so
she's competitive, especially with herself. She'd be ready.

I kept thinking about Ken. My constant cheerleader. He tracked
my progress in my first marathon through Rock Creek Park in
Bethesda in 2005, with Derek and Keyton in tow, and again
following me in Marine Corps and the Harrisburg marathons the
next two years. The Mt. Nittany marathon at Penn State in 2014
was so low-key he was able to drive the actual course and pull over
when I needed water, jelly beans, or dry socks. It poured buckets
for the first eight miles, filling my shoes and demoralizing me, so I
ran that one again the next year to try to redeem myself. For Boston,
I knew he and Oren were studying the course and pinpointing
locations to best find us and cheer us on and then meet us at the
finish to celebrate.

Some days though I just didn't feel like putting on my running
shoes. My training calendar mocked me as I bargained with
switching a day here for a day there, counting the miles to calculate
whether I could fit in a run tomorrow or the next day instead. I
would check my weather app to see when it's supposed to snow or
sleet or rain. Yet again, I started to question everything: Was I
strong enough? Was I too old for this? Was there a rock in my shoe?
And while I loved running outside, with the mountains, the trees,
birds, horses if I went a certain way, my music, and being alone,
running wasn't always poetic.

Whenever I would feel too sorry for myself, I would get a text, email, or call from Keyton. She really had it tough, as she not only was training to run the marathon, her literal job was to manage the team of 20 running and raising money for the same nonprofit. She sent out encouraging messages, info about the pre-race bus ride to the start line in Hopkinton, and details about the post-race party she'd organized at a hotel near the finish line, complete with massages and an array of food.

When we talked, she updated me about her training and how much money the team had raised so far, an amount close to record-setting. She sounded excited, busy, and very stressed out. I worried whether she was sleeping enough.

I'm fine, she laughed. It'll be over soon.

I knew that laugh. It was like a punctuation mark. Or a punch.

♥ ♥ ♥

I sat with Derek as my head bent toward my phone, and I sat with him as I lifted my head toward the television. Focusing past a screen proved difficult.

But I tried.

Yet my efforts at coping were short-lived. On to something else: I tried just about everything out there, perhaps to just make it look like I *was* coping or at least interested in something. Sounded pretty familiar – I tried to sit still and not ask questions my entire life, relying on listening to find out information, including the week in the hospital, to make it *look like* I was coping, calm, *normal*. And I knew very well how to cope: I'd coped with my cleft lip all my life, I coped with feeling alone in high school, with the death of my father-in-law, then one grandparent after another. My mother. But losing my son? That wasn't something anyone knew how to cope with.

Trying to cope led me to pick up the remote and look for a series or a movie that challenged me or took me away for a few hours. But not too far. One night I found *Beautiful Boy*, a dark, depressing film about a loving family. The oldest son was addicted to drugs, and his father tried to do whatever he could to protect him.

How about this one? I asked.

Too depressing, Ken laughed, and put on an old Adam Sandler movie. I smiled and put on headphones and started watching my kind of film: my tears enough to fill a highball glass.

Addiction meant being powerless in the face of whatever you're addicted to. Right? I'd felt absolutely powerless in the face of my emotions since Derek's death, and while I didn't find grief in a needle or a pipe, yeah: feeling powerless over it is spot-on. I sought grief; I let it in, and I invited it to stay. Please, I asked, pour yourself into my veins, fill my lungs with your smoke, warm me from the inside out. *Make me feel something.* Anything. I never could get enough. Grief would fill the giant hole in my heart, and I wanted it poured in to overflowing.

So I looked for it to fill the hole. Everywhere. There's Derek in this movie, a footnote on the edge of every scene, as I watched Steve Carell desperately try to help his son, even walking in his son's shoes in an attempt to save him from drug addiction, an act Ken had tried to do with the brand-new shoes Derek had ordered but never had a chance to wear. What parent wouldn't go to those lengths, for just a chance to fix everything? I'd already bargained with the only thing I had, my life, and now when grief beckoned, I answered, Sure, absolutely yes, I would love another hit, grief there as red pill or blue pill or may I have both please. I craved the tears, the scrawled words I inked onto the corner of a page, the wet sleeve of my sweater. Feeling everything let me know I was still here. And if I was still here, then so was Derek, because he was always with me.

Powerless.

Addicted.

But then there's the withdrawal, when all at once everything grew quiet, yet my mind turned, churned, and thoughts burned constantly right behind my eyes. Thinking about everything, yet feeling nothing.

♥ ♥ ♥

The weeks ticked by until we had just a handful of long runs left, my last one a trek across campus and through the adjacent golf course several times until my watch read 22 miles. Now I had just a few short runs left until race day.

Keyton told me she was feeling pretty good. She'd tallied up 22 miles the day before when Oren drove her out to Ashland and she followed the marathon route back to the city.

Wait till tomorrow, I predicted. Your feet will be sore.

I know. Working from home just in case, she said.

And at the risk of sounding like a mom –

You *are* a mom.

Remember to keep eating. The closer the race gets –

I know, I know. I have a plan written down, don't worry.

And water. Water, water, water.

I know, Mom, Keyton sighed. I'll be fine.

How's work?

Stressful. I don't want to talk about it.

♥ ♥ ♥

I read somewhere that memories and imagination come from the same area of the brain. Makes sense that they're together, since a memory is rewritten every time it's thought about. It's not as if each memory were stored in neat volumes like a library, listed and recorded and easy to pull out and borrow. Memories are collaged together.

So there's Derek, year after year of memories until the years stopped: fire trucks and dinosaurs, chocolate on chocolate, sesame street, dr. seuss and darkwing duck, and Keyton and presents and school and sports, grandparents and great-grandparents, friends and girlfriends, dinners out on the deck and wine and shots, laughter and hugs and hopes and dreams and joy.

I put my pen down and wiped my eyes and my nose on my sleeve.

Now was tangled with then. Then was the conference room filled with people we used to know. Then was seeing Derek one last time. Now was the next day and the next and the next and yesterday and today.

Now was a routine. I checked Derek's email and I texted him, but one day I stopped checking his email and I cancelled his phone. Which was sadder: That I did these things for as long as I did, or that I stopped?

Now was an amended routine. I wrote Derek a note every night and asked him to come home. *I'm not going to make it*, I wrote for the 4,000th, 5,000th, the nth time, knowing I'd write the same thing again tomorrow.

Now was this, a cursive scrawl: *I still miss you. I still use present tense. I still stare at your photos and cry. I still can't believe it.*

I closed my journal, shaking my head at the unreal reality of knowing what happened to Derek, to my family, yet living every day in disbelief. That line between real and unreal, Before and After, blurred and blurred until it blended into an otherworldly grey and simply disappeared.

♥ ♥ ♥

Twenty-two degrees felt even colder when yesterday hit 40. What was left of the snow had melted, leaving squishy mud laced with ice along the shoulder of the road as I ran. I looked for what I thought was a flash of cardinal weaving through the bare branches, and just like that misstepped on the soft ground, and my foot sank just enough to leave a mark – how long would my mark remain on this earth?

The wind picked up when I turned left, and I longed for the comfy couch next to my warm greyhound. Training in less-than-ideal weather wasn't the greatest – snow back in the forecast, grey skies, inevitable frozen hands, then sweaty hands, then more wind, then tears running down my cheeks. Was I crying? I usually did from time to time, which was fine, but now my nose was running and it's hard to breathe, and sometimes my chest was on fire and my quads burned – *why was I doing this again?* Crying was therapeutic, yet running through a fog of tears with snot running down my face, my breath lost in gasps, wasn't. There's a ton of suffering and self-doubt – after all, it's twenty-six-point-two fucking miles – but

Keyton was counting on me, and, trust me, we'd been through much worse.

About a year before the worst thing happened, when Keyton was a senior in high school, she called me from a friend's house.

Can you come pick me up?

What? I can't hear you. Why are you whispering?

Mom. Please. Come pick me up. The cops are here.

What?

Some neighbor called the cops because the music was too loud, and they're making us take breath-a-lyzers, and I failed, so you have to pick me up. Like now.

Fuck.

I had to sign a form along with other parents I recognized from soccer practices, acknowledging that my daughter had been drinking alcohol while underage and thus had to then attend an alcohol awareness program that met once a week for six weeks. Accompanied by a parent. Me.

Keyton told me in the car that some of her friends somehow beat the breath-a-lyzer, learning how to do so from their older siblings. I guess Derek never got busted, she bemoaned.

I guess not, I agreed.

Am I grounded or something?

We'll see, I answered. I'd always told my children to call if they ever needed a ride, that there'd be no punishment for calling.

Ugh, she said and leaned her head back and turned toward me. I'm sorry, she said.

I'm just glad you're okay.

Me too. And I'm glad I didn't kick in another window.

Ha ha, very funny.

What wasn't funny was when she got busted again, but not at a dumb high school party where annoyed neighbors called the cops. This time she was a freshman at Penn State, telling stories about her dead brother to her friends and toasting Derek with red cups full of vodka. In her dorm room, she cranked up the bass and they all sang along to Mac Miller and then Three 6 Mafia. A suspicious RA pounded on the door, and everyone got written up and issued warnings. Except for Keyton. When she pled her case and shared her grief as the reason, she was sent for mandatory alcohol counseling.

I was furious.

You're being punished for grieving! No one else has to go to counseling!

I don't care. Her flat voice told me everything.

I sniffed. Would it help if I called?

Of course it would help. Why do you have to ask? You're my mom – why can't you just know?

Her words stung. And they were identical to what I'd thought about my mom: *You're my mom – why can't you just know?*

♥ ♥ ♥

I didn't know what I didn't know. Along with the writing course that pushed me to write about my grief, I joined a couple of groups on effbook about child loss. I left several almost immediately, so focused they were on angels and plans and reasons and lessons – all of that wasn't for me. But the more secular groups were still difficult. Mostly I lurked, reading other posts and comments, looking for connection. Belonging. And sometimes a word or phrase posted by a complete stranger affected me so much that my thoughts were filled with the weight of it for the rest of the day to the point that I was compelled to write about it, even if I managed to scribble just a few quick sentences. But once in a while a word or phrase was upsetting, and I broke into tiny pieces, splintered beyond recognition. Sometimes what I read was strange, as if written in a language I couldn't understand. Yes, we all grieved differently, our losses were different, but still. *What should I do with my daughter's ashes*, a post read, *they're in a shopping bag in my hall closet.* Another post read, *I started throwing out my son's stuff because it's taking up a lot of room.* And another, *Turns out today was the sixth year of my loss; I had forgotten.* Sentences like these sounded bizarre to me. And I'd think, wow, my son's ashes were on my nightstand. When I went back and forth from Pennsylvania to Maryland I always carried them/him with me and imagined the scenario if I were ever pulled over: Forgive me, officer, these are my son's ashes between my hip and the car door; sorry I was speeding.

And it was this splintered feeling while reading these posts that made me shake my head, perplexed and crying, and feeling like I felt in early grief. I'd try to write down what I thought I understood, but returning to early grief was like a feeling of being transported from a steady state to one that seemed so long ago, but actually once I landed there, it was like I never left. The same exact thing happened when I read about Derek's friends graduating or Derek's friends getting married or Derek's friends buying a house, starting a new job, having a baby: This all-encompassing rush of overwhelm identical to early grief. And again as Keyton graduated college, moved to her first apartment, started a job, introduced us to Oren.

Early grief gripped me, and it's like I never left.

♥ ♥ ♥

My long training runs came to an end. Did any of these long runs afford me an opportunity to find a couple of my grieving heart's broken pieces?

No.

And, as usual, I had my additional corollary doubts.

Running was an endurance sport, just like grieving; and grief was the epitome of a long run – it's the longest run because it never ended. I'd never find the pieces I was looking for. They were lost forever. Grief took and took and took, and all I could do was to just keep running with it. I had to keep going.

marathon

It was still dark when the marathon team filed onto the bus Keyton had arranged. Still chilly, the sun was forecast to warm the coming day. Our start wasn't until 11:15, so there was plenty of time to decide what layer of clothing to keep or shed. We also weren't stuck cooling our heels and standing around until then: one of the team members had a friend who lived near the start in Hopkinton, and she invited us to hang out all morning in her quaint circa-1800s clapboard house.

I sat in a corner of the small living room watching the clock, periodically drinking water. My shoes were off, and I watched everyone else chatting and laughing. Keyton was opposite me, shoes on, water bottle on the floor, and she was standing with her arms crossed. I motioned for her to sit, but she didn't get my meaning right away. I knew her mind was spinning with her responsibilities for the 20 people on the team, ticking through completed tasks and fretting about uncompleted ones as she tried to make this event as awesome as she could. I knew she worried about everyone else's experience more than her own, so I went over to her a few minutes later and offered to braid her hair.

Sit, I whispered. Rest as long as you can. And don't forget to eat.

She sat. I will, she said, touching her ponytail. I don't need a braid. Thanks anyway. My hat will keep my hair together.

Aww – you two look alike – let me take your picture, a teammate exclaimed.

We each had a Penn State hat on, our ponytails threaded through the back, and we wore the marathon team's signature white tank with black compression pants. We stood and smiled, our arms around each other, our heads tilted together.

And then it was time to head out. But first we took a team photo in the front yard.

The start line was a couple of blocks away. As we walked together, Keyton said, I don't think I'm going to use my headphones. I want to experience the whole thing.

Sounds good, I agreed.

Good luck! Good luck! The team shouted to each other as we lined up with hundreds of others in the correct corral. Everyone looked restless, rolling ankles and stretching hamstrings, as we waited. Noise was everywhere. Flags, bright sun, runners in costumes, glittered streamers on headdresses. Someone threw up, so we shifted away. Keyton took a quick selfie with me and then chatted with another teammate while I stood on her other side. The day before we'd promised each other we'd stay together, but I told her if she wanted to go on ahead, then she should go.

And then a cannon boomed.

Go!

And we went.

♥ ♥ ♥

Derek.
Derek…Derek…Derek.
Derek…Derek.
Derek…Derek…Derek…Derek…Derek…
Derek.
Derek.

♥ ♥ ♥

I focused on Keyton. This would be her first marathon! And we'd be running on Patriots' Day for the first time since 2019, since Covid-19 shut everything down, even America's oldest race. Patriots' Day was the holiday we'd never heard of until Keyton moved to Boston: It's the day the battle of Lexington and Concord, the start of the Revolutionary War, was recognized. So historic, momentous, and cool, and I knew I'd likely cry at the start, cry at the finish, and be choked up for the many miles in between.

VERY DARK PLACES

♥ ♥ ♥

I wanted to notice everything and remember everything I'd noticed. The stalwart golden retriever near the start line, the immediate downhill so intense many runners fell under its spell and sprinted but were exhausted by the time the course leveled out again, the constant encouragement from cheering spectators, trotting past Wellesley, their screaming students lining both sides of the road, ticking off each town we passed as we got closer and closer to the city.

I wanted to forget that I lost Keyton as soon as the gun went off. It was just for a few minutes, but I thought she was ahead, then I thought she was behind, and before I panicked completely, there she was, just behind me.

I was trying to go as slow as possible down that hill, she said. Did you see Elvis back there on the roof?

Yes! So funny!

Should we hit every water station? Or every other one?

Let's do every other one at first. At least walk through to stretch our legs.

Sounds good.

We're through Ashland and Framingham already, she breathed. Well, almost.

Maybe we'll see Dad and Oren soon.

Natick and then Wellesley coming up – woo hoo!

You did your long runs out here, right? A couple times?

I did – some of it looks familiar, but remember when I took a wrong turn and had to call Dad? He got me back on the right road.

I remember, I said. I took a deep breath and clenched and unclenched my fists. I shook out my hands and rolled my neck.

You okay?

Yeah, yeah, just stiff and sore and thistlely, I said, using a mispronounced word Derek said when he was little to describe my mom when she tried to get up off the floor. You sound all thistlely, he told her when he heard her bones creak. The word stuck.

Mile eight, then nine. At ten, Keyton started walking.

Just for a sec, she said.

Fine by me. I used the time to take long strides and stretch out my hip flexors. I hugged one knee into my chest, and then the other. I looked back to see Keyton walking slower. Shit, I thought.

We're almost to Wellesley. Downhill. Come on. Let's do this.

All right, she sighed, and shifted into a slow jog.

Slow is good; slow is moving; let's keep moving, I thought. "Born in the USA" blasted nearby amid cheering.

At the next water station, she walked.

Do you want a gel? I offered. I have some from home; they're pretty good. Chocolate.

Nuh uh, she shook her head. I'm so tired.

Me, too, I agreed, But come on, hon, let's keep going. We're not quitting.

I'm not quitting!

I know, that's what I said, we're *not* quitting! Come on, let's walk just a little faster.

By the time we reached the sharp turn at the Newton fire station, we'd seen Ken and Oren four times. As they cheered us on, I didn't want to worry Ken about Keyton's struggle, but I knew I had to tell him how she'd been doing.

I don't know if we're gonna finish, I whispered as he leaned close to brush salt from dried sweat off my cheek. She's very slow and says she felt sick. I don't think she ate much this morning, so she's running on an empty tank.

Ken looked concerned. We'll try to find candy or something till we meet up with you again in a couple miles. Don't they have gels at the water stations?

She won't eat those.

Keep trying and I'll see if I can bring you something she'll eat.

See you soon, I called to Ken and Oren and pulled a gel from my pocket. Eat this, I told Keyton. I mean it. You need your strength: Heartbreak Hill is coming up, I reminded her.

♥ ♥ ♥

I hoped more than anything the mistakes Ken and I made with Keyton were forgivable. When we encouraged her to go back to school just weeks after Derek's funeral, this attempt to fix her by pretending life was back to normal was not helpful at all. She didn't need to be fixed – she needed *us*. When we avoided talking about grief with her because we fell into our learned pattern of not talking about hard things, assuming we'd upset her more, we should have done the opposite: not assumed anything, especially that she didn't want to talk about grieving her big brother. When we isolated ourselves and turned inward, we treated her as if she was included, because we wrongly viewed her grief as identical to ours. Keyton's grief was *different*, and it continued to be, and until we learned how to grieve together, yet differently, I knew she'd feel alone in her sorrow. Even abandoned.

Still, could I ever help my daughter the way she'd helped me? She'd introduced me to a whole other side of grief world when she shared with me what she'd found about the grief writing course. She'd opened my heart to a shy greyhound who deserved love, and when Cairo died very suddenly, she quietly suggested a few months later that maybe we should foster another grey, which we did, and we then adopted a blue greyhound from Ireland named Whisky. What could I do for Keyton aside from listening when she wanted to talk with no hurry or judgment?

But no matter my good intentions, the learning curve was steep.

♥ ♥ ♥

Keyton finally choked down half of the viscous substance and she seemed a little more alert, so I coaxed her to finish the gel packet.

Fuck, she shivered, That's gross. Then she smiled. Hey – look! Push pops! She almost skipped to the curb where a few little girls were handing out the frozen treats. What flavor? She called to me. I got a red one!

Purple, I said.

We sucked on the icy sweet relief and took a selfie, her tongue red and mine purple. She seemed rejuvenated beyond recognition, but I cautioned her, Yo, we still have six miles to go.

We took in the sights as we ambled up Heartbreak Hill, noting boomboxes blasting 80s music, couples in lawn chairs waving us on, teenagers with hand-lettered signs that read, You're better looking than anyone so far!

When we get to the top, let's run to the next water station, I said.

We did, and then we walked as we sipped from paper cups.

I'm hot, Keyton complained. I wish I wouldn't have worn this long-sleeved shirt under my tank. She pushed up the sleeves.

Maybe it's hotter the closer we get to Boston? I guessed.

Are we there yet? She whined and smiled.

But the next moment her smile was gone. I'm done, she said.

She was out of spoons, been out for a while, and I had to insist that she wasn't when I said, No, you're not. Mile 23 is not time to quit. People quit at mile 3, not 23.

♥ ♥ ♥

I could confirm that I knew exactly what to say to Keyton, that we were open and honest about our grief. I could confirm that when we talked about Derek we focused on how grateful we were to have had him in our lives for as long as we did. I could confirm that I forgave myself for failing to protect Derek and for failing to then save him and bring him back. I could confirm that the lawsuit brought swift justice. I could confirm that recently I realized that all of this was a mistake, a huge misunderstanding, that it wasn't us, it wasn't Derek – he's right here – *Look!* – and none of this ever happened. I could confirm that time did help and that peace and healing did arrive to soothe me. I could confirm that I learned how Ken's grief and mine were different, and that when he told me how guilty and sad he felt, I stayed strong and stoic for him. I could confirm I found comfort in distractions even though I thought that nothing could ever comfort or distract me. I could confirm that Derek was still here, just out of order, like he's in the CIA and overseas somewhere in a top-secret location, unable to reveal the truth. I could confirm that my parents talked about their grief and understood mine, meeting my needs, no matter what. I could confirm that prayer helped. I could confirm that I felt stronger and better, so much so that I was able to go back to everything I used to do, especially visiting friends and family who assured me there'd be no memories present that might upset me, so far from that football field. I could confirm that karma worked.

I could confirm all of this. But none of it would be helpful. Or true.

The only truth I could confirm was that Death would come for someone in everyone's life, and because that someone was loved, grief would be there. One of the many, many tragedies of being human.

♥ ♥ ♥

Come on – we're not done; we're at Brookline – look, there they are!

Frantic waving from Ken and Oren lifted the veil of exhaustion from Keyton's eyes, and she jogged to the chain-link fence that separated them from us.

Is she okay?

I think so, I said as I shook my head. I felt like crying. I whispered, I've been practically carrying her since mile 10.

Almost there, hon, Ken said as he patted Keyton's back. You worked so hard and now all that training's paying off, he added.

Yeah, right, she snorted as Oren hugged her.

We stayed close to the fence and Ken and Oren walked with us for about half a mile.

Let's go, I said.

See you at the finish line! Oren called as we jogged away.

Jog, walk, jog, walk.

Try and walk a little faster, honey, I pleaded. The light was starting to slant sharper, and I knew without checking my watch that it was around five o'clock. All the other marathons I'd run, even the one in drenching rain, I'd finished in about four hours, forty or so minutes. This one would be a five-hour-plus-who-knows-how-long one.

How much further?

What would Derek say? Ken and Keyton do that too, play that prosopopoeia game, *What would Derek say?* The longer he's not here, the more I wanted to hear what he had to say.

♥ ♥ ♥

Not too much further. I hope, I said, wondering.

There was hope again, as if it contained the power to pull us to the finish line. Even though I didn't know what might fill a glass of hope, it was everywhere as we ran from Hopkinton to Copley Square. Whatever hope looked like, I picked it up and carried it with me while we ran. Maybe I dropped most of it when I wanted to relent and walk off the course with Keyton when she'd insisted she was done, and yet a tiny bit, a crumb of hope, small enough to fit in the glass I held, maybe, stayed at the bottom of my pocket – as anchor – some hope for me to hold for next time.

Right on Hereford, left on Boylston.

Keyton! There it is! Let's go!

We grabbed each other's hand, and we ran to the finish line, smiling, and we raised our hands up high as we crossed, and I looked at her and she at me, and I knew in that moment, as we ran and walked and struggled through each inch of pavement that made up this storied race, as she'd threatened to give up and I'd never left her side, as we completed the Boston Marathon together and patiently waited while medals were adorned around our necks, as we snapped selfies, as we limped to the hotel where food and massages waited, and as she reunited with Oren and I with Ken, it was in that moment that I had finally, finally, helped my daughter.

final words

I know this is a long book. Believe me, I contemplated and considered massive edits for the sake of shortening the story. But then I thought, *Fuck it! Save the edits for the movie!*

It would be expected, but not honest, to close my story of living with the loss of my son with growth, transformation, and even redemption. That, as I have been promised, it got better. I did get my voice back, here, in writing these pages. But this isn't solely my story, for starters. It's Derek's, too. And what to do when our two stories are mine alone to tell.

That's what I thought about as I stared at the photo on my desk of the two of us smiling under the New Mexico sky, my arms around my little boy, protecting him. Angled just so, the frame was out of the light, but I wondered, what if the colors started to fade? Would my face disappear first, as it should have?

I used to think there's no name for this grief. But there *is* a name for it: Mine.

Is there profound understanding to be found? Lessons, reasons, newfound possibilities? Maybe I could admit to a shift in my grief, that we shared a tacit understanding of sorts. A nod. That when I felt everything all at once or when I felt nothing at all: between these was grief. A fine perfect balance, like a kinetic Alexander Calder mobile, where the slightest breath of air could both move and shift that balance.

It's the same with grief. Grief is a very dark place. Grief is complicated. Grief is whole while it's splintered. Grief is alongside joy and anger, and it's noisy and silent. Grief is all I have left of what I've lost, and I will never let it leave me too.

Grief is love. And grief is all I have left of Derek. I must hold it, so that I can hold him.

Island

Wave of sorrow,
Do not drown me now:

I see the island
Still ahead somehow.

I see the island
And its sands are fair:

Wave of sorrow,
Take me there.

Langston Hughes

acknowledgments

I'm indebted to the wisdom found in the pages of Megan Devine's *It's Okay that You're Not Okay*, its accompanying workbook, *How to Carry What Can't Be Fixed*, and her *Writing Your Grief* course; Dr. Joanne Cacciatore's *Bearing the Unbearable*; and Dr. Mary-Frances O'Connor's *The Grieving Brain*. Other resources consulted were various issues of *Psychology Today*, *The Lancet*, and, of course, Wikipedia.

My partner and best friend offered out-of-this-world patience and invaluable insights as he recorded meticulous notes while reading numerous drafts. No one but you, Ken. I love you.

Please visit www.thedereksheelyfoundation.org to read more about The Derek Sheely Foundation and its mission of raising awareness of traumatic brain injuries and supporting other nonprofits who deliver critical health, housing, and educational services to those in need. If you're interested in receiving Concussion Awareness Kits for your team or project, reach out to me at kristen@thedereksheelyfoundation.org.

I'm honored you found this book and am sorry for the grief you're holding.

Derek Thomson Sheely and his mother, 2010